A History of
SPORTS
CARS

A History of
SPORTS
CARS

G. N. Georgano

Spring Books

London · New York · Sydney · Toronto

First published in Great Britain in 1970 by
Thomas Nelson and Sons Limited

© George Nicolas Georgano 1970
This edition published 1974 by
The Hamlyn Publishing Group Limited
London · New York · Sydney · Toronto
Astronaut House, Feltham, Middlesex, England

Designed and produced by
Rainbird Reference Books Limited
Marble Arch House
44 Edgware Road
London W2

House Editor: Peter Coxhead
Designer: Pauline Harrison

The text was set in Monophoto Century 10/11 by
Westerham Press Limited, Westerham, Kent, who
also originated and printed the colour plates
and cover
The text was printed and the book bound by
Butler & Tanner Limited, Frome, Somerset

ISBN 0 600 34441 X

Printed in Great Britain

Contents

Colour Plates

Acknowledgments

In a book of this nature, the author must rely on many sources of information and photographs and these are listed below. Two people who deserve special thanks for their overall help on the book are Michael Sedgwick and Helen Marshall. Michael has not only answered nearly all the abstruse questions with which I have bombarded him, but has also read the entire manuscript, and made countless helpful comments and suggestions. He has been greatly helped by Helen's meticulous filing of information. I should also like to thank Peter Coxhead of Rainbird Reference Books Ltd for the patience and understanding with which he has borne my last-minute additions and corrections. For my research facilities I owe a tremendous debt to Veteran Car Club of Great Britain, in whose library I have spent hundreds of valuable hours over a period of nearly a year. Others who have given invaluable help and advice include:

Tony Bird, Andy Darley, and John Stammers (Riley Register)
Anthony Blight
Peter Caunt (Crossley Register)
Miss Sue Cobb
John A. Conde (American Motors Corporation)
R. L. Dibben (Singer Owner's Club)
F. S. Derham (Bristol Cars Ltd)
K. J. Fidgen (S.T.D. Register)
Dennis C. Field
David Filsell
Malcolm Ginsberg (Lotus Cars Ltd)
David Hodges
Peter Hull
Bill Jackson (Editor: *Antique Automobile*)
Miss Beverly Rae Kimes (Managing Editor: *Automobile Quarterly*)
T. G. C. Knowlys

Dr João de Lacerda
Dr Alfred S. Lewerenz
D. Linton (Chevron Cars Ltd)
F. Wilson McComb
Hans-Otto Neubauer
John Olorenshaw
S. J. Pearson (Standard-Triumph Motor Co Ltd)
Major W. T. Pitt
William Pollock
Cyril Posthumus
T. H. Rolfe (Alexander Engineering Ltd)
José Rodriguez-Viña
E. F. Timberlake
Michael Wilby
Andrew A. Willson
R. A. Woolsgrove (Lamborghini Concessionaires Ltd)

The illustrations are all credited to their individual sources, but I would like especially to thank the following for their help in providing the photographs, and in suggesting sources:

Peter Burn (*Autosport*)
Dorothy Clendenin (*Road & Track*)
Hugh Conway
Peter Garnier (Editor: *Autocar*)
C. W. P. Hampton
Miss Helga Hansen (*Autocar*)
Maurice Harrison

G. L. Hartner
James Lee (*Motor*)
Dr Alfred S. Lewerenz
Miss C. Rose Maurice (Automobile Manufacturers' Association)
Laurence Morton (*Motor Sport*)
Anthony Pritchard

Cyril Posthumus
Miss Susan Sebesta

Michael Ware (Montagu Motor
  Museum)
E. D. Woolley

It is impossible to give a complete list of books consulted, but among my more regular works of reference have been the following:

W. O. Bentley: *W.O. – an Autobiography*; A. T. Birmingham: *The Pre-1939 Riley Motor Cars*; W. Boddy: *Continental Sports Cars*; *The Sports Car Pocket Book*; *The Story of Brooklands*; John Bolster: *French Vintage Cars*; Colin Campbell: *The Sports Car*; Cecil Clutton and John Stanford: *The Vintage Car*; Cecil Clutton, Paul Bird, and Anthony Harding: *The Vintage Car Pocket Book*; H. G. Conway: *Bugatti*; David J. Culshaw: *'The Motor' Guide to Makes and Models*; Hans-Heinrich von Fersen and Jerry Sloniger: *German High Performance Cars*; Hans-Heinrich von Fersen: *Autos in Deutschland 1920–1939*; Luigi Fusi and Peter Hull: *La Vetture Alfa-Romeo dal 1910*; Gregor Grant: *British Sports Cars*; Richard Hough: *History of The World's Sports Cars*; Peter Hull and Norman Johnson: *The Vintage Alvis*; Raymond Mays: *Split Seconds*; Lord Montagu of Beaulieu: *Lost Causes of Motoring*; Elizabeth Nagle: *The Other Bentley Boys*; T. R. Nicholson: *The Vintage Car*; Anthony Pritchard and Keith Davey: *Italian High Performance Cars*; David Scott-Moncrieff: *Three-Pointed Star*; *The Thoroughbred Motor Car*; John Stanford: *The Sports Car*; David Thirlby: *The Chain-Drive Frazer Nash*; R. J. Wyatt: *The Austin Seven*; Féderation Internationale de l'Automobile: *Yearbook of Automobile Sport* (Annually).

G. N. Georgano
London, 1970

Introduction

More words have been written on the definition of a sports car than on any other kind of vehicle. Practically every car has been entered for a sporting competition of some kind or another, but the definition must surely rest not on how the cars were actually used, but on the makers' intentions. Here one can hardly find a better definition than that of Cyril Posthumus who said that a sports car is one in which performance takes precedence over carrying capacity. This applies to a greater or lesser extent to all the cars described in this book, but one must add that in the modern sports/racing car performance takes such precedence that the cars are unsuitable for ordinary road use.

The emergence of the sports car is described in Part One, and by 1914 there were a number of cars on the world's markets whose performance was exceptional by the standards of the day, and by no means unsatisfactory even in 1970. However, the 1920s really saw the sports car established as a type which was, with its transatlantic cousin, the speedster, regarded as a symbol of the restless new decade.

The most important effect of the war on design came from aero engine practice, as many car firms had been producing such engines in their factories. In England, for example, aero engines were made by the Sunbeam, Rolls-Royce, Napier, Daimler, Wolseley, Crossley, Humber, Siddeley-Deasy, Swift, and Arrol-Johnston factories. The effect on their cars was mixed; Napier's single ohc six showed its ancestry plainly, as did the splendid 37·2hp Hispano-Suiza, but Arrol-Johnston soon abandoned their ohc designs for side-valve engines. Swift built Hispano-Suiza V-8 engines, but there was little evidence of this from their conventional side-valve engines of the 1920s. Two main influences of aero engine design were found in cars within a few years of the end of the war: overhead valves operated by push-rods, or from an overhead camshaft, and the use of aluminium for pistons and cylinder blocks. Neither of these developments was entirely new: inclined overhead valves had been seen on the 1904 Pipe, while Isotta-Fraschini used a single overhead camshaft for most of its sporting models from 1906 onwards. An aluminium crankcase was used in the 1898 De Dion Bouton, while aluminium pistons had been used by W. O. Bentley in his specially prepared 1914 D.F.P.s. However, the 1920s saw such practice becoming generally accepted; overhead valves were seen on fifty-two per cent of cars by 1930, and on a much higher percentage of sports models. Aluminium pistons permitted a much higher piston speed, with consequent increase in power per square inch of piston area. 2,000 feet per minute was near the maximum speed for cast iron pistons, but with aluminium this was increased to 3,000 feet per minute, and in the Bentley to 3,500 feet per minute, a speed seldom exceeded forty years later. Coupled with improved breathing offered by overhead valves, this brought a great increase in engine efficiency.

The supercharger, a device for forcing the mixture into the cylinders at a pressure greater than that of the atmosphere was found on a number of sports cars. European cars used superchargers of the Roots type, in which two figure-of-eight vanes were geared together, giving a pressure of up to 15lb per sq in. The few supercharged American cars such as Auburn, Cord,

The Coupe Boillot at Boulogne in 1928. Christian's Lombard receives attention in the pits while passing it is Marinoni's Alfa-Romeo 1500. (Photo: Montagu Motor Museum)

For Englishmen who could not get to Brooklands the beaches provided an alternative venue for sprints. In this picture, taken in about 1913, can be seen a road-equipped single-seater, possibly a Calthorpe, a distinctly touring Humber which was probably an official car rather than a competitor, and two Talbots with straight-through mudguards.
(Photo: Montagu Motor Museum)

and Graham, used rotary fans with a low pressure of not more than 2lb per sq in. In some ways the value of a supercharger was more psychological than practical, and this was never truer than of the 38/250 Mercedes-Benz SSK whose banshee wail boosted the driver's ego in the same proportion as it disconcerted his competitors. An inevitable drawback of the supercharged car in competition was that it was considered to have a greater capacity than its unsupercharged equivalent. This did not prevent some supercharged racing cars from regularly defeating their larger unsupercharged rivals. The most notable examples of this were the 1½-litre Alfa-Romeo Tipo 158s and 159s, which dominated Grand Prix racing in the period from 1947 to 1951.

The gearbox received more attention than it had in the pre-war period, from both designers and drivers. Previously it had been mainly used for starting from rest, and for climbing hills. In ordinary road work the use of gears for acceleration was scarcely thought of. With large, low-speed engines it would not have been a great advantage, and the very light traffic gave no real occasion for constant gear changing and rapid acceleration. Careful spacing of gear ratios was not a pre-occupation of the average pre-war designer, with the honourable exception of Ettore Bugatti, whose Type 13 was so far ahead of contemporaries that it was a timeless car rather than a typical Edwardian. In the 1920s a close-ratio four-speed box with overlap of speeds between each ratio became widespread on high-performance cars. Ideally, this box was mounted separately from the engine, so that it could be operated by a short, vertical lever. Alas, the gearbox was moved forward so that it could be made in unit with the engine, and the lever became longer, more willowy, and at an angle. However, this was overcome by remote control, as on the M.G. J2, which meant that the lever could once more be short and vertical, although the feel was never as positive as with direct control.

Probably the most notable improvement of the 1920s was the adoption of 4-wheel brakes. This, again, was not a new principle, having been introduced by Argyll and Isotta Fraschini in 1910, and used with success in Peugeot and Delage racing cars just before the war. At the 1919 Olympia Show several cars had front-wheel brakes, and in the following few years the design swept the world, so that by 1927 there were few models that were braked on the rear wheels only. The Austin Seven had front-wheel brakes from the beginning, albeit with minute drums, but Rolls-Royce did not introduce them on their Twenty until 1925. Generally speaking France adopted the system before other countries, and it was only in France that the unusual system of brakes on the front wheels and transmission, but not on the rear wheels, was used. This system was seen on some models of Chenard-Walcker and Bignan.

The narrow, high-pressure tyres of the early vintage period were superseded by wider, low-pressure balloon tyres (35lb per sq in). These together with front-wheel brakes made the front heavier, and in order to prevent the steering from becoming impossibly heavy, lower gearing was employed. The trend towards wider tyres and lower pressures was continued during the next decade.

The variety of sports car available in the 1920s grew rapidly, and within three years of the Armistice the breed was represented in most price ranges and car-making nations. The very name 'sports car' appeared for the first time in this period. An article in *The Autocar* in February 1919 used the expressions 'sporting car' or 'sports car' indiscriminately, but soon afterwards the latter came to be generally accepted. In France the distinction between touring and sports cars was less marked, but the expression 'Type Sport' came to be used for the high performance model of a range, even if it differed little in appearance from the Type Tourisme.

Because of the wide variety of sports cars available, it is difficult to generalize about categories, but certain distinct types begin to emerge. The usual definition of a light car is one of under 1,500cc capacity, and in this category a large number of sports vehicles were found. The genuine cyclecar of the early 'twenties was little better than its pre-war ancestor, although many new makes appeared, especially in France. Practically all were entered in competitions of some kind, such as the Coupe Internationale des Voiturettes at Le Mans, or the Bol d'Or, but in many cases they were simply stripped two-seater touring cars. In England one of the few cyclecars which could be called a sports car was the G.N., and it was from the French-built G.N. that there was developed one of the most successful light sports cars, the Salmson. With its rival the Amilcar, it established France as the home of the cheap sporting two-seater, and these cars and their imitators brought sporting motoring to a wider public than had ever known it before. They were by no means as refined as the Type 13 Bugatti, but then neither were they so expensive. Bugatti himself offered the Type 22 and 23 Brescia sports in the light car category, as well as the larger Type 30 2-litre straight-8. England had few rivals to offer to Amilcar and Salmson, but in a slightly larger category there were 12/50 Alvis, Aston Martin, Speed Model Hillman, and the G.N.'s descendant, the Frazer Nash. Later in the decade came various sporting versions of the Austin Seven. In Germany the cyclecar flourished as never before, and the breed of curious little 3- and 4-wheelers with chassis-less wooden construction, radial engines, and other eccentricities survived into the 1930s, when it was long extinct in other countries. However, with very few exceptions, German vintage sports cars were all in the over 1½-litre category.

The light sports car was, of necessity, a two-seater, but in the larger category, the four-seater tourer body was widely used. The fast tourer was a continuation of the pre-war theme established by Vauxhall, Sunbeam, Crossley and others, and many other makes joined in. France had a great variety of firms making this type of car, although many machines called sports cars in Great Britain were not so thought of in France. They merely offered the kind of performance any buyer expected from a car of their size and price. Their development was encouraged not only by the straight roads, but also by a number of races whose rules excluded all but four-seaters in the larger capacity classes. These included the early 24 Hour Races at Le Mans, and the Touring Car Grands Prix. In England most of the famous sports cars such as the 3- and 4½-litre Bentleys, 30/98 Vauxhalls and twin-cam Sunbeams came into this category, while the same situation applied in Italy.

As in pre-war days the United States was in a position quite different from that of Europe. With the coming of mass production the sporting car played less and less part in the life of the country. Races tended to be either for out-and-out racing cars of the Indianapolis variety, or stock car events in which ordinary tourers and sedans competed. There were no races which in any way encouraged a sporting type of road-going car, as Le Mans or the Mille Miglia were doing in Europe, where a higher proportion of car buyers were interested in sporting qualities. The nearest that American manu-facturers approached to the sports car in the 'twenties was the speedster, a machine in which standard components were combined with bodies of highly sporting appearance. They were nearly always two-seaters with beetle backs, wire or disc wheels, cycle-type wings, and individual step plates instead of running boards. They were created to look fast, even when standing still. On the whole they were bought as second cars, as personal transportation for a man who, on other occasions, might ride behind a chauffeur. Although not intended for motor sport, they were frequently bought by sportsmen, and used for driving to the golf or yacht club, or the local polo ground. They were seldom used for long distance touring, as they had negligible luggage space, while their poor weather protection made them extremely uncomfortable in the winter, except in Florida and Southern California. Like the Mercer and Stutz raceabouts of an earlier era, the speedsters were frequently laid up during the winter months. Thus they were machines of limited practical use, and the fact that they sold at all is a measure of the booming American economy during the 'twenties. Another enemy of the speedster was mass production. The industry was being concentrated more and more in the hands of larger manufacturers for whom a small sideline was unprofitable. During the first twenty years or so of the industry, buyers were relatively few and individualistic, so experiments and oddities (steam cars, electric cars, speedsters, and so on) could flourish. When the bulk of the population became motorized, conformity became much more profitable for the manufacturers. The individualists may have been the same in numbers, but from representing perhaps ten per cent of the buyers in 1910, they had shrunk to less than one per cent by 1925, and to cater for them was quite uneconomic.

Another factor which restricted the use of the speedster was overcrowding of the roads. It was becoming harder to find an empty stretch of well-surfaced road on which to let your speedster have her head, even if that head was only 80mph, while the roads that were still empty had atrocious surfaces quite unsuited to the small ground clearance of the average speedster. The crippling financial blow of the 1929 Stock Market Crash, and the social disapproval of display even by those who still had money, completely demolished the market for the speedster, and there were virtually no sport-ing cars made in America for twenty years.

The Vintage Sports Car Club was formed at the end of 1934, and even at that early date it had no hesitation in choosing December 1930 as the limit for the Vintage car. No other decade in this century has been so clearly marked from its predecessor as the 1930s from the 1920s, whether in politics, economics, or the design of the motorcar. Precarious democracies gave way to Fascism, boundless optimism was swamped by the apathy of the Depression, and motoring became less trouble and less fun, a tendency which has continued to the present day. Most of the world's ills could be traced to the great stock market crash of October 1929, and yet by the end of the decade far more ordinary families owned a car than had done so in 1930. However, the choice of sports cars dropped drastically within a few years, and in the summer of 1934 a correspondent in *The Autocar* wrote nostalgically of the cars of the 1920s which had no current counterpart. Bentley 3-litre, Alvis 12/50, Sunbeam 3-litre, Vauxhall 30/98, the most famous names of the 1920s, had all given way to the closed touring cars of much less character.

Not all changes were for the worse, as the dyed-in-the-wool vintage enthusiast used to claim, but inevitably quality suffered as mass-production spread, and it became less profitable to cater for individual tastes. This was especially noticeable in the world of the custom coachbuilder on both sides of the Atlantic. If the coachbuilder was to pay his craftsmen enough money for them to afford to be car owners themselves, the finished product became so expensive that virtually no one could afford to buy it. The situation was not helped by the fact that wealthy buyers had less money at their disposal because of reduced dividends and increased taxation. Social justice and the hand-crafted motorcar do not go together, a truism in the 1960s which was already making itself felt thirty years earlier. Admittedly this affected the luxury limousine rather than the sports car, but the days when a young man could have a boat-decked body built to his own designs had largely gone by 1935.

Improvements of the decade were gradual rather than spectacular, and technical development was more conspicuous in Europe than in England. Engine design saw no striking developments, but power output even of the cheapest cars rose steadily. This was due to improved cylinder-head design, and the more scientific study of the flow of gases in the combustion chamber. Detachable cylinder-heads became more common, and although gasket trouble was frequently encountered at the beginning, this was soon overcome. Piston design and material were also improved. Overhead valves became almost universal on sporting engines, although some of the fastest sports-tourers such as the Railton used American side-valve engines. The more advanced sporting machinery such as the Bugatti Types 55 and 57, and the 2·3-litre Alfa-Romeo used twin overhead camshaft engines.

Suspension made more notable progress during the decade than any other single part of the car, sporting or otherwise. With a few notable exceptions such as Lancia and Morgan, front suspension of 1930 cars was not unlike that on the cars of twenty years earlier, that is, by semi-elliptic leaf springs. As a result of racing experience in the 1920s friction disc shock absorbers were widely used on sports cars, the most popular being the André Hartford which gave a firm ride. Less sporting cars used the softer Armstrong or Houdaille shock absorbers. However, the great step forward was the replacement of the old-fashioned 'cart spring' by one or another forms of independent suspension of the front wheels. The first British sports car maker to use i.f.s. was Alvis who introduced a transverse leaf system on the Speed Twenty for 1934 and had used all round independent suspension on their 1928–30 front-wheel drive car. Not many sports car manufacturers followed this in England, although the mass-production firms, Vauxhall and Singer, introduced it within two years. Vauxhall were obviously following the example of their American owners, General Motors, who had adopted i.f.s. on all their cars by 1935. In Europe, Alfa-Romeo, Steyr, Citroën, Horch, Lancia, and Mercedes-Benz all used i.f.s. at this time, but in England the classic sports cars such as Aston Martin, Frazer Nash, H.R.G., and Lagonda stuck to conventional suspension. Independent rear suspension was much rarer, although Mercedes-Benz fitted it to all their models from 1935 onwards, and it was widely used by Central European manufacturers such as Austro-Daimler, Skoda, and Tatra, even on their humblest family saloons. The only British car to have i.r.s. was the advanced Atalanta of 1937–1939.

Tyre design changed gradually during the period, the tyres becoming wider and fatter, with an accompanying reduction in pressure from an average of 35lb psi in 1929 to 26lb psi in 1937. By the mid-thirties, tread design had become a scientific study, resulting in new patterns aimed at reduced skidding and more silent running. Although not so vital with sports cars, the latter was becoming an important factor on such cars as the Rolls-Royce, whose silence of engine showed up the noise made by the old knobbly tyres of the 1920s.

One of the most important developments of the thirties was the appearance of the relatively cheap sports car based on a mass-produced chassis, the two most obvious examples being the Wolseley Hornet and the M.G. M-type Midget, both of which were derived from the Morris Minor. On the whole their buyers were those who wanted to look like sportsmen without the expense or the driving ability demanded by the genuine sports car. This led to a proliferation of accessories with which the 'promenader', as he was disdainfully called by the real enthusiast, could deck his small car. Chrome-plated stoneguards for headlamps and radiator, leather straps to hold down the bonnet, fold-flat aero windscreens, 'mechanic's grip' on the passenger side of the dashboard – all made their appearance on the cheaper sporting car. Useful for really fast competition machinery, they had little point on a car which was hard put to exceed 65mph. They were very much a part of the 1930s scene, though, and the two-toned Wolseley Hornet Special festooned with accessories often carried off prizes at the Concours d'Elegance held at Hastings, Bournemouth, Torquay, or Blackpool.

Generalizations are always dangerous, but one can say that there were four main types of sporting motorcar made in the 'thirties. First, the cheap derivation of a mass-produced family car, already mentioned. This was the least attractive to the keen driver, and yet the most successful from the point of view of sales. Their weaknesses lay in their inheritance from the mass-produced saloon which itself was an unsatisfactory car in many ways. The small 6-cylinder engine chosen for the saloon in the interests of smoothness, led in the sports car to immoderately high revving resulting in noise and heavy fuel consumption. Because of the short chassis these engines were often mounted well forward over the front axle, which led to poor steering and roadholding. Nevertheless they gave pleasure to many owners, and set a fashion which has remained particularly British right up to the present day. The success of the British sports car in the United States after World War 2 was almost entirely due to the M.G. TC Midget which was a direct descendant of the M-type Midget of 1930.

Another type which received its share of brickbats, both at the time and from historians, was the Anglo-American Sports Hybrid. These cars, of which Railton, Brough Superior, and Jensen were the best known, combined powerful, slow-revving American engines with traditional British coach-work, and the results often looked very handsome. Unfortunately, their sponsors were, without exception, small firms, and could not afford to make all the desirable changes to the American chassis with its soft suspension and low-geared steering. Although some had remarkable performance, they tended to put on weight as the decade advanced, and became more expensive 'promenade cars', popular with the film and theatrical world.

The third category one can call the traditional sports car, and this included most of the venerated marques such as Alvis, Aston Martin, Frazer Nash, Bugatti, Lagonda, Talbot, the earlier Alfa-Romeos, as well as the new makes of H.R.G. and Squire. These carried on the vintage tradition of sturdy construction, hand finish and firm suspension by semi-elliptic leaf springs, but inevitably they were becoming outdated by 1938, and were giving place to the fourth category. Mostly from the European mainland, this was a new breed of sports car using independent suspension, tubular frame, and light metal construction. Examples were the later, all-independently sprung Alfa-Romeos, Delahaye, the sports Mercedes-Benz, and Type 328 B.M.W. Some of the German cars were using aerodynamic bodies tested in wind tunnels, notable examples being the B.M.W.s built for the 1940 Mille Miglia. An English latecomer to this group was the all-independent Atalanta with 4-cylinder or Lincoln-Zephyr V-12 engines. Some purists moan about the decadance of the sports car in the late 1930s, but cars such as these were encouraging pointers to the direction in which design was going. Had the war not intervened the traditional sports car builders would have brought out modernized designs, and indeed there were some interesting prototypes running, two examples being the Aston Martin Atom, and the Type 64 Bugatti.

After World War 2 these trends continued, and until the mid-1950s sports car design followed logically the pattern set by more advanced cars of 1939. Independent front suspension soon became so widespread as to occasion no special comment, while independent suspension of the rear wheels was increasingly adopted on the higher performance cars of the 1950s. All-enveloping coachwork such as had been seen on the 'tank' Bugattis of 1936 was universal on Italian cars by 1950, and soon the traditional narrow

The start of a J.C.C. race at Brooklands, 9 July 1939, showing the wide variety of cars which took part in such events. From right to left: Aston Martin Ulster, Essex Terraplane saloon, Alvis 12/70, another Ulster, A.C. 16/80, Frazer Nash, 1932 Ford V-8, a 'special', Atalanta V-12, two S.S. 100s and a Lagonda drophead coupé. (Photo: Montagu Motor Museum)

body and separate wings of such cars as the Lago-Talbot were replaced by streamlined designs. The structure of the sports car changed too; the conventional frame with side members was replaced by a built-up space frame of small-diameter tubes which formed the basis of both body and chassis, the former being covered by light alloy panelling. One of the first examples of this was the Tojeiro-designed A.C. Ace, which was also a pioneer of the modern sports car in having all-round independent suspension. Many of the new small firms used moulded fibreglass for their bodywork. This enabled firms of limited resources to produce attractively streamlined designs in quite small quantities. However, fibreglass is not very flexible, and any lack of torsional stiffness in the frame resulted in the appearance of ominous cracks in the bodywork.

In engine design, the twin overhead camshaft layout became almost universal for high performance engines, some expensive V-8s and V-12s having a total of four camshafts, two for each bank of cylinders. A large number of firms specializing in engine tuning sprang up, and the intense rivalry between these greatly advanced the study of gas flow in the cylinder head, camshaft design, and other aids to performance. For the first time, there was a direct 'feed-back' from the world of racing to that of the popular car, as engineers with racing experience modified the design of popular saloons. Cars such as the Lotus-Cortina, Brabham-Viva, Dauphine-Gordini, and Fiat-Abarth were examples of this, a trend which had no pre-war equivalent.

The major development in braking was the introduction of the disc brake derived from aircraft brakes produced by the Dunlop Rubber Company during the war. These were first seen in sports car racing on the 1952 Jaguar, and undoubtedly contributed to that make's success at Le Mans. The Jaguar drivers could delay the application of the brakes to a point 300 yards nearer the hairpin at the end of the Mulsanne straight than their rivals could. The advantage of a disc brake is not that its retardation for one application is better than that of a good drum brake, but that its fade is negligible even after repeated applications. In the 1960s discs became standard on the front wheels even for modestly priced sports cars such as the Austin-Healey Sprite, and most high performance cars had discs all round.

With socialist governments in a number of European countries it might have been expected that the more expensive cars would die out, but this has certainly not happened in the field of the sports car. Though the custom-built limousine dwindled during the 1950s, and all but disappeared in the following decade, a succession of glamorous sports cars has been made. They have seldom sold more than a few hundred per year, but have found enough buyers to keep the firms going. The customer for the top price car has changed from the dowager to the successful younger business man, while the increasing affluence and youth of the entertainment world has undoubtedly helped the sales of the more exotic cars.

It was among the more expensive Italian cars that the first examples of the Gran Turismo coupé appeared. This was not entirely a new type, for fast, closed two-seaters had been made in pre-war days, but mainly as custom bodies on chassis such as the Type 50 Bugatti, and in very small numbers. In performance and handling the new GT coupés were the equals of the open sports cars, and indeed their aerodynamic shape often gave the GTs a slight advantage in maximum speed over the open two-seaters. The increased comfort of the closed body obviously extended the appeal of such cars, and just as the saloon took over from the tourer in the early 1930s, so the GT coupé is replacing the open two-seater in the 1960s. The scope of the high

Finish of the 1956 Mille Miglia, last but one of these classic events. Castellotti's Ferrari is seen leading Cabianca's Osca 1500.
(Photo: Paul Popper Ltd)

performance car is greatly extended, efficient heaters enabling it to be used in below zero winter temperatures. The growth of the motorway system all over Europe encourages the business executive to drive to his appointments instead of being tied to the time-tables of railways or aeroplanes. The GT coupé has been called 'the businessman's express', and while some may object to this definition, there is no doubt that many are bought for business use, part of their cost and running expenses being tax-deductible. This is not to say that they do not make ideal pleasure cars too, but if the makers had to rely only on buyers who paid for their cars out of personal income their sales' picture might be much less encouraging.

In early post-war years, both open and closed sports cars competed in major races such as Le Mans and the Mille Miglia, their engines highly tuned, but their design basically similar to that of the cars which could be bought by the public. In smaller club events, cars like the Jaguar XK 120 and Healey Silverstone were perfectly capable of being driven to the event, raced and driven home. However, in the early 1950s a number of firms began to prepare special sports cars for racing, and their rivals had to follow suit or abandon the struggle. One who took the latter course was Frazer Nash. Their Le Mans Replica had been very successful on road and track from 1948 to 1954, but the small firm found that they could not meet competition from the specialist breed of sports/racing cars, so they withdrew from active support of racing. Other, wealthier, firms such as Aston Martin and Jaguar pursued very successful careers with specialized cars such as the DBR 1, and C- and D-types respectively, but by 1959 they, too, found that sports car racing had become too expensive and divorced from road-going machines, and ceased to make competition cars. In Italy Alfa Romeo and Lancia both built prototype sports cars in the mid-1950s, but soon abandoned them, leaving the field to Ferrari and Maserati. Both these firms built a variety of competition machines, front and mid-engined; Ferrari mid-engined cars were reflected in the Dino production coupé, but so far Maserati have kept the engine ahead of the driver on all their production cars. From the mid-1960s onwards most important competition sports cars have been in the prototype category, quite unsuitable for use on the road. They are often referred to as Group 6 cars, as they fall into Group 6 of the F.I.A. (Federation Internationale de l'Automobile) classification. The Federation divided competition cars into nine groups, ranging from Production cars (Group 1) of which at least 5,000 had to be made, to Formule Libre racing cars (Group 9). In the prototype sports category there was no stipulation about production figures, actual or intended. The regulations went no further than saying that 'their use on open roads may be foreseen, and in that case the cars must include all equipment normally provided, and legally required, for vehicles using public roads.' Thus Group 6 cars all had headlamps and horns, but luggage space and spare wheels were optional. In 1968 there was a capacity limit of 3 litres for these cars. Even more specialized were the Group 7 cars whose all-enveloping bodies gave them the superficial appearance of sports cars, but they were in fact classified as two-seater racing cars, built exclusively for races on closed circuits. In this book they are dealt with only in passing, although some had interesting developments in the field of sports cars. The Chevrolet-powered Lola GT 70 was originally an open Group 7 car, but a closed version was built for sports car racing, and with the necessary equipment and number built (twenty-five) it came into Group 4 ('sports cars', as opposed to 'prototype sports cars'). In 1969 a road-going version was to be offered for sale to the public. For 1970 a slight modification of the F.I.A. classification has been announced. Sports cars (minimum of twenty-five built) will be known as Group 5 instead of Group 4. Prototypes will remain in Group 6, still with a capacity limit of 3 litres.

One of the first sports cars built exclusively for track work was the Cooper-Climax of 1955. This carried its engine behind the driver, following the fashion of Cooper racing cars. With this design, John Cooper and his team at Surbiton started a trend which was completely to alter the layout of high performance cars. Lotus followed suit with Grand Prix cars in 1960, while Ferrari turned to rear engine location for sports racing cars in 1958, and Maserati in 1961. Up to about 1965 road-going sports cars were mostly front-engined, but all recent designs have followed the lead set by Cooper ten years earlier. Strictly speaking, these cars are not rear-engined but mid-engined, as they carry the engine behind the driver but ahead of the rear axle. This layout was originally seen only on the most expensive cars, but the trend has spread to smaller cars such as the Lotus Europa and Matra M.530. The mass-producers have so far avoided the mid-engine, but Fiat are known to be interested in the Autobianchi prototype shown at Turin in November 1968, while collaboration between Volkswagen and Porsche has now resulted in a popularly-priced mid-engined design. Within the next ten years all sports cars worthy of the name will probably be mid-engined coupés, although it will be sad if the front-engined open two-seater ever completely disappears. However, the manufacture of such cars is largely confined to Great Britain, and all the current representatives, such as Austin-Healey Sprite, Triumph TR 6, Morgan and Jaguar E-type, are ageing designs. In America the Chevrolet Corvette continues the tradition, but the 1968 'dream car' Chevrolet, the Astro 2, was a mid-engined coupé, and it is unlikely that the conventional Corvette will survive for more than two or three seasons.

Increasing speed limits in many countries have led people to question the future of the high performance car in any form at all. What is the point, they ask, of building a car capable of 180mph, when the driver is breaking the law at half that speed? It is true that maximum speed figures are becoming increasingly academic, but no-one can legislate against acceleration and road-holding, and the sports car will continue to justify its existence on these attributes. It is often said that we live in an increasingly conformist age, but while the extremes of wealth and eccentricity may be disappearing, there are more people than ever before with the money and leisure to appreciate the kind of motoring which is a sport rather than a necessity.

Part One
The Emergence of
the Sports Car

'In the beginning they were all sports cars' is a popular phrase which people use to stress the sporting character of the pioneer motorists. It is often said that early cars were playthings of the rich, amusing toys for the sportsman who had grown tired of horses. In fact this was probably less true in the pioneer days before the turn of the century than in any later era. Most of the pioneer car builders were middle-class engineers of no great wealth, while the few rich enthusiasts like Sir David Salomons, the Hon Evelyn Ellis and the Comte de Dion took the movement intensely seriously, as indeed they had to, in the face of the fanatical hostility which motors aroused in many influential quarters. There was not much sign in the 1890s of the devil-may-care playboy attitude of Louis Zborowski or L. C. le Champion. Indeed, the early motorists had a good deal in common with the early Christians, spreading the 'gospel' wherever they could, rejoicing over new converts, especially if they were influential like the Prince of Wales, and commiserating with each other on the many persecutions that came their way. They undoubtedly had a lot of fun too, but even when racing had become a regular part of the calendar, it was the utility of the motorcar of which they were most proud. The value of motors to the tradesman, to the commercial traveller, to the doctor and to the farmer was stressed over and over again in the new journals such as *The Autocar, The Automotor Journal, La France Automobile* and *The Horseless Age.* It is significant that until well into the 1900s the lorry and the bus were featured alongside the latest racing cars and voiturettes.

The Paris-Rouen Motor Trial of 1894, known at the time as the 'Concours du Petit Journal', is generally considered to be the first motor competition, and from it sprang the great town-to-town races which spread the fame and notoriety of the motorcar through Europe. Usually starting from Paris, they raced to Bordeaux and back in 1895, to Marseilles and back in 1896, to Amsterdam and back in 1898, while by 1901 the destination was as far away as Berlin, and in 1902, Vienna. The series ended in 1903 with the tragic Paris-Madrid race which was stopped at Bordeaux after several drivers and spectators had lost their lives. During this period the racing car had emerged as a distinct type, much more powerful than the ordinary touring car, but still capable of being driven on the road. The dictum that 'the racing car of today is the touring car of tomorrow' was never truer than in the first five years of this century. Gabriel's 80hp Mors of 1901, winner of the Paris-Berlin race, was fitted with a 60hp engine and a four-seater tonneau body, and used for several years on the road. This practice of making fast tourers out of old racing cars continued up to 1914, examples including a 1905 Gordon Bennett Siddeley, 1908 Grand Prix Austin, 1908 T.T. Darracq, and 1908 Grand Prix Weigel. An example which still exists is the 1908 Grand Prix Itala, equipped with a touring body in about 1909, and today owned by Cecil Clutton. Much rarer was the conversion of a touring car into a racing car; it is appropriate that one of the very few examples of this concerned the famous 60hp Mercedes. The team of three 90hp Mercedes for the 1903 Gordon Bennett Race in Ireland was destroyed in a factory fire less than a month before the race. Three standard 60hp chassis were borrowed from the firm's Paris agent, and on one

A sporting 12/16hp Sunbeam seen at the Caerphilly Hill Climb of the South Wales Automobile Club. (Photo: Montagu Motor Museum)

of these Camille Jenatzy won the race against opposition from nine special racing cars.

These powerful cars, equally suitable for racing or touring, could well be thought of as the first sports cars, although they were never known by that name. Touring Trials, as opposed to races, had been held since before 1900, but in the earliest of these the aim was simply to demonstrate that motor cars could travel distances of 1,000 miles or more with reasonable reliability. Cars of all kinds down to the 25mph 3½hp De Dion-Bouton voiturette took part, and these events did little to develop a sporting breed of car. The same applies to the first series of Tourist Trophy races, in which the cars were stock tourers with four-seater bodies.

Probably the first events which led to the development of a sporting road car were the Herkomer and Prince Henry Tours, held in Germany from 1905 to 1911. The former, to give its full name, the International Touring Car Competition for the Herkomer Trophy, consisted of a road section of some 500 miles, from Frankfurt-am-Main to Innsbruck, a hill-climb at Semmering, and a speed trial over 5½km at the finish. As well as the Trophy, the winner would have his portrait painted by the sponsor of the competition, Professor Hubert von Herkomer, R.A. The competitors in the 1905 event were ordinary heavy touring cars, some with closed bodywork, and the event attracted little attention. It was won by a 40hp Mercedes. In 1906, however, no marks were awarded for coachwork, and competitors were quick to take advantage of this. Canvas flaps appeared in place of doors, seats were sketchy, and some cars had flared wings. H. Massac Buist, writing in *The Autocar*, complained that some of the drivers of Continental cars adopted scorching tactics, 'the drivers proceeding from the very starting line with open exhausts', and emitting clouds of blue, black, and yellow smoke. It was regrettable, he said, that a reliability trial pure and simple, which is laid down in the regulations under which the British amateurs have been induced to enter, should be turned into ungentlemanly racing. Alas for British sportsmanship, the first nine places were filled by German cars, the winner being Doctor Rudolf Stöss, who was driving an 18/20hp Horch. At 2·7 litres, this had one of the smallest engines in the entry list, but it was an advanced unit with overhead inlet and side exhaust valves, and ball-bearings throughout. In appearance it was hardly a sports car, yet it foreshadowed the cars which became so prominent in the next five years.

One of the competitors in the Herkomer Tours was Prince Henry of Prussia, younger brother of the Kaiser. He was a keen motorist and amateur mechanic, and was said to set an example to the scorching type of Continental driver whom English journals were so fond of deriding. The last Herkomer Tour took place in June 1907, and a few months later Prince Henry announced that he would present a trophy for a touring car event. The cars had to be four-seaters, and cylinder bore was restricted to 146mm for 4-cylinder engines, and to 120mm for 6-cylinder engines. Trade entrants were excluded which *The Autocar* thought a very proper step: 'There is unfortunately in the Trade a certain number of men whose ideas of gentlemanly behaviour are crude, which naturally tends to detract from the value of such trials.' In anticipation, at any rate, the first Prince Henry Trial was expected to be such a peaceful, unhurried affair that it was recommended to those who wanted a motoring holiday in Germany without language difficulties and at a reasonable cost. In fact, the event attracted few British entrants, and only one British-made car, a 45hp 6-cylinder Napier driven by Miss Dorothy Levitt. When the competitors assembled at the start, at Berlin on June 7th, 1908, it was evident that many professional drivers had slipped

1. Above: *1911 Vauxhall Prince Henry 3-litre tourer.* (Photo: Vauxhall Motors Ltd)

2. Below: *1914 Abadal 15·9hp sporting tourer. Coachwork by Navarro of Lisbon. Owned and photographed by João de Lacerda.*

24

in despite Prince Henry's stipulations, while the appearance of some of the cars was far more exotic than any of the Herkomer entrants had been. Most distinctive were the Horches; they had four-seater bodies of what came to be known as a torpedo type, with a cowl between front and rear passengers, no doors, and wings so flared that they looked like surf boards. There were no windscreens, or any kind of hood for the passengers. British journalists, used to the high, wide, *Roi-des-Belges* tourer of the time, were most uncomplimentary about the Horches and other 'streamlined cars', not realising that they were being treated to a glimpse of the future. It is interesting that while the British correspondents were so rude about the Prince Henry cars, the German and Austrian papers call them *das idealer Tourenwagen*. Touring cars they may not have been, but embryo sports cars they certainly were. It was the ingenious circumvention of the rules which led to progress. Had Prince Henry's regulations been strictly adhered to, his name would never have been perpetuated in connection with the development of the sports car.

The event was won by Fritz Erle in a 50hp Benz whose body was less startling than those of the Horches, but still had the flared wings and streamlined scuttle of the later sports cars. Willy Poege's Mercedes, which was second, had no wings at all, and looked not unlike a Grand Prix car with a four-seater body. A number of unknown drivers who later achieved fame took part in this first Prince Henry Trial, including Ettore Bugatti, who is said to have fallen asleep at the wheel of his Deutz and driven it into a tree, and young Count Kolowrat, who drove a Laurin und Klement.

The 1909 Prince Henry Tour produced no startling motorcars, and was little more than a leisurely drive, but the 1910 event saw the appearance of two excellent sporting cars, one in Austria and one in England. The Prince Henry Austro-Daimler was the first significant car to be made by the Austrian firm, and was also the first internationally famous design of Ferdinand Porsche who was later responsible for the Mercedes-Benz S-series sports cars and for the Volkswagen. The engine had four separately-cast cylinders of 105×165mm, giving a capacity of 5,714cc. At 1,900rpm the power output was 86bhp, but the engine was capable of speeds of up to 2,300rpm. Inclined overhead valves were operated by a single overhead camshaft, and the specification included twin magnetos and light steel pistons. Altogether the engine was of the best contemporary design, although not in any way radical. The chassis was conventional, although the chain drive was an archaic feature. The Austro-Daimlers were the only chain-driven cars in the 1910 Prince Henry event. No less than eleven cars were entered in the Tour, of which two were works entries, and Austro-Daimlers took the first three places. The winning car was appropriately driven by Porsche himself. The model was put on the market as the sporting side of the Austro-Daimler range, which included touring cars from 16hp to 50/60hp. The earlier Prince Henry cars and other high performance machines dating back to the 1903 Mercedes could be called touring cars with lighter bodywork, or superannuated racing cars, but the Austro-Daimler was a special sporting model, differing noticeably from the side-valve, shaft-drive touring cars, all of which were cheaper, even the massive 120×154mm 50/60hp. About 200 Prince Henrys were made between 1910 and 1914, later models being known as 27/80s in England. Shaft drive was introduced on the 1912 models, and a handsome V-radiator introduced at about the same time distinguished it from the staider touring cars. It was usually fitted with a comfortable open four-seater body, with full weather protection, ideal for long-distance touring. Some two-seaters were also built (not supplied by the factory), but there were few freakish designs mounted on this chassis.

·3. *1912 Austrian Daimler Prince Henry 27/80hp tourer. Owned by C. J. Bendall. (Photo: Charles Pocklington)*

27

The other sporting car to appear in the 1910 Prince Henry Trial was the 3-litre Vauxhall. This was developed from the 20hp car of 1908, designed by Laurence Pomeroy, which won the 2,000 Mile Trial of that year. In itself, this was not a particularly remarkable design, giving about 38bhp and a maximum speed of 50mph, but it was Vauxhall's first L-head engine, and was suitable for tuning. Pomeroy was particularly interested in raising crankshaft speeds, and by 1910 this engine could produce 60bhp at 2,800rpm. To accompany this increase in power, the Prince Henry Vauxhalls had very different bodies from the staid 1908 tourer. Their radiators were sharply pointed, and there was a straight-through line from the bonnet to the scuttle. The low four-seater body had no doors. Their performance in the Trial was not the spectacular success of the Austro-Daimlers, but two of the three cars entered made non-stop runs, while the third was only slightly delayed. A few Prince Henry type cars came into private hands late in 1910, and a four-seater tourer was exhibited at Olympia in 1911. The standard model had no doors and a bulbous back, but a modified version, also supplied by the

The best-known survivor among the converted racing cars is the 1908 Itala. The 12-litre 4-cylinder car is seen here in the hands of J. A. Williamson:
(Photo: Bruce Edwards)

factory, had small doors extending about half way down the body sides, and a straighter back. It was hardly a touring car in which to take maiden aunt or prospective mother-in-law for a country drive, but it offered four seats and as much performance as any sportsman could reasonably expect from a car costing only £580. The Prince Henry Vauxhall soon established a good reputation for sensitive handling, smooth running, and flexible top gear performance. It was one of the first cars to combine docility and power. For 1913 a larger 3,964cc engine was used, giving 75bhp at a slightly lower engine speed of 2,500rpm, and this new engine allowed more comfortable bodywork to be fitted to the Prince Henry, with no loss of performance. The beautiful tourer owned for many years by Laurence Pomeroy Jnr, son of the car's designer, is one of these later Prince Henrys. For ordinary road work, this design would have been quite adequate for several more years, but Vauxhalls supported a sporting programme, not only of Coupe de l'Auto and Grand Prix racing cars, but also entering regularly in hill-climbs such as Shelsley Walsh, Sutton Bank, and Pateley Bridge. By 1913 the Prince Henry

Above: *Dr Rudolf Stöss at the wheel of his 18/20hp Horch with which he won the 1906 Herkomer Trophy. Beside him is August Horch.*
(Photo: Friedrich Heil Collection)

Above right: *Dr Stöss again, this time in a 1908 Prince Henry Horch.*
(Photo: Friedrich Heil Collection)

Two other entrants in the 1908 Prince Henry Trials:
An Opel (below) *with sketchy body and* (below right) *a Rex Simplex with curious flared wings.*
(Photos: Friedrich Heil Collection)

could no longer hold its own in these events, and a larger, more powerful engine was developed at the suggestion of John Higginson, a well-known competitions driver, to be used in the Prince Henry chassis. This had dimensions of 98 × 150mm, and the car was known as the 30/98. The probable explanation for the name is that the engine developed 30bhp at 1,000rpm, and a theoretical 98bhp at its maximum speed of 3,000rpm. It was essentially a competition car, and non-works cars were only supplied to a few buyers who could be relied on to enhance the company's image in competitions. The most successful of these was Higginson who made ftd at Waddington Pike, Shelsley Walsh, and Aston Clinton, all in 1913. Not more than a dozen 30/98s were sold before war broke out; apart from the company's reluctance to sell them to all and sundry, the price of £900 for a chassis compared with £580 for the excellent Prince Henry was an obvious deterrent. After the war, of course, the 30/98 became the standard sporting Vauxhall model.

The Prince Henrys all had V-radiators to distinguish them from the staider Vauxhalls, but the 30/98 reverted to a flat radiator slightly rounded at the top, whose design hardly changed up to the end of production in 1927. This gave better cooling than the pointed version and the Prince Henrys entered for the 1914 Alpine Trial also used this flatter design. Like the 30/98 in the 1920s, the Prince Henry enjoyed good export sales, especially to

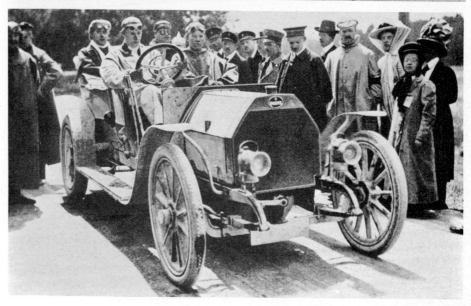

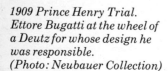
Above: *A 50hp Benz of the type which won the 1908 Prince Henry Trial.* (*Photo: Friedrich Heil Collection*)

Above right: *'... not unlike a Grand Prix car with four-seater body.' Poege's Mercedes storming a hill during the 1908 Prince Henry Trial.* (*Photo: Neubauer Collection*)

1909 Prince Henry Trial. Ettore Bugatti at the wheel of a Deutz for whose design he was responsible. (*Photo: Neubauer Collection*)

Australia. In 1914 a two-seater driven by Murray Aunger made the journey from Melbourne to Adelaide in just under 15 hours, beating the previous record by four hours. Its average speed was nearly 40mph, a remarkable performance considering the appalling roads.

The Vauxhalls and the Austro-Daimlers were notable in that they represented the sporting end of a bread-and-butter range of cars, and in the years from 1911 to 1914 numerous other manufacturers began to develop similar machines. No longer was the fastest car in the catalogue necessarily the largest, as had been the case from the earliest days of motoring. Tuned, high-speed engines and lighter chassis and bodies took the place of sheer size, and so the true sporting car was born. Today the popular conception of a sports car is of a two-seater, but practically all the fine sporting cars of the late Edwardian era were normally seen as four-seaters. Two-seater bodies might be supplied by special coach-builders on such chassis as the Prince Henry models of Vauxhall and Austro-Daimler, Shelsley Crossley, and sporting 12/16 Sunbeam, but they were the exception, and where the car makers also supplied the bodies, they were almost invariably four-seaters. It is dangerous to generalize, but one can say that to a large extent the sporting car of up to 3-litres capacity was inspired by the French voiturette races such as the Coupe de l'Auto, while the larger cars were bred for events such as the Austrian Alpine and Swedish Winter Trials.

The Coupe de l'Auto races were sponsored by the French magazine *l'Auto*, in order to encourage the sporting light car. The early races of the series, from 1905 to 1909, produced very light voiturettes with one or two cylinders, while from 1910 to 1914 new regulations encouraged some excellent 4-cylinder cars of up to 3-litres capacity. The voiturette design was governed by the regulations which limited the cylinder bore to a figure varying between 80mm and 90mm for twins, and to 65mm for 4-cylinder engines. As no limit was placed on the length of the stroke, designers gained maximum capacity by using immensely long strokes. These verged on the ludicrous by 1910, when the 2-cylinder Lion-Peugeot VX-5 had dimensions of 80 × 280mm. The bonnet was so high that driver and mechanic had to peer round it in

*A Prince Henry Vauxhall on the Coppice, near Accrington. At the point where the photograph was taken the gradient was said to be 1 in 2·6, but the Vauxhall re-started successfully.
(Photo: Autocar)*

*One of the few Vauxhall 30/98s built before the war.
(Photo: Montagu Motor Museum)*

The Prince Henry Vauxhall which averaged nearly 40mph between Melbourne and Adelaide. Murray Aunger at the wheel.
(Photo: Montagu Motor Museum)

1907 Sizaire-Naudin two-seater.
(Photo: Montagu Motor Museum)

order to see where they were going. Despite this problem, coupled with a very high centre of gravity, Jules Goux's car was second in the Coupe de l'Auto. These more extreme designs were racing cars pure and simple, and were not offered to the public, but a number of interesting machines built for the Coupe de l'Auto did come onto the market. One of the most successful light cars in racing was the Sizaire-Naudin, first offered for sale in 1905. It had a single-cylinder engine of 918cc, and an old fashioned armoured-wood chassis. A modern feature, and very rare at the time, was independent front suspension by transverse leaf springs and sliding pillars. The marque's first major race was the 1906 Coupe des Voiturettes, in which Georges Sizaire, brother of designer Maurice, drove for the whole race, and won at an average speed of 36·2mph. Another car, driven by Louis Naudin this time, won the 1907 Sicilian Cup voiturette race. Encouraged by this success, the firm entered three cars for the 1907 Coupe de Voiturettes, and took first and second places. They repeated this performance in 1908, and backed up their

1911 de Dion-Bouton type CP Type de Course. This car has completed over 11,000 miles in the hands of its present owner Mr John Dymond. (Photo: John Dymond)

racing victories with numerous successes at hill-climb and sprint events. This was the ideal formula for selling this type of car, besides which the Sizaire-Naudin was very good value at the equivalent of £120 in France and £178 in England. It was one of the first cheap, light, sporting cars with real performance, including a speed of up to 50mph. Kent Karslake has given a charming account of the one which he owned in the 1930s, in the pioneer days of the V.S.C.C. (Vintage Sports Car Club): '. . . in its early stages the opening of the throttle seldom seemed to effect much change in the situation. Suddenly, however, . . . the Sizaire would take a full gulp of mixture which it really appreciated, and with a series of resounding *plop-plop-plops* it would go bounding off down the road.' Sales of the single-cylinder continued up to 1911, the capacity now enlarged to over 1,500cc (120 × 140mm). Four-cylinder cars of less sporting character then came into the range, soon after which the Sizaire brothers left the firm anyway.

The well-known firm of De Dion-Bouton made very few competition cars at any time, but their single-cylinder long stroke engines had been used with success by other makers in the Coupe de l'Auto races, so for 1909 they listed a *Type de Course* two-seater roadster powered by a 100 × 150mm engine developing 18bhp at 2,200rpm. With its raked steering column, bucket seats, and bolster tank, it looked very sporting, but its performance was sluggish compared with that of the Sizaire-Naudin.

A remarkable British car which used the De Dion engine was the Jackson 'Black Demon'. Originally this had an engine with the astonishing dimensions of 104 × 213mm, known as the 7/27hp. The bonnet was slipper-shaped, coming to a sharp point at the front, while it was so high that the driver had almost to peer round it. Six months after its first appearance in November 1909, the firm advertised that 'orders can now be taken for early delivery of Black Demons', but it is unlikely that many orders were forthcoming. Jackson also made other De Dion-engined sporting cars, with dimensions of 100 × 130mm, or 100 × 200mm, the former being known as the 'Little Long Bonnet No. 8'.

Most of the earlier voiturettes were crude machines which went into very limited production, if at all, but a notable exception was the 1908 Isotta Fraschini. Unlike most of the voiturettes, it had a 4-cylinder engine of

Above: *A 'boy's racer' par excellence was the 1909 Jackson Black Demon.* (Photo: Motor)

Above right: *1911 Isotta Fraschini 10hp two-seater, driven by Mrs Bradburne of the Dorset Automobile Club.* (Photo: Autocar)

1,327cc, with overhead valves operated by a single overhead camshaft. Maximum engine speed was 3,500rpm, a quite remarkable figure for the time. It did not attract a great deal of attention, although it was put into limited production in 1908, and was a catalogued model for the next two years at least. The British list price was £285, which does not seem excessive for such a high quality light car, but it probably appeared about five years too early to be properly appreciated. Small cars meant cheap cars to the average buyer of 1908. However a few were sold in England, and a Mrs Bradburne drove one with great success in competitions organised by the Dorset Automobile Club.

It has been suggested that the small Isottas were designed by, or influenced by, Ettore Bugatti, but there is no conclusive evidence in favour of this theory. The overhead camshaft design was not an innovation for Isotta, whose designer Giustino Cattaneo had used it on a 120hp racing car as early as 1905, two years before the link between Isottas and Lorraine-Dietrich which is given as the reason for Bugatti's influence. This link itself is somewhat shadowy, and seems to stem from the slump in the Italian motor industry which coincided with the need by Lorraine-Dietrich for expansion. They planned to have their cars built in England, by Ariel of Birmingham, and in Italy *chez* Isotta Fraschini. Nothing permanent seems to have emerged from either of these arrangements, although some sources claim that some Isottas of 1907 to 1908 were really Lorraine-Dietrichs. Ettore Bugatti was certainly associated with Lorraine-Dietrich a few years earlier, but had severed his connection with them by 1907. However it is very likely that he was able to examine closely the 10hp Isotta, and when the first production car to bear his own name appeared, it bore a striking resemblance to the Italian car.

The prototype of the car was built by Bugatti at his own expense, it is said in the cellar of his home at Cologne, during 1908, and towards the end of 1909 he moved into a disused dye-works at Molsheim, and began production. The engine was a 4-cylinder overhead camshaft unit of 1,327cc, with curved, sliding tappets operating the overhead valves. Three wheelbase lengths were offered, 6ft 6½in (Type 13), 7ft 10in (Type 15), and 8ft 4½in (Type 17). Of these, the Type 13 became the best known, and was the most sporting. In *The Autocar* report on the 1910 Paris Salon, the reporter wrote that 'a little Bugatti and a little Bédélia seemed most delightful looking runabouts.' He evidently did not look very closely, for he continued 'in these, two people can sit one in front of the other'. In any case the comparison of the jewel-like Type 13 with a crude, noisy cyclecar (see page 47) would be enough to cause apoplexy among today's Bugatti-fanciers. Surprisingly little notice was taken of this excellent little car which from the very first had the Bugatti qualities of precision of steering and lightness of control. Cecil Clutton has written of a surviving example, 'it is essentially to be controlled with fingers and toes rather than with the hands and feet. The gear lever is flicked rather than pushed or pulled.' It was streets ahead of any other small car of the time, and of most larger cars, but although Bugatti designs were well up to standard by 1914, there was little sign of the enthusiasm which the marque was to excite ten years later.

Another high performance light car from Germany (people sometimes forget that the Alsatian-built Bugatti was a German car up to 1918) was the Apollo. Designed by Karl Slevogt, the Type B had a small 4-cylinder overhead valve engine which gave 12bhp from its 1,030cc, and had a maximum speed of 45mph. A special racing version gave over 20bhp. Bodies of the Type B, and its larger brother the 2-litre Type R, were elegant torpedos, remarkably effective scaled-down versions of the bodies found on larger Teutonic cars like Horch. A Type R won the 1913 San Sebastian Rally. One or two other German firms, notably Hansa, made small sporting cars, but on the whole the large torpedo tourer held sway in Germany until well after World War I.

From 1911 to 1913 the Coupe de l'Auto Race was for cars of up to 3 litres, and a number of the racing cars formed the basis of medium-sized sporting cars for the public. One of the most notable of these was the 12/16 Sunbeam. The 1911 racing cars were, in fact, based on the standard touring chassis, although the T-head engine was replaced by an L-head layout, and the stroke lengthened from 120mm to 149mm. With a bore of 80mm, the capacity was 2,996cc, the dimensions being similar to those of the post-war 3-litre Bentley. Power was increased from about 25bhp to 58bhp at 2,400rpm. The body was an ugly streamlined affair, not redeemed by Rudge-Whitworth wire wheels. In the race the car retired, but its influence was obvious on the new 12/16

Below: *Ettore Bugatti's first masterpiece. This is a 1914 Type 17 on the largest of three wheelbases available. (Photo: C. W. P. Hampton)*

Below right: *1911 Apollo Type B with streamlined two-seater body. (Photo: Neubauer Collection)*

which was offered to the public at the 1911 Olympia Show. This had the side valve engine, stroke increased to 150mm (3,016cc), and there was a sporting tourer with wire wheels. At £425, it cost £50 more than the ordinary tourer. This model, in turn, was the basis for the 1912 racing cars, although the engine was considerably modified, and gave 73·7bhp at 2,700rpm. 1912 was the *annus mirabilis* for Sunbeam, three cars taking first, second, and third places in the Coupe de l'Auto. They never did as well again, but by the end of 1913 the sporting tourer was definitely part of the Sunbeam range. This was one of the more attractive sporting cars of the immediate pre-war period; its appearance was much lower than that of the ordinary tourers although full four-seater bodywork was available. With its wire wheels, flowing wings and 'lipped' radiator inherited from the racing cars, it had a strikingly light appearance. The bodies were designed by J. Keele Ltd of New Bond Street, London, who specialized in these sporting bodies. About a dozen of the sporting tourers were made up to the outbreak of war, and nothing as attractive emerged from the Sunbeam works for several years after the war.

The 1910 Coupe de l'Auto Race was won by a make new to racing, the Spanish Hispano-Suiza. Unlike previous Coupe de l'Auto winners, this Hispano had a 4-cylinder engine. Its designer, Marc Birkigt, clung to the long stroke principle, as any designer had to, in order to obtain a reasonable engine size. The dimensions were 65 × 200mm, and the capacity 2,655cc. Maximum power was over 60bhp. The valves were arranged in a T-head which was becoming outmoded by this date, but a modern feature was unit construction of engine and gearbox. This car was the basis of the Type 15T Hispano which was put into production in 1911, although for the production car the engine was enlarged to 80 × 180mm (3,620cc). This was the first really distinctive car to come from the Hispano factory, and also the first Spanish car to make any impression in other countries. One of the first customers was King Alfonso XIII who was already familiar with the products of Hispano-Suiza, having bought a 20hp chassis in 1905. In 1910 Alfonso received as a present from the Queen, 'to her august husband', a Type 15T. The model soon became known as the Alfonso, and as such was exported to

King Alfonso XIII leaving his palace in his Alfonso Hispano-Suiza. (Photo: Maurice Harrison Collection)

England, France and other countries. The market for expensive cars was much larger in France than in Spain, and in 1911 a factory was set up by Hispano at Levallois-Perret. Three years later they moved to Bois-Colombes which has been associated with Hispano-Suiza ever since, and where aero engines are still made today. Alfonsos were made in both factories, in France until the outbreak of war, and in Spain for a year or two longer. The Alfonso came in two wheelbase lengths, 8ft 8in, and 9ft 10in and two back axle ratios were available, giving 3·0 or 3·25 to 1 on top gear. The short-chassis cars were usually fairly stark two-seaters but tourer or even saloon bodies were mounted on the long chassis. As a sporting car it was very attractive, with an effortless and unfussy top gear performance, and a maximum speed of over 80mph for the short-chassis car. At £545 it was cheaper than a Prince Henry Vauxhall, and it was much less tiring on long journeys than the smaller two-seater cars. It was not revived after the war, as Hispano's policy turned to touring cars of maximum luxury, but in England at any rate the Alfonso commanded a good price on the secondhand market for a few years. Major W. T. Pitt entered his two-seater in an R.A.C. Rally as late as 1934, and toured Switzerland in it in 1946. Several Alfonsos competed in the early events of the Vintage Sports Car Club, soon after it was founded in 1934.

A lesser-known contemporary of the Alfonso was the Abadal, produced by another Barcelona firm, F. S. Abadel y Cia. Francisco Abadal was one of the leading dealers for Hispano-Suiza cars, and a very aggressive salesman. He constantly wrote letters to the press extolling Hispanos, and seems to have been something of a Spanish S. F. Edge. He is said to have introduced the Hispano to King Alfonso in 1905. Late in 1913, when the Alfonso Hispano was already well established, Abadal introduced a car bearing his own name, examples of which were exhibited at the Paris Salon that year. They had rakish V-radiators, and were fitted with the boat bodies that were so fashionable that year. The engine was remarkably similar to that of the Alfonso, having the same dimensions and T-head design, although the gearbox was separate. A multi-plate clutch was used, as on the earlier Alfonsos, and the semi-elliptic rear springs were also a feature of the early, short-wheelbase Alfonsos, rather than of the later ones. Altogether, there was little originality in the Abadal, although its V-radiator gave it a distinctive appearance. A licence to manufacture it in Belgium was taken up by the Imperia company, and ultimately, more Abadals were made in Belgium than in Spain. The name survived after the war in the Imperia-Abadal sports cars which achieved some success in local sports car races. Meanwhile Sr. Abadal, who was also a General Motors agent, turned to the production of heavily-disguised Buicks. The story of these, however, belongs to the post-war period.

Many other firms entered cars in the 1911–1913 Coup de l'Auto Races, but few of them followed the example of Sunbeam, Vauxhall and Hispano-Suiza in offering catalogued sporting cars. Manufacturers were still content to use racing as publicity for their ordinary touring cars, and the Coupe de l'Auto Arrol-Johnstons, Singers and Vinots had no counterparts in the catalogues. However, a firm that took little part in racing offered one of the best sporting cars of the period, the 15·9hp Shelsley Crossley. The first 15·9 (confusingly called the 12/14 by the makers), appeared in 1909, and had a 4-cylinder monobloc side-valve engine of 80 × 120mm, and a capacity of 2·6-litres. It was in no way a sporting car, although examples were entered in reliability trials and hill climbs soon after its introduction. Its most remarkable feature, and a very rare one at the time, was the use of Allen-Liversidge 4-wheel brakes. These were not satisfactory as the footbrake operated the front wheel brakes only, and to achieve balanced 4-wheel braking, foot brake and hand brake

A Crossley Shelsley two-seater
seen at the Manchester Motor
Club's hill climb at Buxton in
September 1913.
(Photo: Autocar)

had to be applied simultaneously and with equal pressure. This was beyond the average driver, and the application of brakes on the front wheels only resulted in damaged axles and springs, and loss of steering. In May 1913 the Shelsley sporting model appeared. This had a longer stroke (130mm), a rounded radiator, and in standard form, a smooth torpedo body like that of the sporting Sunbeam. Only the rounded radiator cars were called Shelsleys, although some flat radiator cars had sporting bodywork, and some Shelsleys had quite staid-looking coachwork, such as the Alford & Alder drop head coupé which S. F. Edge had built to his own designs. Like the standard 15·9, the Shelsley nearly always had wire wheels, although artilleries could be fitted, as indeed could a flat radiator, if the owner wanted to disguise the performance of his car. With a four-seater body the Shelsley was capable of 60mph, and could average 30 to 35mph over a long period on varied roads. At 30mph a fuel consumption of 30mpg was claimed. *The Autocar* said that the car's steering was 'something approaching perfection'.

The cars described were typical of the better medium-priced sporting cars available in 1914. There were several others, such as the 15hp Straker-Squire and 12/40hp D.F.P. The latter was not regarded as a sporting model by its makers, Doriot, Flandrin et Parant of Courbevoie, but in England it was tuned by W. O. Bentley and fitted with aluminium pistons which con-tributed to increase its power from 25bhp to 40bhp. Many other cars of sport-ing appearance were made between 1912 and 1915, but they were simply sporting bodies on perfectly standard chassis. They were usually torpedo tourers rather than two-seaters, and with wire wheels in place of artilleries,

Sporting bodies on touring chassis at the 1913 Olympia Motor Show. Above: *Mors sleeve-valve 17/20hp*; right: *Spyker 14/20hp.* (Photos: Autocar)

staid cars such as the sleeve-valve Mors, 14/20 Spyker, 14hp Hurtu, and 15·9hp Belsize looked quite sporting. In many cases the makers did not pretend that the sporting qualities went beyond looks. The sporting Briton, for example, was announced as having 'mechanical features almost identical to the standard model, but a greatly modified appearance. It is intended to meet the requirements of purchasers desiring a car of racy appearance.'

In continental Europe sporting bodywork took more extreme forms, notably the boat-shaped bodies of which a rash broke out at the 1913 Paris Salon. These had open bodies of more or less boat shape, and any number of marine accessories and fittings such as dummy copper rivets, portholes for bonnet ventilators, rowlocks in place of door handles, halyards and cleats to hold down the hood. One Alin et Liautard body on a Th. Schneider was clinker built, with alternate planks of light and dark wood, and even had a stern post. All this was a reflection of the snobbery of yacht-owning, just as was the wearing of yachting clothes by German motorists of a later era. On the whole these boat-bodied cars were not bought by serious sporting motorists, and were found generally on obscure, non-sporting chassis such as the D.S.P.L., S.C.A.P., and Vermorel.

The Coupe de l'Auto races bred some very fine medium-sized cars as we have seen, but the machines in the top price and size range were more generally associated with the long-distance road events such as the Austrian Alpine Trial and the Russian Trials of 1910 to 1914. These were the successors to the Prince Henry Trials which ended in 1911, and attracted the same mixture of wealthy, aristocratic amateurs, and professional drivers testing

One of the more striking boat-shaped bodies at the 1913 Paris Salon was this three-seater on a Turcat- Méry chassis built for Count Mandarinoff. (Photo: Autocar)

the latest products of their companies. Russia provided really testing events, for outside the large cities there were virtually no roads at all. One driver likened Russian motoring to driving over the Sussex Downs for hundreds of miles at a stretch. At least one was not likely to meet other motorists, for in 1913, there were only 6,000 cars in all Russia, compared with 132,015 in Great Britain and 1,194,262 in the United States. They were owned by merchants or aristocratic landowners; the latter usually bought their cars on hire-purchase for, although rich in land, they had little ready cash. German cars were the most popular, although the Czar favoured Delaunay-Bellevilles. Two English firms – Lagonda and Austin – entered their cars in the Russian Trials although they took little part in other competitions at the time. The former seem to have sold their products almost entirely in Russia before the introduction of the little 11·1hp monocoque construction light car. Their 20·1hp 3-litre engine developed 58bhp which was comparable with the original Prince Henry Vauxhall, although the Lagonda never achieved anything like the fame of the Vauxhall. In 1910 Austin entered their 40hp car in the Russian International Tour. It was a standard model, with a 4-cylinder side-valve engine of nearly 5·8-litres capacity. The body, named 'Vitesse', was a torpedo type, much more streamlined than the usual Austin tourer, which at that time was a very staid machine. This car, driven by Harold Kendall, won the St Petersburg Automobile Club Trophy. Late in 1911 a new 40hp, with a larger bore and capacity of 6·3-litres, appeared, and a sports-version of this, known as the Defiance, was prepared for the 1912 Czar's Cup. With a high-lift camshaft and larger carburetter, its claimed maximum speed was 95mph, a remarkable figure for a large touring car of the period, if true. It was probably more like 85/7mph, which is still very creditable. The car had a clean sheet throughout the Czar's Cup Trial, but crashed into a telegraph pole a few miles from the finish. The 40hp Defiance was offered for sale to the public at the 1912 Olympia Show. A line of sporting Austins followed, although they never became well-known, and must have been made in very small quantities. From 1913, a 30hp Defiance was listed, with the same tune and body style; the price was £850 in March 1913, and had risen by August to £1,000, or nearly double the price of a Prince Henry Vauxhall. It is not surprising that it was not catalogued after October.

The 1914 Austin 20hp driven in that year's Austrian Alpine Trial by Harold Kendall and Vernon Austin. (Photo: Autocar)

Meanwhile the Defiance type bodies could be obtained on ordinary 15, 20 and 30hp chassis. Perhaps the most attractive sporting Austin of this period was the 1914 Alpine 20hp with tuned engine, wider track, and 'colonial' radiator. The prototype was driven in the Alpine Trial by Harold Kendall and Vernon Austin, Herbert's son. It performed reliably, but they only won a Silver plaque. The production model had a larger bore, giving a capacity of 3,610cc, lighter pistons and con rods, high-lift cams, a modified carburetter and more acutely raked steering column. It might have become a really successful model, but as it was announced only two months before the outbreak of war, very few were made.

The Austrian Alpine Trial took over the Prince Henry's reputation as Europe's leading road event in 1911, although it had been held, largely contested by light cars, for six years previously. The route covered nearly 900 miles including six major passes, and no rest periods were allowed in the four day event. Despite this, the contestants did better than was expected, no less than ten cars completing the Trial without penalty points. These included four Austro-Daimlers, and one each of Audi, Laurin & Klement, Mercedes, N.A.G., Nesselsdorfer, and Puch. The Austro-Daimlers were not the large Prince Henry models, but relatively small cars with 30bhp 2·2-litre engines, capable of 60mph. The other cars were all standard touring cars which, although possessed of a good performance, were hardly sporting machines.

The 1912 Alpine Trial route covered some 1,500 miles, and no less than 23 cars had clean sheets. To determine who should win the various cups and prizes, lots were drawn, and the winner was W. Gutmann's Mercedes. An Opel was second, and this firm also won the team prize. This 1912 event was the first in which Rolls-Royce took part; one example of their London-Edinburgh model Silver Ghost was driven by James Radley, but suffered the the ignominy of coming to a halt on the Katschberg Pass, two of the passengers having to dismount before the car could re-start. This caused immediate complaints that the car was too highly geared, but this model had climbed steeper hills in Scotland, and it was finally concluded that the rarefied atmosphere of the Austrian Alps was responsible. Far from being daunted, Rolls-Royce submitted their cars to intensive testing for the rest of

The 2·3-litre Austro-Daimler driven in the 1911 Austrian Alpine Trial by Ferdinand Porsche, seen here at the wheel. (Photo: Neubauer Collection)

1913 Austrian Alpine Trial. James Radley's Rolls-Royce Continental tourer. (Photo: Friedrich Heil Collection)

that summer, and the following year entered four of their new model, known as the Continental. This model has since been called the Alpine Eagle, but this was never Rolls' own name for it. It had a four-speed gearbox, and the engine was tuned to give 75bhp compared with 60bhp of the standard Silver Ghost. These cars had the largest engines of any in the 1913 Alpine Trial and they dominated the event. Once again, lots had to be drawn to determine the winners, and the most important cups were won by Rolls, Minerva, and Horch. The Rolls team only missed winning the team prize because of a minor accident to one of the cars. The team prize went to the German firm of Audi, who also swept the board in 1914. Designed by August Horch, who had left the firm that bore his name in 1909, these Audis were quite conventional, but very reliable cars. They had bi-bloc 4-cylinder engines of 3,538cc, giving about 40bhp at 2,000rpm, not a spectacular figure when compared with the 58bhp of the smaller-engined Prince Henry Vauxhall, but with a lightweight aluminium body, the special Alpine Trial cars were capable of over 60mph. They won the team prize in 1913 and 1914, when five Audis finished with clean sheets.

Apart from the makers who were directly concerned in the Alpine Trials, there were many who made large, powerful touring cars whose performance was sufficiently above average to take them into the category of sporting

*1913 Austrian Alpine Trial.
Prince Ely of Parma's Austro-
Daimler; The Horch team;
one of the Puch cars at Vienna.
Note the curious arrangement
of 'Puch' on the radiator.
(Photos: Friedrich Heil
Collection and Autocar)*

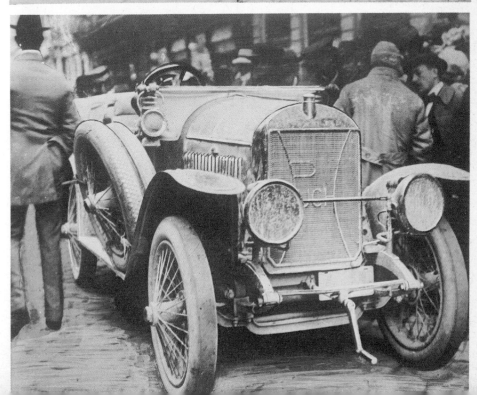

vehicles. It is impossible to be dogmatic about categories of this kind, but among the more noteworthy high-performance tourers were the big 6-cylinder Napiers, the 90hp Mercedes, the 200hp Benz, and the 100hp Isotta Fraschini. Until about 1910 Napier was the best-known British make for both quality and performance, and S. F. Edge advertised that the cars could be had in two forms, 'carriages for town work', and 'Napier Racing Cars, designed for speed and taking part in competition'. The most notable of the latter was the 'Sixty', whose 7·7-litre 6-cylinder engine actually developed about 75bhp, and gave it a maximum speed of nearly 70mph. More striking than speed was its flexible top gear performance, for it could pull away from a standstill in top gear, and with this model Edge set a fashion for long distance top gear runs. Like all the 6-cylinder Napiers, its engine was considerably over-square (127 × 102mm), and set far forward in the frame, with the radiator well ahead of the front axle. Because of this, the large Napiers had an appearance which was aggressive and purposeful rather than handsome. Edge used a special version of the 'Sixty' with lengthened stroke for his famous 24 hour run at Brooklands in 1907, when he covered 1,581 miles at an average speed of just over 65mph. The long-stroke model (which, in fact, had exactly square dimensions of 127 × 127mm) was put into production as the Sixty-Five in 1908, and was made until 1912. Even larger was the Ninety, with a capacity of over 14-litres, and dimensions of 156 × 127mm. With a wheelbase of 11ft 11in, this model was more suited to formal than sporting coachwork and was popular with Indian potentates, of whom the Nizam of Hyderabad was the most regular customer. The introduction of the Rolls-Royce Silver Ghost marked the end of Napier's dominance of the luxury car trade, for the Rolls combined Napier's assets of speed and top gear flexibility with greater refinement, and, in the eyes of most people, better appearance. Napier's sporting reputation was much higher, but there were inevitably few buyers of a fast tourer at over £1,700, and the really big Napiers had been dropped before the outbreak of war. The company's boom period was 1909 to 1911, when 1,800, or more than a third of the total output of cars, were made. Of course these included smaller sixes, fours, and even a 10hp twin-cylinder car.

Ever since the famous Sixty of 1903, Mercedes had always had a powerful car at the top of its range, which with light bodywork was capable of high performance. These included the 70hp and 90hp T-head chain-driven cars of the Wilhelm Maybach era, and the 90hp L-head model, also chain-driven, designed by Paul Daimler and made from 1910 to 1914. Known in England as the 'Ninety', and in Germany as the 37/90PS, this was the first Mercedes to

A brace of Napier tourers taking part in the R.A.C. 1000 Miles Trial, c. 1908. (Photo: Montagu Motor Museum)

wear the V-radiator as standard (from 1913), and this sharply-pointed prow combined with its size certainly gave it a sporting appearance. The 9·5-litre engine had one inlet and two exhaust valves per cylinder, and drove the car at up to 75mph, provided a light body was used. In fact, many of the 90s were fitted with heavy limousine coachwork bringing the total weight to over 2½ tons which, with the vast frontal area of limousines of the day, naturally limited performance. Wheels could be either wire, artillery or disc, and the sporting models frequently used the latter. The 90 was superseded in 1914 by the smaller and more modern 28/95PS, which had a single overhead camshaft 6-cylinder engine of 7,273cc, and shaft drive. This model was re-introduced after the war, and achieved most of its fame in the 'twenties.

Like Mercedes, Benz also produced a wide range of powerful cars which were successful in Russian Trials, but their most remarkable car was the 200hp, catalogued in 1912 and 1913. The engine of this model had originally been used in the 'Blitzen Benz' racing cars which had first appeared at a Brussels Speed Trial in 1909, and later that year had covered a flying half mile at Brooklands at 127·9mph, driven by Hemery. The Blitzens had a great racing career in the United States, and in 1911 Bob Burman drove one at 142mph at Daytona, this being an unofficial Land Speed Record. The over-head valve engine had dimensions of 185 × 200mm, giving a capacity of 21½ litres. It seems extraordinary that the firm should have offered such a vast machine for sale as a road-going car, but in 1912 it appeared in the cata-logues at about 30,000 marks (a 90hp Mercedes cost 25,500 marks) for the chassis alone. In England, the RAC rating was 84·9hp and the chassis cost £1,800. Nevertheless a small number was sold, and Field Marshal von Hindenberg was said to have used one as a Staff Car during the First World War. Captain Alistair Miller raced a four-seater tourer at Brooklands as late as 1930 and this car survives today.

The small ohc Isotta Fraschini has already been mentioned, but Cattaneo's range extended to much larger cars, including the Type KM, known in England and the US as the 100hp. This had a 4-cylinder engine of 10,618cc which developed 140bhp at 1,800rpm. Like other Cattaneo designs, it had a single overhead camshaft, which in this case operated four valves per cylinder. Final drive was by double chains but a much more modern feature was the use of four-wheel brakes. Unlike the Crossley's system already mentioned, the Isotta's rear wheel and transmission brakes were operated by pedals, while the front wheel brakes were operated by the big outside lever. The latter were in fact described as emergency brakes, and the overall stopping

Below: The 200hp Benz at Brooklands in 1928. (Photo: Montagu Motor Museum)

Below right: Another large Benz with streamlined body seen at Gaillon Hill Climb in 1911. (Photo: Montagu Motor Museum)

power of the three brakes does not seem to have been much better than that of the Isotta's contemporaries which relied on rear wheel and transmission brakes only. The later KMs usually carried a handsome V-radiator, and were almost certainly the first Italian cars to do so, although this largely Germanic fashion was later copied south of the Alps by Fiat, Itala, S.P.A., Bianchi, Alfa Romeo, and possibly other makers. A smaller version of the KM, the 6,234cc Model TM was also made, this being the sporting model of a large range which included many side-valve models. The little 10hp ohc car had been dropped in 1911, but the KM and TM continued until the outbreak of war.

Apart from Isotta, there were very few Italian cars which could be called specifically sporting models. Several firms had built Grand Prix racing cars, notably Fiat and Itala, and many makes were entered in the Targa Florio, Coppa Florio, Coppa della Velocita, and other races, but these were stripped touring models which looked highly sporting, but did not have any note-worthy engine or chassis modifications. The Edwardian Bianchi was nor-mally a staid touring car, but a few sporting versions of the big 4-cylinder 42/70hp car were made. These had handsome V-radiators, wire wheels and light doorless four-seater bodywork. Like the KM Isotta, they had double chain final drive, and since they were made until 1916, they must have been among the last cars in the world to use this system.

1916 Bianchi 42/70hp sporting tourer.
(Photo: Autocar)

The Sporting Cyclecar

We have seen that the early Coupe de l'Auto races bred a crop of light racing cars, many of them freakish in design, but they did not result in sporting cars for the general public. In 1910, however, there appeared the first of a new breed of motorcar which soon generated world-wide, if short-lived, enthusiasm. This was the cyclecar, a four-wheeled vehicle whose mechanism owed much more to the motorcycle than to the car as it was known at the time. Two of the earliest, and also the best-known, cyclecars were the British G.N. and the French Bédélia, which appeared almost simul-taneously in the year 1910. The G.N. began as a home-built machine, the work of two young engineers, Archie Frazer-Nash and H. R. Godfrey. Like many amateur enthusiasts of the time, they wrote an article about their car in *The Motor Cycle*, and this led to so many enquiries that they began production the following year. The engine was a 90° V-twin of 1,100cc capacity mounted in line with the chassis. In the prototypes this was a proprietary make, a J.A.P., but soon Godfrey and Nash fitted their own engine, using Peugeot cylinder barrels, pistons and valves up to 1912, and thereafter their own design entirely. Transmission was by a two-speed chain and dog-clutch system, and final drive by twin belts. The simple frame was of ash, and the total weight of the car was only 400lb, compared with 800–1,000lb for the conventional light car. The price was only 95 guineas, again significantly less than was asked for most other cars. It is not surprising that the cyclecar soon began to attract customers, mostly motorcyclists who wanted greater comfort and carrying capacity.

Across the English Channel, two Frenchmen, Bourbeau and Devaux had devised a cyclecar strikingly similar to the G.N. They used a V-twin engine initially, although later they offered singles as well. This drove by chain to a countershaft about half way down the chassis, whence the power was taken by very long, exposed belts to the rear wheels. Instead of the side-by-side seating of the G.N., the Bédélia's seats were in tandem, with the driver at the rear. Steering was by wire and bobbin, and the whole front axle turned with the wheels, a crude and dangerous system which had been abandoned on most cars by 1895. However the Bédélia, like its British equivalent, was cheap to buy and to run, and relatively fast, being capable of 45mph in its standard form, and up to 60mph in its later sporting versions.

By the end of 1912 the cyclecar movement had become well established in England and France. No less than 70 makes of car of under 1,500cc were shown at Olympia that year, and the new magazine, *The Cyclecar*, sold 100,000 copies of its first issue. 'The New Motoring' as its supporters called it, soon became a crusade; just as the early motorists boasted the advantages of motor over horse, so 'The New Motorists' gleefully related stories of how the cyclecar scored over the large car. It was manoeuvrable in traffic, it could be driven through the garden gate of a small suburban house (which would not have had a drive and garage at that time), and it could negotiate the narrowest country lanes, thereby introducing the delights of the countryside to the motorist of modest means. *The Cyclecar* radiated a charming aura of infectious enthusiasm which the more general motoring magazines never had. It preserved this even through its changes of name to *The Light Car and Cyclecar*, and then *The Light Car*. To its demise in 1956, *The Light Car* seemed to be produced for amateurs by amateurs (in the best sense). Although most cyclecars could not be called sporting machines, the humblest cyclecarist was always something of a sportsman, and needed patience and a sense of humour to cope with the vagaries of belts that slipped or broke, steering cables that snapped, and so on. Road trials were immensely popular with 'The New Motorists', and a number of firms began to offer sporting models. Some were sporting only in their bodywork, such as the Speed Model Zendik which had a torpedo-type body and disc wheels, and looked just like a Coupe de l'Auto racer in miniature. During 1913 and 1914 numerous makes of cyclecar were raced at Brooklands, including an A.C. Sociable 3-wheeler with canoe-shaped body, and the prototype Carden monocar. This engaging vehicle had a rear-mounted 4hp J.A.P. engine driving direct to the rear axle. There was no clutch, and the driver had to push-start his machine, and then vault into it as the engine began to fire. More serious than these were the sporting G.N.s. In 1913 the engine was mounted transversely, the cylinder heads peeping out of holes in the bonnet sides. This gave excellent cooling. The Grand Prix model was designed for the 1913 Amiens Grand Prix des Voiturettes, but the models sold to the public under this name were suitable for ordinary road use. More sporting was the Vitesse which had a tuned engine with steel pistons, and a staggered two-seater body. Maximum speed was 62mph, and the price £155. By the outbreak of the war the G.N. had established an excellent reputation in the cyclecar world, although less than 200 had been made. Leading members of the Cyclecar Club such as Frank Thomas and Osmond Hill owned and competed in G.N.s, the former's car having an outsize engine and being known as the 'Hippopo-Thomas'.

A number of G.N.s were exported, and thus introduced the cyclecar movement to countries which had not developed it themselves. Austrian motorists took to the G.N. in some numbers, and a special cyclecar hill-climb was held at Semmering in September 1913. In addition to G.N.s, a number of local makes took part, including Mullner, K.A.N., a single-seater streamlined version of the Phänomobil 3-wheeler, and several Austros. The latter was the only specifically sporting cyclecar to be made in Central Europe, and was built in small numbers largely for competitions. Powered by a 6hp N.S.U. engine, it had a four-speed gearbox and double-chain final drive. Front suspension was independent by sliding pillars, on the lines of the Morgan. Its maximum speed was over 55mph, and it was described as very noisy, but that was a price which the cyclecarist had to pay for speed. Germany, Italy and Spain showed little interest in the cyclecar, probably due to poor roads outside the towns, but the United States, paradoxically, had over 100 makes during a short boom period from 1913 to 1915. None of these was particularly sporting, however, and there were few special competitions held for cyclecars.

In 1913 the Automobile Club de France held two races for cyclecars, the Grand Prix des Voiturettes at Amiens, and, three weeks later, the Grand Prix des Cyclecars at Le Mans. Motorcycle combinations competed alongside the cyclecars, and 3-wheeled cars ran in the former category. The Amiens event was, in fact, won by a 3-wheeler, the Morgan driven by W. G. McMinnies, with Frank Thomas as his mechanic. This success resulted in a range of sporting Morgans known as the Grand Prix models being offered in the catalogue the following season. There were three variants, the Grand Prix No 1 with side valve J.A.P. engine and narrow body at £105, the No 2 with similar specification and wider body, also at £105, and the No 3 with ohv engine, identical to the G.P. winner, at £115. The so-called Sporting Model Morgan was really a touring model. The Morgan was the only sporting 3-wheeler made in England before the War, and was certainly the outstanding one throughout the 1920s as well.

The 4-wheeler section of the Amiens Grand Prix was won by a Bédélia, with disc wheels, driven by Bourbeau, and the Le Mans event by a Ronteix, another French make of more conventional layout with 4-cylinder engine. These cyclecar races were very light-hearted affairs; in the Amiens event Frank Thomas became thirsty and asked his driver to stop by the crowd, one of whom handed Thomas a wine bottle. McMinnies scorned to join him at first, but the sight of Thomas drinking was too much for him, and, there being no breathalysers at Amiens in 1913, he, too, took a long gulp. Francis Samuelson who drove a Marlborough had a female mechanic; much was made of this phenomenon by the press, but no one seemed to realise at the time that she was his wife, and moreover, that they were on their honeymoon. Now Sir Francis and Lady Samuelson, they are still keen sporting motorists, and Sir Francis is an active member of the Vintage Sports Car Club.

A sporting cyclecar. The V-twin Bédélia built for the 1913 Cyclecar Grand Prix. Production Bédélias usually had wire wheels. (Photo: Autocar)

A 1912 45hp Mercedes with Gordon Watney aluminium body. At the wheel is Count Zborowski who became celebrated after the war as the builder and driver of the Chitty-Chitty-Bang-Bangs. (Photo: Autocar)

Apart from the sporting cars mentioned, there were many highly sporting looking cars around in 1914, many of which were re-bodied touring machines. Probably the best-known specialist in this line was Gordon Watney who had a small workshop near Brooklands. To these premises came second-hand Mercedes tourers, limousines or landaulettes whose bodies were removed and replaced by sporting coachwork of Watney's own design. They were mostly aluminium doorless shells with red leather upholstery which were made for Watney by the Ewart Geyser Company. He also tuned the engines of some of the cars, and many were raced by their new owners at Brooklands. Another emporium of sporting machinery was Charles Lane & Co Ltd of 311, Euston Road, London. Here one could buy a re-bodied 59·6hp Grand Prix De Dietrich, a Fiat saloon with tiny portholes in place of windows, or a 48hp Daimler two-seater with shortened chassis, disc wheels, and Vauxhall-like V-radiator. Many of these cars had only an indifferent performance, but they were bought by young amateur drivers for whom anything over 50mph was an exciting speed, and who cared nothing for handling ability, simply because they had driven nothing better. Bright colours, a funny name on

the side of the bonnet, and the appearance of a 'racer' satisfied many of the young 'knuts' of the day. One journalist at any rate held that the motorcar had effected a very desirable change in masculine fashion, or should one say affectation. 'Motoring', he said, 'has done a great service to society by eliminating the long haired type of effeminate nondescript that once upon a time had endeavoured to set the fashion. Nowadays long hair and manners *en suite* are not suitable for motoring. . . . A knowledge of mechanism has effected a more manly type of youth.' World War 1 which was so soon to break out not only reinforced the manliness, but spread the 'knowledge of mechanism' more widely than anything else could have done, and so helped to bring about a wider market for sports cars in the 1920s.

4. *1913 Sunbeam 12/16hp sporting two-seater. Owned by J. F. Olorenshaw. (Photo: A. E. Coe & Sons Ltd)*

2. The Sporting Car in the United States of America

In the period up to 1914 the development of sporting cars in Europe and America were almost entirely separate, and virtually none crossed the Atlantic in either direction. This did not apply to racing cars, for Wintons took part in the Gordon Bennett races, and Christie and Thomas in the Grands Prix, while Peugeot and Mercedes competed at Indianapolis, but one looks in vain for a Mercer, Lozier or Stutz in the Alpine Trial entries, or for a Prince Henry Vauxhall in the Glidden Tours.

In America more than Europe, poor roads dictated the design of early cars. In 1900 most country roads were dirt or corduroy, a surface of logs laid across the road as close as possible. Summer was the only suitable time for travel; in spring and autumn the roads were feet deep in mud, and in winter there was deep snow over much of the country. In 1905 a traveller said that the average American rural road was worse than its equivalent in eastern Poland. Moreover, these roads started a mile or two outside the large towns, and in many cases the building of suburban houses preceded the laying of paved roads (not that America was unique in this respect – a similar situation could be found in parts of Middlesex in the 1930s). In Washington one third of the city streets were of untreated dirt in 1890, and the figure in New Orleans and Kansas City was four-fifths dirt. These conditions encouraged a car which was light, powerful, and simple, not a bad formula for a sports car, although it was some time before any such machines were built. Simplicity was essential so that the average village repairer could keep the car going; the factory-trained mechanic was still a long way off. When the sporting car did appear, it was a simple design with a large, slow-turning T-head engine and minimal body composed solely of two bucket seats. The engines were usually the same as those employed in the firms' touring cars and were not specially tuned.

Probably the first sporting car built for sale in America was a steamer, the Stanley 'Gentleman's Speedy Roadster'. Steam cars had been built in considerable numbers since the turn of the century, but were mostly light runabouts with no claims to high performance. By 1906 most of the smaller makes had disappeared, or turned to the internal combustion engine, but Stanleys were just getting into their stride, producing larger touring cars and also raising the Land Speed Record to 127mph with a boat-shaped machine powered by an engine of only 30hp. The roadsters came in three models, all with light two-seater bodies with no weather protection. The Model EX had a 18-inch boiler and 10hp engine; the Model H, known as the 'Gentleman's Speedy Roadster' with 23-inch boiler and 20hp engine; and the Model K with 26-inch boiler and 30hp engine. The latter was developed from a special roadster built for R. W. Stanley, son of F. E. Stanley. All the members of the family were keen motorists, and ideas incorporated on a personal car would frequently find their way into the following year's production models. The weight of the roadsters was under 15cwt, and performance was startling for 1906. The model H claimed the title of Fastest Stock Car in the World after achieving 68·18mph over a 15-mile handicap race at Ormond Beach, while a flying $\frac{1}{2}$ mile was covered at 75mph. F. E. Stanley was once arrested near Boston and charged with driving at nearly 60mph. In court

5. *1910 Cutting Model A-40 Tourabout. Owned by Philip S. Baumgarten. (Photo: William S. Jackson)*

1908 Stanley Gentleman's Speedy Roadster owned by Mr Carl Ansley of St Thomas, Pennsylvania. (Photo: Kenneth H. Stauffer)

next day he pleaded not guilty, and when the judge asked him how he could do so when the evidence was so clear against him, he replied; 'I plead not guilty to going 60 miles an hour. When I passed the officer my speedometer showed I was going 87 miles an hour.' He was fined five dollars!

The first roadster of classic layout was the B.L.M., a little-known machine made in Brooklyn by James Breese and Charles L. Lawrence, two young men barely out of school. Listed from 1906 to 1908, it had a fairly small 4-cylinder engine of 24hp, said to be 'French-built', and shaft drive. The radiator was set well back from the front axle, and bodywork consisted of the usual two bucket seats behind which was a tool-box and two spare tyres. They admitted that their car was expensive, and at $3,500 it attracted few customers. A Stanley roadster cost only $1,000, and the famous T-head Mercer of a few years later was not more than $2,500. James Breese's younger brother Robert later made a few light sporting cars in Paris, one model of which used a single ohc engine.

Between 1908 and 1914 a large number of American manufacturers listed a two-seater sporting car in their catalogues. They called them runabouts (although this term was also used for a light, cheap two-seater), raceabouts, roadsters, or speedsters. Some won lasting fame for their makers, establishing them in the eyes of the public as sporting manufacturers, while others were merely sidelines. Often a local dealer would strip and tune a car in order to take part in races, hill-climbs and endurance runs, and so boost the sales of touring cars. Success might lead to a demand for replicas, which would be passed to the factory, and would result the following year in a roadster model in the catalogues. An example of this was the Maxwell 'Sportsman'. A few 22hp cars were built for demonstration by the company's branches in the sporting events of 1909, the original car averaging 54·3mph in the Long Island Motor Derby. This led to requests for replicas, and a small series of roadsters called Sportsman were made in 1910, although Maxwell was not generally thought of as a sporting marque. Other makers who listed sporting models included Apperson, Peerless, Kissel, Marion, Marmon, Midland, Stoddard-Dayton, National, Locomobile, Scripps-Booth, Sharp-Arrow, Overland, and Thomas. Above these stood the makes which are largely remembered for their sporting cars – Mercer, Stutz, Lozier, Chadwick, and Simplex.

1907 Thomas 40 runabout.
(Photo: Automobile Manu-
facturers' Association)

The Mercer company was founded in 1909 as a successor to the Roebling-Planche company who had made cars for a few years previously. Roebling was a well-known firm of wire manufacturers, and members of the Roebling family were on the board of Mercer throughout the best years of the company. In 1910 appeared the Type 35, of which the Raceabout soon became one of the most famous, as well as the most graceful, of pre-war American cars. It was designed by Finlay Robertson Porter, who later made his own cars under the names F.R.P. and Porter. So much has been written about Type 35 Raceabout that it is sometimes forgotten that not all Type 35s were Raceabouts. The 35 range also included a Runabout, a much staider vehicle with windscreen, doors and hood, a Touring, and a Limousine which was used as a taxicab in a number of cities. The Raceabout was known by the following suffixes during the years that it was made: 1911: 35-R, 1912: 35-C, 1913 and 1914: 35-J. The engine was a 4-cylinder T-head type, with dual ignition, giving 60bhp from 4·9 litres. This was a small unit as American engines went, but thanks to high gearing and low weight a maximum speed of 75mph was obtainable. The bodywork was classically simple; two low bucket seats, a bolster tank behind them, and behind that a small tool-box and two spare

1914 Mercer 35-J Raceabout,
seen in England during the
1954 Anglo-American
Vintage Car Rally.
(Photo: Motor)

tyres. The 35 Raceabout never had a windscreen, but a monocle bolted to the steering column was available, and has become a symbol of the make. In fact its effectiveness as a windbreak must have been very limited, and a pair of goggles which the sporting driver wore anyway, would have been of much more use. The usual colours of Raceabouts were Canary Yellow, Azure Blue striped with white, or Maroon striped with black and gold. Some cars were supplied in pure white. The price varied between $2,250 and $2,600 according to the year, which was reasonable considering the performance offered. Steering was beautifully precise, and the delicacy of handling complemented the fine lines of the Raceabout to give an overall impression of jewel-like quality. As a result it has become one of the most sought-after antique cars today, and one recently realised $45,000 at an auction, the highest price yet paid for an antique. It had its faults, although they were not such as to deter the average buyer of the day. Braking was poor and emergency stops impossible – by the time the car had stopped, the emergency was twenty yards behind. The light chassis was rather fragile, and most of the surviving Raceabouts have had their chassis re-welded at some time or other; but then the builders never thought that their cars would be driven and enthused about nearly 60 years after they were made. Another drawback was the hard ride and wind buffeting, but the sporting car of that time was not intended for long distance work anyway. They achieved innumerable successes in races, mostly with stock cars in private hands, although there were a number of special racers such as the Type 45 150bhp car raced by Eddie Pullen. Even in 1911, the Type 35's first year, they won several stock car events and came 12th and 14th in the Indianapolis 500 Mile Race. Both cars were then driven home by their owners! In 1912 a Type 35 Raceabout was 3rd at Indianapolis, although it had the smallest engine in the race. Like many successful small firms then and now, there was a great deal of enthusiasm among the employees. When Eddie Pullen won the Grand Prize in February 1914, the whole works closed down for a half-holiday.

The greatest days of Mercer were over by the end of 1914. The youngest and ablest member of the Roebling family, Washington Roebling III, had been drowned in the 'Titanic' disaster in 1912, and his drive was sadly missed. Because of the war, high-grade Belgian steel was no longer available, and the company cut down their racing programme. In 1915 F. R. Porter left the company, and a new range of cars replaced his T-head designs. This was the L-head 22-70 series, designed by Erik H. Delling, who had been with Mercer since 1913, and had designed a special racing car called the Deltal in that year. The 22-70 was in fact based on the Deltal design. The engine was a monobloc four with a remarkably long stroke, the dimensions being 95×171mm, giving a capacity of 4·9 litres, or about the same as the Type 35's. Power was quoted at 72bhp at 2,700rpm. Again a wide range of bodies was available, including a Raceabout on the short wheelbase of 9ft 7in (the standard wheelbase was 10ft 10in). It was a much less stark machine than the old Raceabout, with sides to the body (though no doors yet), wire wheels and electric starting. A windscreen was standardized from 1919. It was faster than its predecessor but was raced much less, largely because the era of the privately entered car which could be driven home after the event was practically over by 1915. A single ohc special racing car was driven by Joe Thomas in a number of events but was nothing like the standard cars. By 1918 all three founding members of the Roebling family had died and the company was sold to a Wall Street syndicate headed by Emlen S. Hare. The rest of the Mercer story belongs to the post-war era.

Harry C. Stutz had been associated with the design of the American

Underslung car from 1906 to 1909, when he formed Stutz Auto Parts to manufacture components, notably transmissions and axles, for other car makers. He graduated to complete cars in 1911, with the foundation of the Ideal Motor Car Company, of Indianapolis. The first car was completed in only five weeks, and entered in the Indianapolis 500 Mile Race in May. It finished 11th after a completely trouble-free run and Stutz made a great deal of publicity about this, calling it 'The Car That Made Good in a Day'. In fact it was not particularly remarkable in an era when many stock cars were entered successfully in major races, but it was an encouraging start for a new make, and within two months Stutz was advertising three models for sale: a roadster, and four- or five-seater touring cars, all with the same engine as the Indianapolis car. This was the 6·3-litre T-head Wisconsin 4-cylinder unit which was used by a number of other manufacturers. The roadster model became the Bearcat in 1914, by which time two alternative engines were available in all the Stutz models. These were the Wisconsin four, which produced 60bhp at 1,500rpm, and a slightly smaller 6-cylinder unit which was smoother but less powerful. The majority of Bearcats used the 4-cylinder engine, with which the total price was $2,000 as compared with $2,125 for the 6-cylinder Bearcat. The roadster with doors was continued but the starker, doorless Bearcat soon claimed most of the public's attention as the glamour car of the Stutz range. In conception it was very like the Mercer Type 35 Raceabout, and much has been written about the rivalry between the two cars. The Stutz was heavier in appearance and, in fact, 3,000lb compared with 2,500lb, and the larger engine was hardly more powerful. Enthusiasts for each make produce impressive lists of their respective racing successes,

1914 Stutz Bearcat roadster. (Photo: Alfred Lewerenz Collection)

but, as many of these were achieved with special cars such as the ohc Mercer or 'White Squadron' ohc Stutzes, one cannot draw any useful conclusions from these. One point is that the Mercer Type 35 was in its last year of production when the Bearcat appeared, whereas the latter continued to be made until 1925, so new Bearcats would have been competing against Mercers which had already seen several years' hard use.

As well as the Bearcat, Stutz made a smaller sporting model known as the H.C.S., after the founder's initials. This had a similar body to the Bearcat, but a much smaller 4-cylinder engine, and cost only $1,475. It does not seem to have been a great success, and only lasted for the 1915 season. It should not be confused with the later H.C.S. of 1920 to 1925, which was a separate make formed by Harry Stutz after he had left his original company. Another model was the Bulldog, normally seen as a four-seater tourer, although a few Bulldog Special roadsters were made in 1917. The Bulldog was available only with the 4-cylinder engine.

One of the finest cars built in the United States in pre-war days was the Lozier, made at Plattsburg, N.Y. from 1905 to 1910, and thereafter at Detroit until 1918. H. A. Lozier Jnr spent two years examining the finest European cars before he put his own car into production in 1905. Designed by John G. Perrin they were initially high-quality, chain-driven, touring cars costing $5,000, but stripped chassis were entered in races from 1906 onwards. The really great period of Lozier came after the introduction of the shaft-driven models of 1908. These came in two forms, the 4-cylinder 45hp Type H and the 6-cylinder 50hp Type I. Both carried a variety of bodies, of which the open styles bore names evocative of the wealthy East Coast world in which they found many of their buyers. The Riverside seven-seater touring car, the Meadowbrook two-seater roadster, the Briarcliff four-seater toy tonneau, and the Lakewood four/five torpedo tourer, were named after Riverside Drive, New York City, the Meadowbrook Hunt Club, Long Island, Briarcliff Manor Lodge, New York, and the Georgian Court, Lakewood, New Jersey. The Meadowbrook and Briarcliff were the most suitable for competitions, and were intended to be stripped for racing. Catalogues frequently showed them in racing trim with large capacity fuel tanks installed, these being available from the works. Many racing successes were achieved from 1907 to 1911, including the 24 hour races at Philadelphia and at Brighton Beach, the Elgin National Championship, and the Havana Stock Car Race. Their most successful driver was Ralph Mulford who had been a tester for the firm even before their car building days, when they built motor-boat engines. Mulford came second (officially) in the 1911 Indianapolis 500 Mile Race and won the Savannah Vanderbilt Cup the same year. Many of these victories were achieved with standard cars which, after the race, would be fitted with their wings, headlamps, and handsome Meadowbrook or Briarcliff bodies, and driven home. This was not too unusual at the time, but Loziers somehow combined their sporting character with an aristocratic cachet which Mercer and Stutz never achieved. They were, of course, far more expensive, for a 6-cylinder Briarcliff cost over $5,000. After 1911 the factory raced no more, but the same models were continued until 1917, the 4-cylinder car being renamed the Type 46 and the 6-cylinder the Type 51. They were powerful, 'long-legged' cars in which 3rd gear was direct, and was good for speeds of 4-60mph. Fourth was an overdrive, and, in the words of the catalogue, was 'only needed when excessive speeds of over 60mph are required'. As with so many of the great makes, changes of leadership and an incursion into the lower-priced market with an L-head Light Six at a $3,250, and a four at $1,575, signified a decline, and all production ended early in 1918.

1909 Lozier Briarcliff four-seater toy tonneau.
(Photo: William S. Jackson)

A minor Pennsylvania make which achieved considerable sporting fame was the Chadwick. It was a high-quality car which had been made in small numbers since 1904, but it was the introduction of the Great Chadwick Six in 1907 which gave the firm a car suitable for competitions. It had a vast 6-cylinder ohv engine of 11·2-litres capacity, whose cylinders were cast in pairs, each pair surrounded by a copper water-jacket. The usual touring models were made, but there was also a short-chassis runabout which was capable of over 60mph. The price was $6,500, and only a few were sold. Total Chadwick production was only 235 cars. This runabout was more successful in hill climbs than in races, winning numerous events at Wilkes Barre, Cleveland, Skippard Hill, Norristown, and the Ohio Valley Hill Climb. The driver in many of these successes was Willy Haupt, and it was he who suggested the supercharger which has brought Chadwick immortality as the first make to use this device. At first he used three carburetters, which boosted the speed from 65–85mph, but he then found that the valve area was a limitation to further power. The valves could not be enlarged because of the copper water-jackets, so he conceived a compressor which would force the mixture into the cylinders at a greater pressure than that of the atmosphere. First he used one, and then three compressors, driven by a leather belt from the flywheel at a speed of up to six times engine speed. This blower (the word supercharger was not used at this time) enabled the Chadwick to beat the Stanley Steamers at hill climbs, but it was never a great success in racing. Haupt drove one in the 1908 Vanderbilt Cup, but retired. The blowers

*1910 Chadwick Great Six
Runabout owned by Mr
William Pollock of Pottstown,
Pennsylvania.
(Photo: William Pollock)*

were never used on cars sold to the public, and, in fact, Haupt had many disagreements with the design staff in getting his ideas adopted on the works cars.

The story of the Simplex is remarkably similar to that of Lozier and Chadwick in that they all came to prominence in 1907, built fine cars and enjoyed sporting successes for a period of about five years, after which a decline set in, at least as far as competition cars were concerned. The Smith & Mabley Simplex was a high quality Mercedes-like car made from 1904 to 1907, when the firm went bankrupt and was acquired by Herman Broesel, a banker and textile importer of New York. He renamed the cars Simplex, and concentrated on the 9·8-litre 50hp chain-driven 4-cylinder car; this, in fact, developed more than 60bhp. Like Lozier, Simplex also made engines for motor-boats, and the 11-litre 90hp engine designed for these was mounted in a car driven with great success by George Robertson in the events of 1908. Replicas of this model were sold to a number of friends of the Broesel family who could be trusted to do the cars justice. Herman Broesel Jr and his brother Carl had been students at Princeton when their father went into car manufacture, but they left straightaway to join the firm. A number of their

*1915 Simplex 75hp T-head four.
This was one of the last chain-
driven cars made in America.
(Photo: Briggs Cunningham
Automotive Museum)*

Princeton classmates became customers for the 90hp; one was Gerard B. Lambert who entered every possible race and hill climb while still at college, and did much for the reputation of the car. The 50 and 90hp roadsters continued to be made up to 1913, in which year electric starters were fitted. Touring models were made as well, and coachwork was contracted out with some of the best firms in the country, such as Quimby, Holbrook, Demarest, and Brewster. The last chain drive model was the 1913 75hp, a four of about 10-litres capacity. Some of these cars were fitted with sharply pointed radiators resembling those of the 90hp Mercedes, although the usual Simplex was a flat design similar to that of the older-type Mercedes, Fiat, or Locomobile.

In 1912 Herman Broesel Sr died, and the company was sold in 1913 to the Wall Street firm of Lockart, Goodrich and Smith. In the reorganisation, designer Edward Franquist, who had been responsible for all the chain-drive T-head cars since 1907, was replaced by Henry M. Crane. Doubtless the Simplex was due for re-designing, for the days of the chain-driven T-head monsters were over, but the change meant the end of Simplex as a sporting car. The new Crane-Simplex was a magnificent touring car, and so it should have been at $10,000, but it was not the sort of machine that a youngster like Gerard Lambert could strip and enter for his local hill-climb on a Saturday afternoon. The same change was eliminating all the old-style roadsters. National, whose nearly-stock cars had won at Indianapolis and Elgin, turned to smooth 6- and 12-cylinder tourers, Chadwick was dead and Lozier nearly so. The next generation of the American sporting car was to be the Jazz-Age Speedster, exciting to look at, and sometimes to drive, but very seldom raced, for there were no races held for the road-going Speedster.

Part Two
The Twenties

3. Great Britain

Before the Great War ended in November 1918, a number of British manufacturers announced their post-war programmes, but no sporting models were mentioned until well into the following year. It was soon obvious that there was a great demand for the sporting car, and in the absence of new ones, the only alternatives were to make do with pre-war examples, or to build a car yourself. The former led to greatly inflated prices, and a Rolls-Royce Continental tourer which cost £1,145 new in 1914, commanded £3,000 in February 1919, while the latter alternative resulted in a number of extraordinary aero-engined cars. Aircraft engines were readily available from the Ministry of Munitions, at prices from £30 up; the most common being the 225hp V-12 Sunbeam, 300hp 6-cylinder Maybach, and 275hp V-12 Rolls-Royce Falcon. Fitted in an old touring car chassis, and with a four-seater touring body, these engines gave great power and flexibility, and the cars could outperform anything then on the road. Considering the optimistic atmosphere of 1919, it is surprising that no one tried to make such cars commercially, but in fact all the British machines were private ventures. (In America a few small firms such as Wharton of Dallas and Prado of New York did offer cars with Curtiss OX-5 aero engines, but this was a smaller unit of about 8 litres.) The first aero-engined hybrid was probably that of Harry Hawker who used a V-12 Sunbeam engine of 18 litres capacity in a lengthened Mercedes chassis. With a four-seater torpedo body the car was capable of over 90mph. It took the road in January 1919, and was followed by a number of similar machines, such as Colonel G. H. Henderson's Rolls-Royce/Napier, powered by a 14-litre Falcon engine. With the re-opening of Brooklands in 1920, this type of car naturally became a favourite for track work, and as new and more refined road cars came onto the market, the aero-engined monsters were more often found at Brooklands than on the road. Some were used for both kinds of work, notably the original 'Chitty-Chitty-Bang-Bang', which had a four-seater body, and was always driven up by its owner Count Zborowski from his home near Canterbury. It had a 23-litre Maybach engine mounted in a chain-driven Mercedes chassis, and retained the Mercedes radiator, clutch and gearbox. It was later fitted with a two-seater body, but its successor, the 19-litre Benz-engined Chitty II, always carried a four-seater touring body, and does to the present day. These aero-engined cars were undoubtedly sporting, being built entirely for pleasure and competitions, but their popularity was short-lived. Their fuel consumption was very heavy, brakes were negligible for the speeds of which they were capable, and they were hardly refined by the standards of a Silver Ghost or the new 6-cylinder Hispano-Suiza. The introduction of the £1 per horse-power taxation rate meant that Chitty I would have cost over £100 per year to tax, which is probably why Zborowski drove her on the road with trade plates, while even the smaller Chitty II cost £78 per year.

In February 1919 *The Autocar* carried an article which called for sporting cars in every class from £200 upwards. Within a few months British manufacturers began to answer this call, the first announcement of a sports car coming from Hillman who produced a sporting version of their 11hp light car in May 1919. Lightened pistons and connecting rods, and larger valves

1928 Invicta 4½-litre tourer. It was not yet thought of as a sports car, but this one is engaging energetically in driving tests during the 1928 Boulogne Speed Week. (Photo: Montagu Motor Museum)

increased power from 18bhp to 28bhp. In appearance it was utterly different from the touring Hillman, with its narrow, high aluminium body, pointed radiator, disc wheels, copper exhaust pipe, and outsize Klaxon horn. Its 10-gallon petrol tank had twice the capacity of the touring car's. However, its striking appearance was not matched by a very startling performance: it had a speed of 60mph in second gear, but could only manage 56mph in top, as there was not enough power for the $3\frac{1}{2}$:1 top gear. Later models were improved in this respect, but the high gearing was always a drawback, the 9:1 bottom gear giving trouble starting on steep hills. Raymond Mays in his autobiography *Split Seconds* says that it was the outstanding $1\frac{1}{2}$-litre sports car; in fact, in the summer of 1919, it was virtually the only $1\frac{1}{2}$-litre sports car on the market. The bore was reduced from 65mm to 63mm in order to bring it within the $1\frac{1}{2}$-litre class for competition work, and a tuned model driven by George Bedford achieved a number of successes at Brooklands. Bedford's advice was available to private owners who wanted to improve the performance of their Hillmans, and the car remained in production until 1922.

A much more significant announcement of May 1919 was that of the 3-litre Bentley. It was accompanied by a striking drawing by F. Gordon Crosby, an *Autocar* artist, but no photograph, for the simple reason that there was no car in existence, nor was there to be for several months to come. The drawing was Gordon Crosby's idea of what the car should look like; W. O. Bentley had told the artist the kind of car he had in mind, and had given him a free hand. So the famous Bentley radiator and the winged B emblem were both the creations of Gordon Crosby. Like many successful designs, the Bentley was in no way radical, although it was up to date. The 4-cylinder engine had dimensions of 80×149mm, giving a capacity of 2,996cc, or just under 3 litres. It was the first British car to be described in litres, and many enquiries were made about the meaning of this by motorists who were only familiar with horsepower. The four valves per cylinder were operated by a single shaft-driven overhead camshaft. The cylinder head was fixed, and brakes were on the rear wheels only. With a four-seater body a Brooklands lap speed of 75mph was forecast, and when the car did take the road, this was justified. The most remarkable feature of the announcement was the price of £750 for the chassis.

A chassis was shown at the first post-war show at Olympia in October 1919, but, like others at that show, it was not a running car; among its drawbacks was the rather serious one of having no crankshaft. The starting handle was pinned onto an empty crankcase, and the flywheel was supported by a stub shaft a few inches long. Nevertheless another car was running by Christmas 1919, being assembled at New Street Mews, Baker Street, where a plaque commemorates the fact to this day. Orders came in at the show, and deliveries were promised for June 1920 but in fact the first sale was not made until September 1921, when Noel van Raalte, a friend of W.O.'s took delivery of a four-seater. The price had risen to £1,050 for the chassis, and £1,350 for an open four-seater. Once deliveries began, the car started to fulfil the promise which had been built up during those two years of waiting. 141 cars were made in 1922, 204 in 1923, and 402 in 1924. This was almost the peak year of Bentley production, and although the range was later supplemented by the $4\frac{1}{2}$- and $6\frac{1}{2}$-litre cars, annual production never exceeded 408 for all models (in 1928).

By the mid-1920s the Bentley had already gathered the mystique which has lasted to this day. At the time many laymen thought of any sporting tourer as a Bentley, while today it is the car which springs most readily to mind

6. *1911 Mercer Type 35-R Raceabout. Owned by Hyde W. Ballard.*
(Photo: William S. Jackson)

7. Overleaf, left: *1909 Lozier Model H Briarcliff fourseater toy tonneau. Owned by Dr Russell B. Hunsberger.*
(Photo: William S. Jackson)

8. Overleaf, right: *1928 Bentley $4\frac{1}{2}$-litre four-seater sports car. Coachwork by Jarvis of Wimbledon. Owned by Robin Hames.*
(Photo: Charles Pocklington)

when the phrase 'vintage sports car' is used. It is difficult to explain this mystique exactly, but it probably results from two main factors. First, the persistence and success with which Bentleys were raced, and the glamour attached to the 'Bentley boys', the group of wealthy young sportsmen led by Woolf Barnato. This meant that the Bentley was 'news' to a greater extent than any other sporting car. The Le Mans victories in 1924, 1927, 1928, 1929, and 1930 resulted in front page headlines in *The Daily Express* and other papers, in which patriotism, snobbery and the worship of speed were equally mixed. The second factor was that the circle of customers and potential customers for Bentleys was relatively small, but close-knit, and the news of an outstanding new car was quick to be passed around. The early customers were the best advertisers of the car, and once a certain reputation was established, the wider world of business men and society figures took the car up. Prince George, later H.R.H. the Duke of Kent, exchanged his D.F.P. (with cash adjustment) for a 3-litre, and became a staunch Bentley customer.

The original 3-litre chassis had a wheelbase of 9ft 9½in and usually carried two- or four-seater open bodies, but in 1923 a long wheelbase (10ft 10in) model was introduced to carry the saloon coachwork that customers wanted, although W.O. never envisaged them. More interesting was the Speed Model introduced in 1924, which had the short wheelbase, higher compression ratio (5.3:1 compared with 4.3:1), front-wheel brakes, and a speed of 90mph. This was the Red Label model, perhaps the most famous of all the 3-litres, of which 507 were made between 1924 and 1929. The demand for anything still faster was strictly limited, but Bentley did produce a small number (15), of the extra short-chassis Green Label model, with 6·1:1 compression ratio, for which over 100mph was guaranteed. Not unnaturally, most of the bodies were two-seaters, although a four-seater ran at Le Mans in 1926.

By 1926 the 3-litre was no longer really competitive, in particular being beaten by the 3-litre Sunbeam. The 4½-litre which was announced in June 1927 was a logical development of the earlier car, having a generally similar engine layout. Cylinder dimensions were 100×140mm, the same as those of the 6-cylinder 6½-litre car. Capacity was 4,398cc, and maximum speed 85mph. It was available in two wheelbase lengths, the same as those of the 3-litre, 9ft 9½in and 10ft 10in. However, very few of the shorter model were made. When it was introduced, the 4½-litre was thought of as the sporting model, while the 6½-litre catered for the touring and 'fast town carriage' trade. However, the 4½ soon found itself carrying heavy saloon coachwork just as the 6½ did, although usually with less handsome results, because of its shorter bonnet. A 4½ driven by Woolf Barnato and Bernard Rubin won at Le Mans in 1928, but the firm's last two victories, in 1929 and 1930, were achieved by the Speed Six.

The fastest model of the 4½ was the supercharged version, or 'Blower Bentley' as it came to be known. This was the result of Sir Henry Birkin's desire for extra performance, and was built in the workshops of the Hon Dorothy Paget at Welwyn, as W.O. never approved of the principle of super-charging. It developed a remarkable 240bhp at 4,200rpm, but was unreliable, and never won a race. The supercharger was only really effective at constant high speeds, which meant that it should have been happier at Brooklands than on a road circuit. In fact, a special single-seater, driven by Birkin, did twice take the Brooklands Outer Circuit Record, raising it to 137mph, but this was in 1931, after the old Bentley company had closed down. The other drawback of the Blower Bentley was that it was very heavy on plugs; 'the blower eats plugs like a donkey eats hay', said Nobby Clarke, one of the leading Bentley mechanics. Only fifty-four blown cars were made in all, and

9. 1925 Vauxhall 30/98 Velox tourer.
(Photo: Vauxhall Motors Ltd)

Top left: *Special touring car built by Harry Hawker.* (Photo: Montagu Motor Museum)

Top right: *1921 Hillman Speed Model, on test in Yorkshire.* (Photo: Autocar)

Above left: *Woolf Barnato poses with a 3-litre Bentley.* (Photo: Montagu Motor Museum)

Above right: *A 4½-litre Bentley tourer, seen in Ireland during the 1967 F.I.V.A. Rally.* (Photo: Montagu Motor Museum)

they did more harm than good to the Bentley image, because, although not works-approved cars, the general public thought of them as such, and judged the firm accordingly.

Just as the 4½ was introduced to take over from the ageing 3-litre, so the Speed Six was intended to back up the 4½. It was based on the 6½-litre 6-cylinder car which had been in production since 1925. Differences from standard were relatively few, and were originally confined to a slightly different radiator shape, and a Green Label badge in place of the Blue Label on the standard 6½. All 6-cylinder Bentleys had a system of coupling-rod drive to the overhead camshaft in place of the vertical shaft of the smaller cars. The 1929 Le Mans Speed Six had a compression ratio of 5·3:1 and improved 'breathing' which increased power from 140bhp to 180bhp, and these modifications were incorporated in the production cars for 1930. The Speed Six had perhaps the most successful racing career of any Bentley, winning Le Mans twice, in 1929 and 1930, the 1929 Six Hours Race at Brooklands, the 1930 Double Twelve Hour Race, and 1931 500 Mile Race, both at Brooklands. The successful drivers included most of the Bentley boys,

1929 Speed Six Bentley, with two-seater body by Freestone & Webb. (Photo: Montagu Motor Museum)

Barnato, Birkin, Dunfee, Clement, and Kidston. 545 6½-litre cars were made, of which 177 were Speed Sixes. The majority of the latter were open cars, although a number of coupés were built, including a striking streamlined three-seater (the rear seat faced sideways) for Woolf Barnato. An unusual use of the Speed Six was for police work in Western Australia; the Perth police had two cars, with rather ugly six-light saloon bodies and equipped with wireless.

The logical development of the 6½ was the 110×140mm 8-litre which was introduced at the 1930 Show. It was the smoothest, most silent and most luxurious Bentley yet made, a far cry from the 1921 3-litre, and capable of 110mph. A price of £1,850 for the chassis put it in the class of the Phantom II Rolls-Royce, and indeed it was a worthy rival to 'The Best Car in the World'. Frank Clement thought it was a better car than the Rolls, but it is doubtful if it could have made serious inroads into the latter's sales. By 1930 the Rolls was firmly established in everybody's minds as the luxury car *par excellence* whereas the Bentley image was still that of the open sports car. As it happened, the 8-litre had been on sale for less than a year when its makers went into receivership. Only 100 were sold. The last Bentley was a hybrid model using the 8-litre chassis with a new engine, a 4-litre 6-cylinder unit with pushrod operated valves, the only real Bentley to use pushrods. W.O. was bitterly opposed to this step, but money was so short that economy was the prime consideration. The car had a very poor performance compared with earlier models, and former Bentley buyers were seriously disappointed, for the first time in the company's history. Would-be buyers of new Bentleys were fewer anyway, because of the Depression, and at this crucial moment, Barnato withdrew support, for even his vast wealth was reduced by the Depression. After an abortive bid by Napier, the Bentley company was taken over by Rolls-Royce, and when a new Bentley appeared in 1933, only the name remained.

The post-war 30/98 Vauxhall was announced at about the same time as the 3-litre Bentley, and had the advantage of going into production almost straightaway. The engine had, of course, been developed before the war, while the chassis was a shortened version of that used in the 25hp D-type tourer which had been in production throughout the war as a military staff car. The E-type 30/98 soon established a fine reputation as a fast touring car which could hold its own very satisfactorily in competitions. It was tractable in town, and could be driven in top gear at less than 10mph. Speeds of up to 65mph were possible in 3rd, with a top gear maximum of 80mph to 85mph with the standard four-seater Velox body. Fuel consumption was 22mpg at average speeds, coming down to 16–17mpg with really hard driving. The 30/98 was not a particularly quiet car, with noisy tappets and a booming exhaust, but the latter was a feature which endeared it to many owners, one of whom called it a 'particularly pleasant note'. Apart from the T.T. races, Vauxhalls did not support competitions very much, but private owners achieved many successes with the 30/98. G. D. Pearce-Jones entered his tourer in hill-climbs at home and abroad, winning his class in the Gaillon event, near Rouen, in 1920 when he was one of the very few British entrants present. With the same car he took the standing start record for the Brook-lands Test Hill, at a speed of 24·86mph.

In 1922 the side-valve E-type was replaced by the ohv OE-type. Laurence Pomeroy had designed prototypes of a single ohc engine as the E-type's replacement, while the 3-litre twin-ohc engine built for the 1922 Tourist Trophy racing cars further whetted the public's appetite for a really advanced

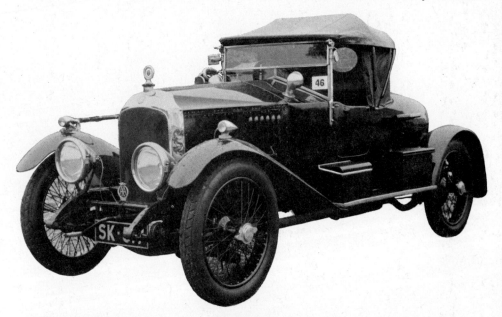

1920 Vauxhall 30/98 E-type two-seater.
(Photo: G. N. Georgano)

sports car. The cost would have been excessive, and such a complicated engine might well have lessened enthusiasm, in the long run. The new engine was quieter than the E-type and developed 115bhp compared with 90bhp from its predecessor. A lower top gear ratio meant that maximum speed remained at around 85mph. Braking had always been the weak spot of the 30/98, and a year after the OE-type was introduced, cable-operated front-wheel brakes were offered as an extra at £25. This was some improvement, although the cables needed constant adjustment under hard driving, and the drums were still on the small side. The cable system was probably thought of as an interim measure for, even before they were announced, the company was already studying a hydraulic system. This was put into production in 1926, together with much larger drums as used on the 25/70 touring car. However, by 1926 the whole conception of a large, slow-turning four-cylinder engine was becoming outdated, and the acquisition of Vauxhall by General Motors spelt the end of the 30/98. It did, however, survive all the other 'old school' Vauxhalls, and one or two 30/98s were still being turned out in the autumn

Vauxhall 30/98 OE-type, c. 1924, with the very handsome Wensum four-seater body. This was a works option, and cost £150 more than the standard tourer. (Photo: Montagu Motor Museum)

of 1927, alongside the new 20/60 saloon. About 580 30/98s were made altogether, of which over half were exported to Australia. It was not to be expected that General Motors would sponsor a new sporting car, and the 30/98 had no successor. However, a sporting body known as the Hurlingham was offered on the 20/60 chassis with no modification to the engine.

Like Vauxhall, Sunbeam had built staff cars during the war, and so were well-equipped to go into production with touring cars within a few months of the Armistice. The excellent sporting 12/16 was not re-introduced, however, and the first sporting models did not appear until August 1921. These were based on the side-valve 16/40 four and 24/60 six, and had inclined overhead valves, four per cylinder, operated by a single overhead camshaft, and aluminium pistons. The 16hp engine was said to develop 60bhp at under 3,000rpm. Known as the OV engines, they were theoretically available in 1922 and 1923, but in fact very few were made. Had they been, the 24hp model would have been a worthy rival to the Vauxhall 30/98. As it was, both models were given push-rod operated overhead valves for the 1922 season, and the 24/60 was listed with a Light Sports Tourer body, but did not have a very remarkable performance. The first really new post-war Sunbeam was the 14hp of 1921, re-named 14/40 for the 1924 season. This 4-cylinder ohv engine had aluminium cylinder block and pistons as standard, but a tuned sports version, developing a claimed 50bhp, appeared towards the end of 1923. It had wire wheels and Hartford shock absorbers, and a deeper radiator than the ordinary model. None of these cars could establish Sunbeam as a truly sporting marque, but in 1925 there came the twin-cam 3-litre, its engine derived from the 1923 Grand Prix car which had won the French and Spanish

A twin-cam 3-litre Sunbeam tourer, stripped for racing. (Photo: Montagu Motor Museum)

G.P. events. Designed by the Italian, Vincent Bertarione, this car gave Britain her last victory in a major Grand Prix until that of Tony Brooks in a Connaught at Syracuse in 1955. To use a twin overhead camshaft layout in a car sold to the public was most unusual at this time, although Ballot made about 100 twin-cam cars from 1921 to 1925. Before the car was available to the public, one was entered in the 1925 Le Mans race, and finished in second place, behind a Lorraine-Dietrich, but ahead of the Bentleys. After this auspicious start it would be pleasant to be able to list a string of sporting successes but in fact they did not come about. This was not the fault of the car, but rather that of company politics. Sunbeam was the British part of the Sunbeam-Talbot-Darracq group, and after 1926 the sporting activities of the group were transferred to the Talbot works at Suresnes, near Paris. Louis Coatalen, designer of the twin-cam, and indeed of all Sunbeams since 1909, turned his interest to the French firm, and Sunbeam went into a decline from which it never really recovered. Nevertheless, the twin-cam was a fine car, capable of 90mph with an open four-seater body. Sir Henry Segrave was the London manager of the firm at the time, and he had a specially tuned model capable of 100mph. The four-seater body was the most commonly seen, usually with cycle-type wings, but a six-light saloon was also available from the factory, while special bodies included open two-seater and fixed-head coupés. Because of its advanced design, it was not originally intended as a serious production model, and the original sanction was for only 25 cars. However, a total of ten times that number were made between 1925 and 1930, including a few Cozette-supercharged cars in 1929. The Sunbeam's weakness was its chassis, which was too long (10ft 10½in wheelbase) and too frail for a high-performance car. Had the makers produced a short-chassis version of about the size of the Red Label Bentley they might have had a first class sports car.

Apart from Bentley, Vauxhall, and Sunbeam, there were very few large British sports cars, especially in the early 1920s. The 24/90 Straker-Squire appeared in 1921, and was unusual in having its cylinders separately cast, and exposed overhead valve gear. Though untidy looking, this engine was light, and the 4-litre unit propelled the car at over 70mph. Light sporting-tourer and two-seater bodies were available, but the price was very high (£1,150 for the chassis alone) and production was interrupted by difficulties with finance and the supply of components. A more successful car was the 20/70 Crossley. This was a sporting version of the 19.6hp tourer which had been in production since 1921. It had knock-off wire wheels, lightened pistons, and a higher compression ratio, and was capable of 75mph. Perrot front-wheel brakes were optional in 1924, and standard from 1925. As originally supplied, it had no hood, but provision was made for one, and most buyers, not surprisingly, asked for one. The standard body was the typical open four-seater, although a two-seater was also made. At £875 complete it was nearly £300 cheaper than a 30/98, and yet not many were sold, nor did it figure very much in competitions. Leon Cushman entered two tuned and stripped tourers at Brooklands during 1924, and one of these lapped at 91mph.

Invicta did not achieve real eminence as a sports car maker until the appearance of their S-type 4½-litre car in 1930, but the marque had its origin in 1924. Captain Noel Macklin had made a few examples of a little sports racing car called the Silver Hawk (see page 88), and was also an enthusiast for the steam car. When he decided to build a new car of his own design, his main concern was with flexibility rather than flat-out maximum speed. With the brothers Oliver and Philip Lyle he set up a 'factory' in the garage of his house at Cobham, Surrey. Three prototypes were made using the 2-litre

1926 Crossley 20/70 sports, seen here at Hainberg hill climb in the hands of its German owner, Frau Liliane Roehrs. (Photo: Autocar)

6-cylinder Coventry-Simplex engine, but the first production cars of 1925 were powered by the 2½-litre Meadows engine. These early Invictas were rather ponderous cars with artillery wheels, and were not capable of more than 60mph, although the top gear flexibility was there from the start. For 1927 the engine was bored out to 3-litres, and it was with this car that Miss Violet Cordery went in for a series of demonstrations that first brought fame to the make. After taking records at Monza, she drove 5,000 miles at Montlhéry at an average speed of 73·8mph, for which she was awarded the Dewar Trophy by the R.A.C. in 1926. She won this Trophy again in 1929 when, in a 4½-litre car, she covered 30,000 miles in 30,000 minutes at Brooklands; meanwhile she had driven a 3-litre equipped with a collapsible tent on a 1,000-mile trip through Africa, India, Australia, Canada, and the United States. The 4½-litre Invicta which appeared at Olympia in 1928 still had a Meadows engine, with the bore increased from 72·5mm to 88·5mm, giving a capacity of 4,467cc. The chassis members were deepened and strengthened, and the brake drums were increased in diameter. This first 4½-litre was not thought of as a sports car, and no racing programme was undertaken as yet, but it was a fine fast tourer. It was by no means cheap, the chassis costing £985, while £1,345 was asked for the four-seater tourer. In 1929 came the NLC, which had a wider track, lower floor, still stiffer chassis and cost £1,050 for the chassis. For 1931 it was known as the A-chassis and was joined by the low-chassis S-type, but this, the most famous Invicta, belongs to the 1930s. In six years, the firm had emerged from being one of the most obscure assemblers to the position of a respected marque with a small but keen band of owners, most of whom were personally acquainted with Macklin and the factory staff. Practically all the cars were collected by their owners from the works, and were frequently returned there for servicing and modifications.

The vintage Rolls-Royce was never thought of as a sports car, but one could hardly imagine a better Grand Touring car than a Silver Ghost with lightweight four-seater tourer body, capable of 2–78mph in top gear, and, as one of *The Autocar* correspondents said 'pulling sweetly and in absolute silence up the Grande Corniche out of Nice without hinting that a change to 3rd would be appreciated, and holding 50–60mph for mile after mile without a sound but the wind and the noise of the tyres.' A sporting model of the

Phantom I, the Continental, was made in 1928, but it is doubtful if any were sold. It had a pointed-tail four-seater body and flared wings, but this sporty appearance did not accord with the Rolls-Royce image.

If there were relatively few makers of large sports cars in Britain in the 1920s, the number of firms offering sporting machinery in the under 2-litre class was enormous. Not only were there more potential buyers for the smaller cars, but it was comparatively easy to turn a 10hp touring model into a sports car of sorts, although, as in pre-war days, many were more sporting in appearance than anything else. The cyclecar flourished for a few years until the Austin Seven showed that four wheels, four seats, and shaft drive could be had at no greater cost than the crudities that the cyclecarists had contented themselves with. Just as before the war, the G.N. was almost the only cyclecar which could also be called a sports car. In 1919 Godfrey and Nash acquired a much larger factory at Wandsworth, and within two years were making 50 cars per week, compared with less than 200 altogether at the old Hendon factory. The post-war G.N. had final drive by chains, this being the chain and dog-clutch system with a separate chain for each ratio, driving to a solid back axle. The chain final drive was originally used on a 'works special' built by Sheret, one of the more talented G.N. employees, who later joined Arnott & Harrison Ltd of Willesden, makers of the New Carden, and gave his name to a simplified and cheaper version of the New Carden. The post-war sporting model was the Vitesse, with alloy pistons and both valves in the head, as compared with the ioe layout on the pre-war Vitesses. With a staggered two-seater doorless body, the overall weight was only 7½cwt and the maximum speed 65mph. Steering ratio was less than half a turn from lock to lock. In 1922 there came a new Vitesse with a camshaft above each cylinder, whose output was about 35bhp. This was more than that of many cars which weighed twice as much as the G.N., and performance was remarkable. However, the engine was far from reliable, and even noisier than other G.N.s, and the ohc Vitesse was only seen in small numbers on the road. During 1921 the control of the firm had passed into new hands, and the sporting models were neglected in favour of touring models with quieter de-tuned engines and a door for the passenger (heresy to Archie Frazer Nash). In 1923 a shaft-driven light car with 4-cylinder Chapuis-Dornier engine appeared. As a sporting cyclecar the G.N. was dead, and it had only a year or two to run before the make itself disappeared. Nevertheless over 3,000 were made from 1919 to 1924, and the marque gave rise to two sports cars whose fame became much greater than that of the G.N., the French Salmson which was derived from the licence-built G.N., and the Frazer Nash.

The G.N.'s Grand Prix rival in pre-war days, the Morgan, flourished during the 1920s, and was the only British three-wheeler which appealed particularly to the sportsman. They were very quick to get into production, and by March 1919 were already making about twenty cars per week. The Sports model now had an air-cooled Swiss M.A.G. engine but was still the ordinary touring model, being re-named more appropriately the Standard in 1922. The Grand Prix had a water-cooled J.A.P. engine, and was joined by the faster, Blackburne-engined Aero for the 1921 season. This long-tailed model was renamed the Super Sports Aero in 1929, and was the fastest vintage Morgan. Overhead valves were introduced in 1923, and standardized in 1925. By 1927 the Aero could reach 80mph, and at touring speeds fuel consumption was about 45mpg. Three-wheeler enthusiasts were always out of the mainstream of sporting motorists, but there were undoubted attractions in the high geared steering and 80mph performance for an outlay of only £145. Two-speed transmission was employed until 1932.

In the light car category (up to 1½ litres), the days of the 2-cylinder engine were numbered, but two firms, Douglas and A.B.C., made sporting twins for a few years. Like many light car makers, Douglas regularly entered their products in the Long Distance Trials such as the London-Exeter-London, and the London-Lands End, and private owners also raced stripped examples at Brooklands. Encouraged by their successes, the London agents, Vivian Hardie and Lane, offered a sports version of the flat-twin light car, with aero screens, bolster tank in the style of the Mercer Raceabout, and no doors. The bodywork, such as it was, was said to have been designed by Miss Daisy Addis-Price who entered at least one of the cars at Brooklands. In 1922 Douglas abandoned the manufacture of cars for motorcycles, but in the same year a new 2-cylinder sports car appeared. The 1,200cc flat-twin shaft-driven A.B.C. light car was something of a compromise between the cyclecar and genuine light car and had been in production for two years. The sporting model of 1922 had enlarged valves and special valve springs, and external copper exhaust pipes running the full length of the car. This feature, also seen on the sports Warren-Lambert and other cars, was usually the sign of the pseudo-sports car and was not continued on the Super Sports A.B.C. which appeared in 1924. This had a larger bore, giving a capacity of 1,326cc, and a more attractive body with pointed tail. A clover-leaf sporting body was made by Gordon England. The Super Sports had a maximum speed of 70mph from a 40bhp engine. The two seats were slightly staggered, and wheels were either artillery or disc. It might have been a rival to the light French sports cars such as Amilcar which were just appearing in England, but the early cars had acquired a bad reputation for throwing pushrods about the countryside, and although this was cured in the later cars, including the Super Sports, the slur lingered. Also the public were coming to demand four cylinders by 1925 even on the cheapest cars (which at £275 the A.B.C. was not), and from 1926 sales fell off very sharply.

One of the more attractive 4-cylinder sporting cars was the 10·4hp Calthorpe. The makers had entered cars in the pre-war Coupe de l'Auto races without success, and some sporting bodies had been mounted on the 10·4hp chassis in 1914–15. The 1920 Sporting Four had drilled connecting rods and aluminium pistons, giving the car a speed of about 60mph even with four-seater bodywork. The usual sporting bodies were two- or four-seaters, in polished aluminium, made by Mulliners who had a factory next to Cal-

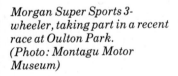

Morgan Super Sports 3-wheeler, taking part in a recent race at Oulton Park. (Photo: Montagu Motor Museum)

thorpes in Bordesley Green, Birmingham. At their best period, in 1921–22, Calthorpe were making between fifty and seventy Sporting Fours per week.

Wolseley has never been renowned as a sporting make (except for their enormous Gordon Bennett racers of 1902 to 1905), but in 1919 they had a promising engine in their single ohc Ten, itself inspired by the Hispano-Suiza aero engines which Wolseley had built during the war. In 1921 a Competitions Department was set up under Captain Alistair Miller, and streamlined versions of the Ten and Fifteen were entered for racing and record breaking at Brooklands. The Sports Ten was the outcome of this and appeared in 1922. It had an aluminium body with pointed tail, and disc wheels, and cost £610. The following year a more highly tuned car known as the Speed Model appeared, now with artillery wheels and costing £695. It had a top speed of over 70mph, but was very stark; there was no hood, and *The Autocar,* in a left-handed compliment, called it 'practically a road-going racing car'. Because of this and the high price, few sports Wolseleys were sold, and they disappeared from the catalogue the following year.

Numerous other firms offered small sports cars, some with mildly tuned engines, some with no tuning, in which case any improvement in performance could only come from fitting a lighter body. Typical of this group was the Bayliss-Thomas, a light car powered by an 8·9hp Meadows or 10·8hp Coventry-Simplex engine. The sports models had lower seats, more inclined steering columns, tapered aluminium tails, twin aero screens, and doorless bodies, but no modifications to the engines at all. Unlike many other such cars, the prices (£275 and £310) were identical to those of the tourers. By 1924, the makers of such cars were discovering that there were more buyers for the all-weather family four-seater, and the field of the light sports car was abandoned to the specialists.

Foremost among these was Alvis. This was a brand-new post-war firm, headed by T. G. John, and its first car was the 10/30 which had a 4-cylinder engine of 1,460cc, which developed 'something over 30bhp' at 3,500rpm. It was a conventional side-valve unit, but had aluminium pistons. Bodywork was in light aluminium, and at 14cwt the 10/30 was the lightest production Alvis ever made. It was thought of as a sporting car from the start, although

Below: 1923 Wolseley Ten Speed Model, *being tested by* The Autocar *in distinctly uncomfortable conditions, considering its lack of weather protection.*
(Photo: Autocar)

Below right: A typical sporting adaptation of a family car was this 1922 10hp Seabrook. The engine was a side-valve Dorman unit as used in many assembled cars, but the appearance was pleasantly rakish.
(Photo: Autocar)

Alvis 12/50 with unusual body by Offord & Sons Ltd. (Photo: Montagu Motor Museum)

overshadowed in memory by the much more celebrated 12/50. In 1921 came the 11/40, with shorter wheelbase and larger bore giving 1,598cc and 40bhp. On this chassis was seen the first of the polished aluminium 'duck's back' bodies, although most 11/40s had touring two-seater bodies. Racing was begun in 1921, the leading works driver being Major C. M. Harvey who retained this position for many years. The 11/40 racing cars were not very successful, retiring in the Coupe Internationale des Voiturettes, and finishing no higher than 17th and 20th in the 200 Mile Race at Brooklands. The works sponsored no racing in 1922, but Alvises achieved many successes in trials. The first overhead valve Alvis, the 10/30 Super Sports, with duck's back body and outside exhaust pipe, was announced in June 1923. Very few were made apart from prototypes because development soon began on the 68 × 103mm (1,496cc) car known as the 12/50. This was the work of Captain G. T. Smith-Clarke who had recently become chief engineer, and it was on a tuned version of this that Harvey won the Brooklands 200 Mile Race in October 1923. The building of this special car took no more than 14 days. Although widely hailed at the time (it was Britain's first victory in this race), it is difficult to estimate how much influence Harvey's success had on sales.

Mrs Dykes' Alvis 12/50, seen at St Martin's corner during the 1928 Coupe Boillot at Boulogne. (Photo: Montagu Motor Museum)

However, by January 1924 about 50 per cent of production was devoted to the ohv 12/50, the rest being the sv 11/40s, which were dropped in 1925. The most sporting model was the SA 12/50 with a short wheelbase of 9ft 0½in, and a maximum speed of over 75mph. The price was £550, which was by no means cheap, but a similarly bodied 11/40 cost only £450.

The 12/50 continued in production until 1932 (with a brief break), being supplemented in 1931 and 1932 by the 12/60 with twin carburetters, a higher compression ratio (5·8:1 compared with 5·35:1), and close ratio gearbox. Front-wheel brakes were introduced in 1924, and the chassis was stiffened. The separate sub-frame which had carried the engine and gearbox was given up. For touring cars the larger 1,645cc engine was used, often in conjunction with ponderous, touring bodies, but the smaller engine was retained for competition in the 1½-litre class. The duck's back style was gradually replaced by the sloping tail beetle back and there was also a very attractive sporting four-seater tourer with narrow body and wire wheels. About 7,000 12/50s and 12/60s were made altogether, of which about 650 are still on the road today. It was one of those happy designs which combined a useful performance with reliability and durability.

In September 1927 came the 6-cylinder 14·75hp with an ohv 1,870cc engine of similar design to that of the 4-cylinder car. The name was taken from the actual R.A.C. rating of 14·75hp, in contrast to previous Alvises in which the second figure represented the brake horse power. The 6-cylinder car never developed 75bhp and the often quoted designation 14/75 is therefore wrong. The same applies to its successor, the 16·95hp Silver Eagle. Body styles on these 6-cylinder Alvises were similar to those on the 12/50s. The Silver Eagle had a 72bhp 2,148cc engine; the short-chassis SE four-seater could reach 85mph with ease.

An interesting, though not very profitable, sideline to these conventional Alvises was the series of front-wheel drive cars sold between 1928 and 1930. The first fwd Alvises had been racing cars, made since 1925, and a production sports car had been put on the market in February 1928. Its engine was basically that of the 12/50 turned back to front but with a gear-driven single overhead camshaft; a Cozette supercharger increased power from 50bhp to about 75bhp. Front suspension followed that of the 1927 Grand Prix car, and was independent by eight transverse quarter elliptic springs, two upper and two lower on each side. Rear suspension was also independent, by longitudinal torque arms and reversed quarter elliptics. These 4-cylinder fwd cars were capable of about 85mph, and achieved a number of racing successes in 1928. In the Le Mans 24 Hour Race they won the 1½-litre class and finished 6th and 9th overall, while in the Tourist Trophy Leon Cushman came second behind Kaye Don's Lea-Francis. However, the fwd cars were noisy and temperamental and were hardly suitable for ordinary road work, although one was bought by a clergyman who intended to use it for parish visiting! About 150 fwds were made, two- and four-seaters, as well as a saloon, their prices being slightly less than £100 above those of the equivalent 12/50. Ten straight-8 fwd cars were also made but these were even more complicated than the fours, and nearly all were retained by the works for research and racing. In one of them Cyril Paul won the 1½-litre class in the 1930 T.T. For a short time in 1929 the 12/50 was dropped in order to concentrate on the 6-cylinder cars and the front-wheel drive cars, but it was hastily re-introduced in 1930 and continued in production well after the more exotic machines had been banished from the catalogue.

In a similar class to the 12/50 Alvis was the Meadows-engined Lea-Francis sports car. Lea and Francis Ltd had been making a complicated range of cars

10. Above: *1927 Amilcar CGSs Surbaissé sports car. Owned and photographed by F. G. Lyndhurst.*

11. Below: *1928 Alvis FA 1½-litre front-wheel drive 'Le Mans' two-seater. Owned by A. Faulkner. (Photo: Roger McDonald)*

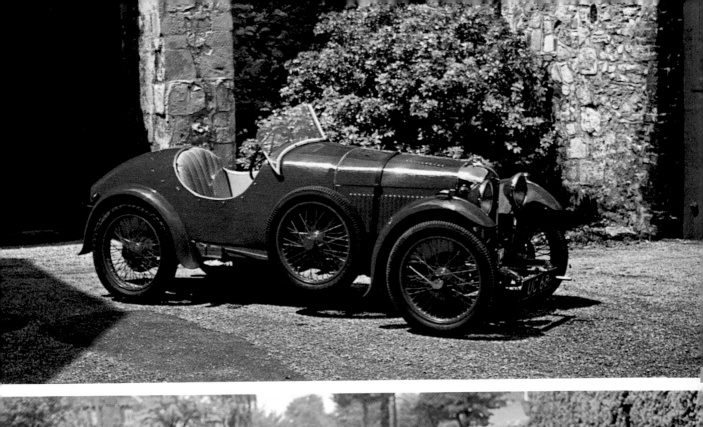

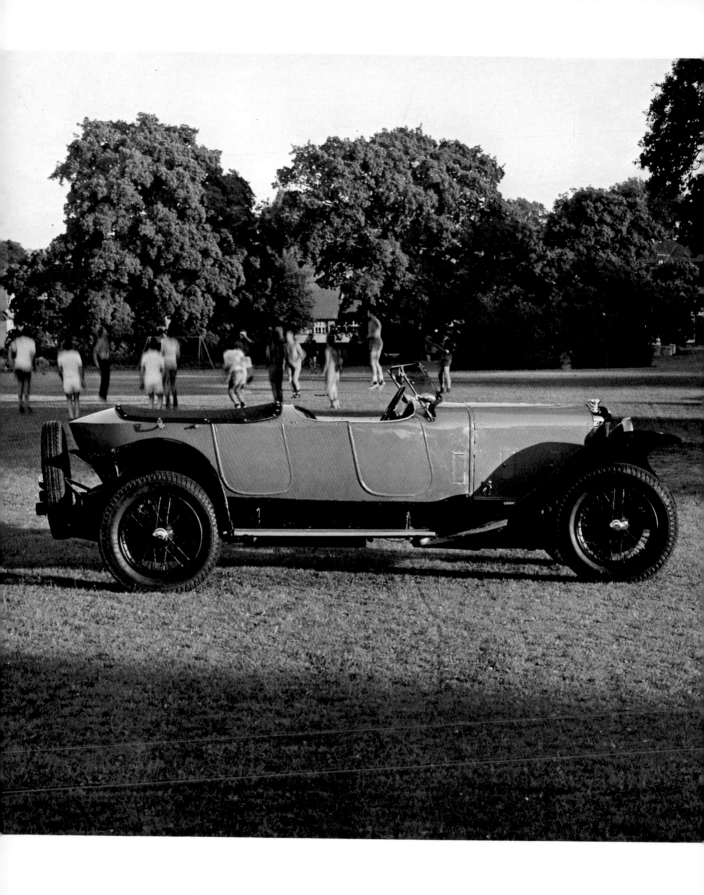

since 1921, and in 1925 announced the 12/40 L-type, powered by the 1,496cc Meadows 4ED engine. This was the most sporting Meadows engine, and was also used later by Frazer Nash and in the French Derby front-wheel-drive sports car. The Lea-Francis sports had a polished aluminium duck's back two-seater body, not unlike that of the 12/50 Alvis, which was not surprising as both were made by Cross and Ellis. The Lea-Francis 'tail' was rather more sloping, however, and carried the spare wheel above the bodywork, while the Alvis' spare wheel was tucked beneath the tail. The Lea-Francis was appreciably cheaper at £375. For 1928, the 4ED engine was used in the new P-type tourer, while the sports model used a special 52bhp version of the engine. Nearly all these Type Os had four-seater bodies, and it was not until the 1928 season that a Lea-Francis appeared which was capable of winning races in the 1½-litre class. This was the S-type, otherwise known as the Hyper. The engine was still the Meadows 4ED but power was boosted to 61bhp by a Cozette supercharger, while the frame was lowered and the radiator sloped at an angle of 15 degrees. The open tourer cost £495 and was capable of 90mph, while the competition two-seater cost £550. These prices were not excessive when compared with those of the 12/50 Alvis, but the Lea-Francis never achieved the popularity of its rival. The earlier cars did not have any of the sporting flavour of the Alvis, while the Hyper model was not renowned for reliability. Lubrication of the supercharger was a very weak point, and an oil-starved blower could not only damage itself but the front of the crankcase as well. Perhaps the Hyper-Leaf was more comparable with the front-wheel drive Alvis, in which case Lea-Francis did well to sell 189 of them, albeit this was over a five-year period, 1927 to 1932, as compared with Alvis sales of 150-odd in two years. The only outstanding racing success of Lea-Francis was Kaye Don's victory in the 1928 Tourist Trophy, which he won by only thirteen seconds from Cushman's fwd Alvis. Leafs also finished fairly well in the Brooklands 'Double Twelve', at Le Mans and at Phoenix Park, all in 1929.

Like Lea-Francis, the Riley was strictly a touring car for the first few years after the war, but in 1922 sporting two- and four-seater bodies were available on the 10·8hp chassis. Originally they had disc wheels like the tourers, but later cars had wire wheels, while colour scheme was usually polished aluminium for the bodies and red wings. This led to the unofficial names Redwing or Redwinger, which have come to be associated with all side-valve sporting Rileys. They were very successful in trials, and Victor Gillow raced a stripped version at Brooklands in 1924. A short-chassis competition version of the Redwing was made in 1925, and at the 1926 Olympia Show there appeared a supercharged ohv model with longer wheelbase, said to be capable of 80mph. However this never went into production, because of a patent infringement concerning the overhead valve gear, and anyway a few months earlier there had appeared a much more interesting Riley. The prototype Riley Nine was announced in the summer of 1926, and immediately caused a sensation. It had a 4-cylinder 1,087cc engine, with large inclined overhead valves which were operated by twin camshafts mounted high in the engine, but not overhead. This layout was shared by the Lea-Francis engine of 1937 to 1953 designed by Hugh Rose, who had previously worked for Riley. It was retained by Riley until they ceased to make their own engines in 1957. The cylinder head featuring hemispherical combustion chambers was known as the PR Head after Percy Riley, and was probably the greatest single factor in the success of the Riley Nine. By the end of 1926 J. G. Parry Thomas was working on the Brooklands sports version of the Nine, and after his death at Pendine in March 1927, the work was carried on

12. 1924 Ballot 2LT 2-litre sports tourer. Coachwork by Lagache et Glaszmann. Owned by G. H. Taylor. (Photo: Charles Pocklington)

83

1929 front-wheel drive Alvis, seen in action at Kalorama in 1964.
(Photo: Montagu Motor Museum)

Above: *1926 Lea-Francis 12/40 sports. The Cross and Ellis aluminium body bore some resemblance to that of the duck's back Alvis.*
(Photo: Montagu Motor Museum)

Above right: *1925 Riley Redwing sporting tourer.*
(Photo: The Riley Register)

by Reid Railton. The Brooklands Nine was one of the prettiest of any small sports car, with very low appearance and steering column so raked that it was almost horizontal. With high compression pistons and special cams, the power was boosted from 32bhp on the touring Nine to 50bhp at 5,000rpm. The price was only £395. The first few cars were assembled by Thompson & Taylor at Brooklands, but production was later taken up by Riley themselves. With an 80mph maximum speed the Brooklands Nine was effective competitition for the light French sports cars such as Salmson and Amilcar which had had few British rivals up to 1927. The Brooklands Nine won the 1,100cc class in the 1928 Six Hours Race at Brooklands, and also in the 1928 and 1929 Tourist Trophy Races. In the next decade they went on to even greater triumphs.

Two makes with rather more specialized appeal than that of Alvis and Lea-Francis were Aston Martin and Frazer Nash. Lionel Martin had built a prototype light car in 1913, consisting of a Coventry-Simplex engine in an Isotta-Fraschini chassis, and after the war he used the same 1½-litre engine in the sports car which he and Robert Bamford announced in 1921. The name came from that of Martin combined with Aston Clinton, the famous Buckinghamshire hill-climb. The car was an orthodox and simple design,

Above: *Riley Brooklands Nine two-seater.*
(Photo: Montagu Motor Museum)

Above right: *1925 side-valve Aston Martin.*
(Photo: Maurice Harrison)

with a side-valve engine, but it had four-wheel brakes from the start. Although the engines came from Coventry-Simplex, they were finished at Bamford and Martin's small works in Kensington, London. They handled well, and had a speed of over 70mph, but were very expensive at £850. Financial backing for the little firm came from Count Zborowski for whom they built some twin-overhead camshaft racing cars which were also driven with success by Clive Gallop, S. C. H. Davis, and B.S. Marshall. When Zborowski was killed in 1924, Bamford and Martin could no longer keep going, as a side-valve sports car at £850 was hardly a competitive product. About 50 had been sold when the original company went into liquidation at the end of 1925. A. C. Bertelli of the Enfield-Allday company designed a new single ohc engine of 1½-litres capacity and 50bhp, and with W. S. Renwick built a car called the R & B Special. Instead of producing it under this name, they acquired the assets of Bamford and Martin, and in 1927 the R & B was put into production at Feltham as the Aston Martin. This new car was much lower than the previous Aston Martin, and had really powerful brakes. It was mostly produced in two-seater form at first, although a few ugly and angular saloons were made. Until 1930 production was very limited, and only about 25 cars were turned out in over three years. It is surprising that Renwick and Bertelli were able to keep going, but it is fortunate that they did so, for in 1930 they produced the International model, so called because it was 'equipped for road racing under International rules in any part of the world.' It was basically similar to the 1927 car, but had dry-sump lubrication, and a close-coupled two/four-seater body. With this car, the makers began to enter competitions, and production rose markedly in the next few years. For the first time, the Aston Martin car was making a profit for its creators.

One of the most individual sports cars made anywhere in the world was the Frazer Nash. This was a direct descendant of the G.N. cyclecar, and when the first Frazer Nash was announced in July 1924, a few G.N.s were still being assembled at Wandsworth. Indeed there was a hybrid car called the Frazer Nash-G.N. which consisted of the chain-driven G.N. chassis into which Archie Frazer-Nash installed a French-built 4-cylinder Ruby engine. Not more than twelve of these were made, and they are interesting only in being a link between the two makes, produced as a short-term measure to provide an income while Frazer-Nash was preparing his own car. This went into production in a small factory at the bottom of Kingston Hill, and seven cars were turned out before the end of the year. They used 1½-litre ohv Plus-Power engines, and retained the three speed chain and dog-clutch transmission which had been developed for the G.N. This system was used on all genuine Frazer Nashes until production ended early in 1939, although four forward speeds were available from 1929. The system was light and made for very rapid changes, and coupled with well-chosen ratios was responsible for much of the appeal of the car. It has been suggested that chain-drive was outmoded even when the first Frazer Nash appeared, but this system had nothing in common with the pre-1914 chain-driven cars, in which gears were changed in a conventional gearbox, and the chains used simply to transmit power to the rear axle. The Frazer Nash system was so unusual that one could never say that it had been 'in the mode', so that it could hardly have been outmoded by 1924. It was a brilliant and original system which worked admirably in the type of car for which it was designed. Early in 1925 the Plus-Power engine was replaced by the cheaper side-valve Anzani unit of the same capacity. This developed 40bhp, and with an all-up weight of 13cwt, the car had excellent performance. On some models the top ratio was too high for maximum revolutions to be reached, but an advantage of the chain transmission was that ratios could easily and quickly be altered. When the supplies of Anzani engines threatened to dry up Frazer Nash considered buying 12/50 engines from Alvis, but nothing came of this, and a newly organised Anzani company continued to supply engines until 1932.

A make firmly associated with the sports car is the M.G., although it had its origins in that most prosaic of touring cars, the Bullnose Morris Oxford. The very first sporting model Oxford had appeared in 1914, and was a single-seater. It must have been the largest road-going monocar ever offered for sale, as most of the few monocars were minuscule cyclecars such as the Carden or Lester. In 1921 a sports Morris Cowley was introduced. It had aluminium pistons and a higher top gear, and achieved some success in trials, but was discontinued in 1922 as it was no longer competitive. An Oxford Sports was made in very small numbers in 1923 and 1924, using both the 11·9hp and 13·9hp engine. It was said to have been 'specially tuned', but no details are available. The Cowley sports was a works model, but the shadowy Oxford was prepared by the Morris Garages in Oxford, and it is here that the story of the M.G. begins. In 1922 Cecil Kimber had become manager of the Morris Garages, and provided the impetus towards a sporting car which William Morris had never displayed. Early in 1924 six sporting

Below: *1928 Frazer Nash Sportop three-seater, with Meadows engine.* (Photo: Montagu Motor Museum)

Below right: *1927 M.G. 14/28 two-seater.* (Photo: Autocar)

two-seater bodies were ordered from the Oxford coachbuilders Raworth & Company, and mounted on Oxford and Cowley chassis. The steering column was raked, and there were modifications to the carburetter and springs. The result was called the Morris Garages Super Sports Morris. The Oxford was later fitted with four-seater aluminium bodies, and the result called the 14/28 Morris Garages Super Sports Morris. Not surprisingly, this was soon abbreviated to 14/28 M.G. Production started at the Alfred Lane works of Morris Garages (who had several premises in Oxford) in the spring of 1924. The chassis were brought in from the Morris works and modified as described above. Hartford shock absorbers were fitted, and two- or four-seater bodies in polished aluminium gave the cars a sporting air, although the familiar 'bullnose' radiator was still worn. The makers described the cars as being for 'motorists of sporting proclivities and cultivated tastes.'

Annual changes made to the Oxford were reflected in the M.G., and the 'bullnose' gave way to a flat-fronted radiator for 1927. This model was the first to carry the M.G. octagon on the radiator.

Cecil Kimber's philosophy was that if a car were 10 per cent better than normal, it could cost 50 per cent more and still sell. The early M.G.s cost between 12 and 46 per cent more than the equivalent Morris cars, and if their performance was no more than 10 per cent better, their handling and appearance were far superior to the standard product. Kimber sold about ten cars in 1924, and over 300 in 1928 which was the year in which two new models appeared, the M-type Midget, and the 18/80. The Midget has been hailed as the first 'real' M.G., and certainly its appearance was distinctive, but mechanically it was very similar to the Morris Minor announced earlier in the year. The 847cc single overhead camshaft engine was mounted in a chassis with lowered suspension and raked steering, and the car was clothed with a very light fabric pointed-tail two-seater body. It was no more a sports car than the 1921 Sports Cowley or many of the adapted cars of the early 1920s, but it was remarkable value at £175. The 20bhp engine drove it at 65mph, and it had the sporty appearance that hundreds of young buyers wanted. In its first year, more were sold than of all the previous M.G.s put together, and the following September the works were moved to much larger premises at Abingdon. The 18/80 M.G. was based on the 2½-litre ohc Morris Six, but Kimber designed for it a completely new cylinder head. It was more of an original design than the Midget, but in its early form was a tourer rather than a sports car.

The M.G. Midget was the first serious rival to the Austin Seven in the smallest sports car class. The first sports Seven appeared in 1924, and had a pointed-tail body and raked steering column, but no modifications to the engine. Much more exciting was the Brooklands Super Sports which was based on the racing cars developed by E. C. Gordon England. These had polished aluminium bodies with a thin aluminium undershield beneath the chassis, and staggered seating. The engine had a high compression head, high lift cams, and double valve springs, all of which were derived from the racing cars. A Brooklands certificate of 75mph was supplied with each car, which cost £265, compared with £175 for the 'tamer' factory-prepared sports model. The Brooklands model was not really intended for road work, but nevertheless over 350 were sold, and innumerable sporting successes were achieved, including first three places in their class in the 1925 200 Mile Race. For the owner who was not interested in racing, Gordon England made the 'Cup' model which had a less powerful engine and domed back to the body which contained the spare wheel. By 1925 many other firms were supplying sporty-looking bodies for the Seven, while owners found that some extra

*1928 Austin Seven Gordon England Cup Model, showing the characteristic domed boot which concealed the spare wheel.
(Photo: G. R. Greinig)*

*1929 Austin Seven Ulster two-seater.
(Photo: Montagu Motor Museum)*

performance could be obtained by a moderate advance in ignition timing. Some over-advanced it, and the result was very rough running. Apart from Gordon England there were very few tuned sporting Sevens offered for sale, as the general practice was to have a sporting body built by Burghley, Cole & Shuttleworth, Duple, or any of a dozen other firms, and either tune the engine oneself or have it done by a firm such as Bassett & Dingle of Hammersmith whose standard 'tune-up' cost only £7 10s.

In July 1928 the Austin works introduced the Super Sports at £225; its Cozette-supercharged engine developed 33bhp, and drove the car at 70mph. Four of these were entered in the 1929 Tourist Trophy, and Archie Frazer-Nash finished 3rd, behind Caracciola's 7·1-litre Mercedes-Benz, and Campari's 1½-litre Alfa-Romeo. A few of these cars were sold to the public, but in 1930 there appeared a new low-chassis sports car, roomier than the earlier model, and available with, or without, a supercharger.

In passing one might note that while the Seven was the most important sporting Austin, it was not the only one. A wire-wheeled Sports Twenty was offered in 1921 with two-seater aluminium bodywork and mildly tuned engine, while various sporting versions of the Twelve appeared. One of these was the Allen-Bennett sports saloon of 1925, which had a four-door body of sporting lines, with a V-windscreen, Hartford shock-absorbers, and a speed of over 60mph. The price was £575, compared with £455 for the ordinary Twelve saloon.

Two interesting examples of small specialist producers of sports cars were Silver Hawk and Arab. The former was the work of Noel Macklin who had built the Eric-Campbell light car, and the Silver Hawk was, in fact, a sporting Eric-Campbell built by Macklin after he had severed his connection with

Arab 2-litre sports car. (Photo: Montagu Motor Museum)

the original company. It had a tuned Coventry-Simplex engine of 1,498cc, with lightened connecting rods and aluminium pistons, and was said to be capable of 70mph. It was designed entirely as a competition car, and no touring versions were listed; the chassis alone cost £495, and without a cheaper car to back it up, it is hardly surprising that only about twelve cars were sold. Nevertheless, with G.N., Silver Hawk was the only British make to compete in the 1920 Coupe des Voiturettes, and two cars finished in 6th and 7th places.

The Arab was a later attempt to make a purely sporting car, and was produced in a small factory at Letchworth. Its designer was Reid Railton who later worked on the Brooklands Riley Nine, and through Railton it is likely that Parry Thomas had an influence on the design. The engine was a long-stroke four of 70 × 127mm having a capacity of 1,960cc. The inclined overhead valves were operated by a single overhead camshaft, and closed by leaf springs as on Thomas' Leyland Eight and Marlborough-Thomas. This engine was developed in 1925, and powered a car which won the Unlimited Novices' Class at the Southport Speed Trials that year, but the official announcement of the Arab did not take place until November 1926. Two- and four-seaters were available at £525, capable of 80mph, and a 90mph Super Sports two-seater cost £550. Parry Thomas' death in March 1927 ended his connection with the Arab, and by then both he and Railton were more concerned with the Brooklands Riley, so the Arab project was dropped. Probably not more than six cars were built.

The only sports car to come from Scotland was the Beardmore, a product of a firm better-known for aero-engines, taxicabs, and general engineering. The 2-litre Sports was developed from the Eleven, which had a single overhead camshaft 4-cylinder engine. In the Sports the bore was increased, compression ratio raised, and stronger valve springs were used. They were handsome cars with wire wheels, V-windscreens, and two- or four-seater aluminium bodies. Maximum speed was 70mph, although acceleration was on the slow side because it weighed nearly a ton. The Sports Beardmore first appeared at the Sorn hill-climb in April 1923, driven by Cyril Paul who was the leading exponent of the car. It was he who drove a special Beardmore at Shelsley Walsh in 1925, and took the record for the hill.

The A.C. was made in 1½- and 2-litre form, and both models could carry sporting bodywork. Up to 1925 the 1½-litre 4-cylinder engine was made by Anzani, and the regular order for about thirty engines per month was the mainstay of the British Anzani Engine Company. When S. F. Edge decided that A.C. should make their own 4-cylinder engines, British Anzani nearly went out of business, thereby threatening the nascent Frazer Nash company. The new A.C.-built four followed the lines of the 2-litre six in having steel liners in an aluminium block, and a single overhead camshaft. The three-speed gearbox was attached to the rear axle. In 1927 a tuned sports model of the six was announced, known as the Montlhéry. Capable of 80mph, it was the only true sports A.C. of the 1920s.

Two firms whose fast tourers of the 1920s led on to sports cars in the next decade will be dealt with in Part Three; they are Lagonda and Talbot.

1922 A.C. 1½-litre, with aluminium two-seater body. (Photo: Montagu Motor Museum)

4. France

The sporting car scene in France was curiously different from that in England. There was a host of machines in the 1,100cc class which was scarcely represented in England, and many fine fast tourers capable of sustained high speeds, and yet the decade ended with most of these makes in decline. In England many sports car makers were late to establish reputations, but once they had done so they consolidated them in the thirties; Aston Martin, Frazer Nash, Invicta, Lagonda, Riley, and Talbot all added to their reputations after 1930, whereas the turn of the decade had almost the effect of the guillotine on their French equivalents. An exception was Bugatti, but practically all generalizations are torpedoed by the cars from Molsheim.

Probably the most typical French vintage sports car was the light machine of under 1,100cc capacity. This figure had more significance in France than in England, for not only was it a sporting category, but the owner of the small car paid much less annual tax, 100 francs per annum as compared with 400 francs for anything over 1,100cc. In the immediate post-war years there were two kinds of small car, those built up from the motorcycle, and those built down from the car. The former were cheaper to make, but very crude, and by 1922 most of the cyclecars had disappeared to make way for the genuine small car with four cylinders and shaft drive.

Most of these small cars were entered in competitions, the most interesting of which was the Bol d'Or. This had the distinction of being the first 24 hour race held in Europe, for the first Bol d'Or was held a year before the more famous sports car event at Le Mans. It was instituted by Eugene Mauve, who was himself a car builder, though his products never distinguished themselves in the race he founded. Mauve was also the president of the Association des Anciens Motocyclistes Militaires, and the entries included motorcycle combinations as well as cars of up to 1,100cc capacity. The rules were very simple; one driver per car was allowed, although a passenger could be carried to keep the driver company if he wished. A rest period of four hours was allowed, and the cars had to have covered at least 90km at the end of the third hour to qualify. This meant an average of nearly 20mph, which does not seem an excessive demand, but one must remember that some of the cars had a capacity of no more than 350cc. Mudguards were not obligatory, and many of the competitors in the later events of the series looked indistinguishable from racing cars. The first race was held in 1922, on a 5km circuit in the forest of St Germain, passing through a number of villages, including some atrocious road surfaces. When these were resurfaced in 1926 so much fresh tar was thrown up that some drivers had to receive medical treatment during the race. An unusual feature of the early Bols d'Or was that the cars started behind a pilot car, as at Indianapolis. In 1923 the pilot was one of the 'tank' Grand Prix Bugattis, driven by Pierre de Vizcaya. A wide variety of cars competed in the Bols d'Or, from well-known sports cars like Amilcar, Salmson, and Sénéchal down to obscure miniatures like the 350cc Viratelle or d'Aux with a maximum speed of 36mph. The regulations separated 3- from 4-wheelers regardless of capacity, which was illogical, for a 4-cylinder 1,100cc Sandford was classed as a cyclecar, whereas the 350cc d'Aux was considered a car on the strength of its four spidery, cycle-type

Typical of the light sports cars which competed in the Bol d'Or was this 1923 Benjamin. (Photo: J. A. Sebesta)

wheels. However a great deal of enjoyment was had by competitors and spectators, and these events did allow small companies the chance to compete in a long-distance race, and gave drivers good practice for the more internationally famous races.

The French 3-wheeler has been largely forgotten, but there were at least three makes which deserve the name of sports car. The Darmont and the Sandford were based on the Morgan, while the d'Yrsan was a home-grown design. The Darmont first appeared in 1924, and followed the Morgan specification very closely. Two side-valve models were made, the air-cooled 'Etoile de France' capable of 66mph and a water-cooled version with a speed of 72mph. The most powerful was the overhead-valve Darmont Spéciale which was available with a supercharger. This was strictly a competition model, and could reach nearly 100mph. The engines were very close copies of the Blackburne as used on the more sporting Morgans. The Darmont enthusiast was of the same rugged breed as the Morgan owner, but a more comfortable 3-wheeler was provided by Stuart Sandford. Sandford was an Englishman resident in France who had driven Morgans in competition on both sides of the Channel. His car retained the Morgan independent front suspension, but had from the start a three-speed gearbox (not adopted by Morgan until 1931), and offered front-wheel brakes in 1924. The most striking difference was that the Sandfords all had 4-cylinder water-cooled engines, and consequently in place of the exposed V-twin engine of Darmont and Morgan one found a handsome pointed radiator. The engines were all made by Ruby (except for a short-lived Sandford-built flat twin in 1934), the most powerful being the 3-bearing crankshaft Model K, which developed 50bhp from 1,088cc. The Sandford was more luxurious and reliable than the Darmont, but prices were up to two and a half times as high, and production was never very great. In his peak period of 1926/27, Sandford was only turning out about 50 cars per year.

Like the Sandford, the d'Yrsan 3-wheeler used a Ruby engine, originally of 972cc, and a three-speed gearbox. It had a tubular chassis, and independent front suspension by transverse springs. Front-wheel brakes were used, but a decidedly old-fashioned feature was that of acetylene lighting. The sports model had an ohv engine, flared wings, and a pointed tail, and looked a typical sporting car of the period. It was capable of 70mph, while there was also a special streamlined racing model called the Scarabée, said to be good

1929 Darmont 3-wheeler.
(Photo: Guy Burnat)

for 85mph. In 1927 a 4-wheeler was introduced, and the following year the 3-wheelers were dropped. The 4-wheeler used the same Ruby engine as its predecessor, supplemented by an 1,100cc version, and made in racing form with a supercharger. They were low and attractive-looking cars, and two competed at Le Mans in 1929, but did not distinguish themselves. A 6-cylinder model was announced, using a twin-ohc engine built by Michel Aviation of Strasbourg, and based on a Vagova design, but the car was never seen in competition.

The two most successful light sports cars were the Amilcar and the Salmson, and for nearly ten years they competed fiercely for sales and sporting successes. The Amilcar appeared slightly earlier than its rival, towards the end of 1920. It was built by a company whose directors were Joseph Lamy and Emil Akar; the name has been suggested as either a combination of both surnames, or as a contraction of Emil Akar. On phonetic grounds the latter seems the more likely, and Akar was, in fact, the senior partner. The designer was Edmond Moyet, while sales were looked after by Mme Lamy. At first the Amilcar was an economy car with no sporting pretensions, although it was more powerful than most of its rivals, giving 18bhp from 904cc. In 1922 came the C4 model, with 1,044cc 23bhp engine, and on this was mounted the first sporting body. Amilcar entered two cars in the 1922 Bol d'Or, and

Sandford 3-wheeler.
(Photo: Montagu Motor Museum)

André Morel's 904cc model won at an average speed of over 40mph. Salmsons were 2nd and 3rd. Morel's car was the basis of the CS, whose 985cc engine developed 23bhp, giving a maximum speed of 60mph. The most typical body was the Petit Sport, a staggered two-seater with pointed tail. Later came the CGS, with front-wheel brakes and redesigned cylinder head giving 30bhp and 75mph. The final development of the 4-cylinder Amilcar came in 1926 with the CGSs, or Surbaissé model, which had lowered chassis and radiator, and looked a much more modern car than the CGS, although both were made side by side. The Surbaissé usually had cycle-type wings, in place of the spindly, flowing wings of the earlier Amilcars, although the later CGS also had cycle wings. At their peak period Amilcar were turning out 35 cars per day, mostly sporting models, from a factory employing 1,200 workmen. The CGS and Surbaissé models were still being made in 1929, but in reduced numbers, and after that the firm concentrated on touring cars. The straight-8 carried some very handsome coachwork, but lacked power and was never a successful sporting car. The 4-cylinder Amilcars were made under licence in two countries; in Austria as the Grofri and in Germany as the Pluto, the latter available with a supercharger. In addition, the Italian firm, S.I.L.V.A. of Verona, assembled the Amilcar and fitted it with locally made bodies. A 6-cylinder twin-cam racing car was offered for sale in 1926, but although a few were fitted with sketchy road equipment, it could not be considered a sports car in the usual sense.

The Salmson had its origin in the G.N. which was built under licence by the Salmson aero-engine company from 1919 to 1922. About 3,000 were made, the same number as in England, but the makers wisely decided that a 2-cylinder car was not a good foundation on which to plan their future. Accordingly, in 1921 they introduced a 4-cylinder light car, after which G.N.-Salmson production tailed off rapidly. The 4-cylinder car had an 1,100cc engine set very far back in the frame, a two-seater body, and no differential. An unusual aspect of the engine, inherited from aero-engine practice, was that a single pushrod per cylinder also acted as a 'pull-rod' for the inlet valve. In a road test on the first model, *The Autocar* remarked on the noisy valve gear, but praised the willing engine. Maximum speed was about 50mph, and fuel consumption 45mpg. A special car built for the 1921 Cyclecar Grand Prix had twin overhead camshafts, and this layout followed on road cars in 1923. The first twin-ohc model was the 1·2-litre 10/15, but in 1925 the smaller 1,100 followed suit. Salmsons came 1st and 2nd in the 1923 Bol d'Or, in which race they carried specially light bodies made of papier maché. The sports Salmson reached its peak in 1926 with the Grand Prix, a rival to the CGSs Surbaissé Amilcar. By now it had front-wheel brakes and a cowled radiator. It cost £265, compared with £285 for the Surbaissé and £250 for the simpler Sénéchal. The most powerful model was the San Sebastian which cost £475 with a supercharger, but in this form the Salmson could out-perform any Amilcar. They won the 1926 J.C.C. Production Car Race at Brooklands, and the Biennial Cup at Le Mans in 1926/27 and 1928/29. When Amilcar introduced their twin-cam six, Salmson replied with a 140bhp Straight-8 but this was too complex and unreliable to be a success. However, on balance, of all vintage models, the Salmson was better than its rival, in that the cheapest model was considerably cheaper, and that if the buyer was willing to pay for performance he could get it. The twin-cam Amilcar Six was not really comparable, being a racing car which was not eligible for all events in which the 4-cylinder cars of both makes competed.

The Sénéchal was probably the next most successful light sports car, largely because of the keenness of its maker, Robert Sénéchal. The 1921

13. *1924 Delage DISS 14/40 sports tourer. Owned by Nigel Arnold-Foster.* (Photo: Montagu Motor Museum)

14. Overleaf, above left: *1928 Bugatti Type 44 3-litre sports tourer. Owned by Ken Purdy.* (Photo: Ken Purdy/Montagu Motor Museum)

15. Overleaf, below left: *1928 Mercedes-Benz Typ S 6·8-litre sports tourer. Owned by C. W. P. Hampton.* (Photo: Charles Pocklington)

16. Overleaf, above right: *1925 Ceirano S.150 tourer taking part in the 1964 V.S.C.C. Welsh Rally. Owned by N. Sloan.* (Photo: Roger McDonald)

17. Overleaf, below right: *1930 O.M. 2·2-litre sports car. This car was re-bodied and exhibited as a new model at the London Motor Show in 1933. Owned by Charles Metcalfe.* (Photo: D. V. Ward)

model was a simple design with 904cc Ruby engine, two-speed gearbox and single transverse leaf spring at the front. The 1922 Grand Sport model had an ohv engine of 985cc, also by Ruby. Sénéchals came 1st and 2nd in the 1,100cc class in the Grand Prix de Boulogne in 1924, and 3rd in the 1923 Bol d'Or. Robert Sénéchal usually drove himself in races, and later became a team driver for Delage in Grand Prix events. In 1926 he won the Bol d'Or, and came 2nd in 1928. Production of Sénéchals was never very large, and few were exported. Those that went to England were imported in chassis form (being driven from Courbevoie to Boulogne, and from Folkestone to London), and fitted with London-built bodies. For a short time British sales were handled by Jean Georgano, the author's father, before being taken over by the Automobile Service Company of Great Portland Street. In 1925 Sénéchal's firm was bought by Chenard-Walcker, and in 1927 the Sénéchal acquired a wide body somewhat reminiscent at the rear of a 'tank' Chenard-Walcker (see page 102). In 1928 there was a streamlined coupé with 1½-litre engine called a Chenard-Sénéchal.

Another car in the 1,100cc class was the B.N.C., made by Bollack, Netter et Cie of Levallois-Perret. Originally it was a light tourer like Sénéchal or Amilcar powered by a 904cc Ruby or 894cc S.C.A.P. engine, although a few cars had Chapuis-Dornier engines. In passing one might mention that these frequent changes of proprietary engine which characterised the smaller makers in many countries were not the result of the designer's whim. Often when a financially shaky, little firm had exhausted their credit and the supplier's patience, they would turn to another, hoping for a little more credit to tide them over. Sometimes the engine maker himself would be in difficulties, as when a valuable customer went out of business or decided to buy elsewhere. Motor manufacture for the small man was a hazardous business, and many men whose names were carried on the radiators of cars would have been better off as employees of larger concerns. That is what most of them became in the end anyway, as the Depression drove the small firms out of business. To return to the B.N.C., a new model appeared at the end of 1925 which was said to be the first production French car to use a supercharger. This was a Cozette whose shaft was mounted vertically. The car became known as the Montlhéry, other models being the Monza un-supercharged short-chassis, and the Miramar long-chassis. The B.N.C. was now a fully fledged sports car, made more attractive-looking than its rivals with the introduction of a sloping radiator in 1927. They were raced widely in that year, taking first two places in the Bol d'Or. The winner on this occasion was Mme Violette Morris, whom *The Autocar* rather unchival-rously described as 'a very masculine lady'. She came 3rd in the 1928 Bol d'Or, and also drove in the Coppa Florio. Like other makers, B.N.C. abandoned the sports car at the end of the decade, and turned to making large luxury cars with American engines. This policy put them out of business within two years.

Associated with B.N.C. was the Lombard, a beautiful little sports car designed by the Salmson racing driver André Lombard, and built in the B.N.C. works. The 1927 AL-3 model had a twin-ohc 4-cylinder engine of 1,095cc, giving 45bhp at 4,800rpm, Perrot-Piganeau four-wheel brakes, and a speed of 85mph. With a Cozette supercharger, power went up to 70bhp at 5,500rpm and speed to 105mph. This from a car of under 1,100cc was quite remarkable. Single-seaters were sold, as well as sports two-seaters and drop-head coupés. Dhome won the 1929 Bol d'Or in a Lombard, and Girod twice won the Circuit de Picardie in a 115mph single-seater. However the cars were very expensive and in 1929 André Lombard ceased to sell the cars under his

18. Above: *1927 Isotta Fraschini Tipo 8A open four-seater sports car. Coachwork by Cesare Sala. Owned by C. W. P. Hampton. (Photo: Charles Pocklington)*

19. Below: *1918 David 8/10hp cyclecar. Owned and photo-graphed by Enrique Rodriguez-Viña.*

1927 Amilcar CGSs seen during an Ilkley Club Trial. (Photo: Montagu Motor Museum)

An early Salmson in the Scottish Six Days Trial. (Photo: Montagu Motor Museum)

A scene during the 1926 J.C.C. High Speed Trial at Brooklands. Left: Grand Prix Salmson and (right) Frazer Nash. (Photo: Autocar)

1927 B.N.C. This was the first of the make to have a sloping radiator.
(Photo: Lucien Loreille Collection)

Lombard AL-3 during the 1929 Brooklands Double Twelve Race.
(Photo: Montagu Motor Museum)

name. For a few months B.N.C. sold the AL-3 under their own name, with their radiator. Ninety-four AL-3s were made in all, of which four survive. The AL-4 was a faster model with 100bhp blown engines and hydraulic brakes. 115mph was claimed, but the car was never completed. Neither was the AL-5, a projected 3-litre 8-cylinder car.

In its origins the Rally was more like a cyclecar, with a V-twin Harley-Davidson motorcycle engine, but soon this was replaced by the usual 4-cylinder units by Ruby or C.I.M.E. At first the Rally had a narrow body with staggered seats like a Grand Prix Salmson, but in 1927 this was replaced by a new wider model which was lower than almost any of its rivals. A Roots-blown twin-ohc car was seen at the 1926 Paris Salon, but not made for sale. Later Rallys had Chapuis-Dornier or S.C.A.P. engines, always in the 1,100cc class. They were not raced very much, but were more successful in rallies(!) winning their class in the Tour de France and the Rallye Feminin Paris-St Raphael. As a sports car Rally lasted longer than any of its rivals, being made until 1933. By this time it had a Salmson S4C engine.

One of the most successful 1,100cc cars in competitions was the 'tank' Chenard-Walcker. These had streamlined bodies with front wheels recessed in fairings, and partially recessed headlamps. The competition cars had vertical radiators set well back, but the cars sold to the public had 'airflow' grilles (eight years before Chrysler). Open two-seaters and fixed-head coupés were made. Not very many were sold for everyday use, perhaps because of their advanced appearance, but they were highly successful in racing. In the 1926 Spanish Touring Car Grand Prix they defeated three Mercedes-Benz 33/140s, whose capacity was over 6 litres. Admittedly the German cars had notoriously poor brakes, but other larger cars were defeated by the little Chenards as well. They won their class in the Georges Boillot Cup at Boulogne, also in 1926, and the Rudge-Whitworth Cup at Le Mans. The competition engines had very small exhaust valves, but extra exhaust ports at the bottom of the stroke controlled a rotary valve turning at one quarter of the engine speed.

There were many other light sports cars, for almost every car maker offered a Type Sport with ohv engine (practically all the engine makers offered ohv units) and sporty body. One cannot list them all, but among the more unusual was the Ballot-engined Soriano-Pedroso which used double-chain drive like a pre-war Grand Prix car and was built by two Spanish noblemen, the Marquis Ivanrey de Soriano and the Marquis de San Carlos de Pedroso. The S.A.R.A. used an air-cooled engine of the firm's own make. An 1,100cc model was driven in the 1923 Bol d'Or by W. F. Bradley, *The Autocar*'s continental correspondent, but crashed into a tree before half the 24 hours were completed. Later, larger S.A.R.A.s with 1,800cc 6-cylinder engines competed at Le Mans, one finishing 3rd in the Biennial Cup in 1926/27, after

Below: *A. S. Gordon's Rally on the approach to the Members' Bridge at Brooklands. J.C.C. Members' Day, July 1929. (Photo: Autocar)*

Below right: *An air-cooled S.A.R.A. at Le Mans in 1924. (Photo: Autocar)*

its team mate had been involved in the famous pile-up involving Bentleys at White House Corner. The G.A.R. lasted throughout the period, running the whole gamut from spidery cyclecar through Amilcar-like sports car with S.C.A.P. or Chapuis-Dornier engines up to a 1,492cc straight-8 with 16 plugs. The Tracta was interesting in using front-wheel drive, designed by Jean Grégoire. The engine, gearbox, and final drive were placed in a row instead of having the gearbox ahead of the axle. This made for a very long bonnet, handsome to look at, but adding to the weight of the car. Nevertheless, they won the 1,100cc class at Le Mans in 1929 and 1930. The engines varied from a 1,100cc S.C.A.P. to a 3-litre Hotchkiss, but only the smaller cars were raced. As we have seen, the minutest cars were raced in the Bol d'Or, but one of the smallest sporting models sold to the public was the Sima-Violet, with a flat-twin 496cc engine, and rear-axle gearbox. The Type Sport had staggered seating.

The other category in which France excelled was the fast tourer, developed on and for the straight roads free of speed limits (in England there was a theoretical limit of 20mph until 1930). Many races were held for this class of car, of which Le Mans is the best known and the only one to have survived to the present day. Others were the Touring Car Grand Prix, the Georges Boillot Cup at Boulogne and the Circuit des Routes Pavées. In the early 1920s there were a number of long-distance road trials, but with increasing traffic the high speeds obtained were becoming dangerous. No one wanted a repetition of the Paris–Madrid tragedy which had taken place only 17 years earlier. Thus the sporting car contests moved from the open road to the circuits, although these were held on ordinary roads, often with very poor surfaces. The Corsican Grand Prix was one of the first such events, and the rules stipulated four-seater bodies, windscreen, and mudguards. This was to ensure that the cars were the sort of machines which could be bought and driven for ordinary touring purposes. In fact, in this and the events on the French mainland, competitors tended to mount special lightweight bodies, often of exotic shape, which the average motorist would not have dreamed of buying, even if he could have done. However, the competition cars had a direct influence on standard design, often being the prototypes of next year's models. The Corsican Grand Prix was won by a Bignan driven by Albert Guyot, while second place was taken by a Turcat-Méry driven by Henri Rougier. Both these men had driven in major events before the war; one of the features of these touring car races was the number of retired Grand Prix drivers who kept their careers going on the slower cars. In other events one finds the names of Szisz, Porporato, Gabriel, and Duray. Incidentally, the prize for the Corsican race was 100,000 francs, the highest up to that date for a European event.

The Touring Car Grands Prix attracted much attention for a few years, partly because they were held either the day before, or the day after, the Racing Car Grand Prix, and on the same circuit. There were separate classes for two-, four-, and five-seater cars, and while no mechanics were carried, each car had to have stone ballast equivalent to the weight of one, three, or four passengers. There was usually a fuel consumption limit as well. Most of the competitors were from the well-known firms such as Peugeot. Voisin, Chenard-Walcker, and so on, but anyone could enter a car if he wished. One private entrant was Alfred Maridet, a wealthy landowner who built a number of cars for his own use. The A.M. which he entered in the 1922 Touring Car Grand Prix at Strasbourg was a large sports car powered by the old-fashioned T-head Janvier engine of 4,850cc. Alas, it caught fire soon after the start; Maridet drove it off the road into a field where it burnt itself out.

As the 120-litre fuel tanks were nearly full, the blaze lasted for most of the race. By 1925 the appeal of the Touring Car Grand Prix was shrinking. The meeting was held at Montlhéry that year, but hardly anybody turned up to watch. In the stands that could hold 10,000 people, it was estimated that there were only 60 spectators, including soldiers and attendants. A local hotel had 400 plucked chickens left on their hands, and special trains and buses were empty.

The first Le Mans 24 Hour Race was held in 1923, again for four-seater cars except in the 1,100cc category where two-seaters were allowed. It was won by a Chenard-Walcker driven by Lagache and Leonard. Second was another Chenard driven by Dauvergne and Bachmann. Lagache and Bachmann were coachbuilders who made the bodies used on the winning cars. The Georges Boillot Cup Race was another event designed to encourage the touring car. It was the final event in the Boulogne Speed Week, a fascinating occasion which included speed trials, a hill climb, a concours d'elegance, and a Light Car Grand Prix. Similar events were held elsewhere in Europe, such as Baden Baden and Freiburg. For a whole week the town would be taken over by sporting motorists; not only competitors but spectators would pour in, in every kind of exotic machine. The events were good tests of versatility, for prizes were awarded on the aggregate performance in speed trials and hill climbs as well as the concours.

Road surfaces were none too good anywhere in the early 1920s, but one race whose organisers deliberately sought out poor conditions was the Circuit des Routes Pavées, or Bad Roads Race, as it was bluntly called in the English Press. Held in the suburbs of Lille in North-Eastern France, the surface was entirely of granite pavé, similar to the cobbled setts of Lancashire. There were eight miles to a lap, the small cars (under $1\frac{1}{2}$ litres) having to cover 22 laps and the large cars 24. The first race in 1923 was won by a Georges Irat, and this make made something of a speciality of the event, winning again in 1925 and taking a class win in 1927. Other makes which did well on the pavé were Chenard-Walcker, Darracq, Lancia, and the big Belgian Excelsior. Even in the early days, speeds were as high as 54mph, which is very creditable considering the surface and the number of tight corners on the circuit.

A very large number of makes produced sporting tourers, and it is hard to select examples. One of the most promising new makes to appear after the war was Ballot. This firm had made engines for many years, and their first cars were 5- and 3-litre racing cars designed by the Peugeot engineer, Ernest Henry. They had twin-ohc engines and this layout was used on the first Ballot sold to the public, the 2LS 2-litre sports car developing 75bhp. This was one of the most advanced sports cars of its day, and in two-seater form could reach 92mph, but it was also very expensive. Not more than 100 were made between 1921 and 1925, and to keep solvent the firm introduced a touring car, the 2LT. This had a single ohc engine of 1,995cc and was typical of the smaller quality touring car. In original form it was not very fast, but when Ballot dropped the twin-cam in 1925, they introduced the 2LTS with hemispherical combustion chambers and larger valves. This gave an extra 10bhp and a speed of 72mph. More important was its ability to cruise comfortably at 60mph for hours on end. In 1928 Ballot introduced a series of straight-8s of 2·6, 2·8, and eventually 3 litres. They were among the best-looking vintage cars, but were too heavy, and their performance was hardly better than that of the 2LTS.

Another new post-war make was the Bignan. Like Ballot, Jacques Bignan was already making proprietary engines when he announced his first car in

3-litre Bignan, winner of the 1921 Corsican Grand Prix; Albert Guyot at the wheel. (Photo: Autocar)

One of the makes which did well in the Circuit des Routes Pavées was Ariès. Here is Laly's 3-litre car which won its class in 1927. Note the full-width bodywork at the rear. (Photo: Autocar)

1919. These had large side-valve engines of 2·9 and 3·4 litres at first. The cars looked sporting, but were not particularly fast until the introduction of a 3-litre overhead camshaft engine in 1921. This engine was based on that of the special car which had won the Corsican Grand Prix; it was designed by Causan, a brilliant engineer who was also responsible for high-performance engines used by La Licorne, La Perle, and Vernandi. Causan also experimented while with Bignan with desmodromic valves; these were closed positively instead of relying on the action of a spring; this was supposed to provide quicker action and avoid spring breakages, but with relatively low-engine speeds it is hard to see its value. The system was not used in production cars, and the competition Bignans did not use it for long. 2-litre Bignans won their class in the 1924 Belgian 24 hour sports car race, and were 3rd and 4th in the first Le Mans race. They had many other successes including leading the 24 hour race at Monza, ahead of two Peugeots and an O.M., for 19 hours before retiring. In fact Bignans were better known on the tracks than on the road, although a 2-litre saloon did win the 1924 Monte Carlo Rally. It is said that an expensive racing programme was responsible for the firm's end. Their final models were small sports cars with Salmson or C.I.M.E. engines and the inevitable small straight-8.

One of the greatest individualists among motorcar builders was Gabriel Voisin. In addition to being a pioneer of aerodynamic bodies, he probably obtained greater performance from the sleeve-valve engine than any other designer. The first Voisin had a 4-cylinder sleeve-valve engine of just under 4-litres capacity. Power output was 80bhp, but this was increased to 90bhp in the sports model and up to 150bhp in the special competition cars entered in Touring Car races. These engines had a compression ratio of 8:1. With light aluminium four-seater bodies they were very successful, taking first three places in the 1922 Touring Car Grand Prix which Rougier won at a speed of 66mph. For the 1924 event, Voisin produced cars of frameless construction similar to that of the Lancia Lambda, using wood, steel, and duralumin. They had streamlined wings, their appearance being not unlike that of the Grand Prix racing Voisins which had run (unsuccessfully) the year before. Four-seater and two-seater cars were entered in the Touring Car race, but they did not have the success of 1922. Voisin also made smaller cars, the 8CV with 1·2-litre engine, and 10CV of 1½ litres. One of the latter won its class in the Circuit des Routes Pavées in 1925. After 1925 Voisin gave up racing, but continued to make fine touring cars, one of the best (in 1932) being the 100bhp 3-litre six. One of the shortcomings of the sleeve-valve engine was that it could not safely maintain a high engine speed, and to keep the revolutions low Voisin introduced an overdrive for the 3-litre. This was originally vacuum-operated, but later the Cotal electro-magnetic system was used. In 1930 a very low saloon and coupé were announced, powered either by a big six of 5·8 litres or a smaller V-12 of 4·8 litres. Unfortunately they were very expensive and perhaps too avant-garde for the average buyer, and hardly any were sold.

Two of France's greatest car builders, Panhard and Peugeot, made sporting cars in the 1920s, which have tended to be overlooked. Like Voisin, the vintage Panhards all used sleeve-valve engines; most cars sold were ponderous tourers, ranging from a 1·2-litre 10CV four to the enormous 6·3-litre 35CV straight-8 luxury car. The latter appealed to the quiet, conservative buyer who thought the Hispano-Suiza too flashy, and who in England would have bought a Daimler in preference to a Rolls-Royce. The Panhard used as a basis for a sports car was the big four, the 30CV 4·8-litre, which, when fitted with light, sporting bodywork, could exceed 85mph. They were not raced as Voisins and Peugeots were, but an enlarged 5·3-litre model won the over 5-litre class at the 1927 Boulogne meeting, beating a 36/220 Mercedes-Benz on an aggregate of two sprints and a hill climb.

Peugeot took an active part in Touring Car races, mainly with sleeve-valve cars. For the 1922 Grand Prix they entered three 3·8-litre 4-cylinder cars, with thinner sleeves than standard, wooden boat-type bodies, and aluminium bonnets. They were beaten by the Voisins, but the following year Peugeots won both the four- and five-seater classes, the former with a 2·4-litre car, the latter with the 3·8. For 1924 they had streamlined bodies, with faired-in rear wheels, and scuttle-mounted headlamps which could be wound down to reduce wind resistance, as on the 1936 Cord. With one of these cars, they won the five-seater class. They won again in 1925, this time using a Weymann saloon body.

In 1927 a special car designed by Louis Dufresne, who had been lured away from Voisin, won the Coupe de la Commission Sportive. The driver was Georges Boillot.

Peugeots continued to do well up to 1928, winning the Coppa Florio, and 24 hour races at Monza and Spa. The big sleeve-valve model, the Type 174, was sold as a sporting tourer and as a saloon, being good for 90mph, and able to cruise comfortably at 75mph for long distances. It was a fine example of the attractions of a large, slow-turning engine; at 60mph it was only doing

1926 Peugeot 18CV sporting tourer.
(Photo: SA Peugeot)

1,960rpm, and only 3,800rpm at its maximum speed. R. C. Symondson says that the tourer he owned for eight years was more than a match for most 4½-litre Bentleys he encountered on the road. In 1928 Peugeot abandoned the sleeve-valve range and turned to smaller cars of no sporting pretensions whatsoever.

There were numerous other cars in the sporting tourer class. Chenard-Walcker, as well as their small 'tank' cars, made 3-litre tourers with brakes on the front wheels and transmission only. These came 1st and 2nd in the 1923 Le Mans 24 Hour Race, and also won the 1924 Circuit des Routes Pavées. A 4-litre straight-8 was also made, but proved too heavy and lacking in stamina for racing success, and too expensive for the general public. Its best performance was 4th place in the 1925 Georges Boillot Cup. Ariès raced both 1,100cc and 3-litre cars at Le Mans and on the Circuit des Routes Pavées. A 3-litre single ohc four-seater nearly won the 1927 Le Mans event, but fell out during the twenty-third hour, leaving the famous Bentley 'Old Number Seven' to take the lead. Although nearly all the small sports cars were made in, or near, Paris (conveniently near their component suppliers), many good touring cars were made in the provinces. In Lyons were Cottin-Desgouttes who entered a team of 3-litre tourers in the 1924 Touring Car Grand Prix. The 4-cylinder pushrod ohv engine had three valves per cylinder, and the cars carried long-tailed fabric four-seater bodies. Replicas of this car were sold to the public. In 1926 a new range of cars with all-independent suspension was introduced, using the same engine, and a new 1,700cc engine in 1927, but these were mostly saloons, and were not raced. The Georges Irat was a well-made 4-cylinder 2-litre car with pushrod-operated overhead valves

3-litre Cottin-Desgouttes, one of a team of three which ran in the 1924 Touring Car Grand Prix.
(Photo: Autocar)

Above: *Piccioni's Voisin which finished 5th in the 1922 Touring Car Grand Prix. A similar car driven by Rougier won the race.*
(Photo: Montagu Motor Museum)

Above right: *André's Georges Irat at St Martin's Corner in the 1928 Coupe Boillot at Boulogne.*
(Photo: Montagu Motor Museum)

1927 Hispano-Suiza H6C 8-litre sports tourer.
(Photo: Montagu Motor Museum)

and Perrot front-wheel brakes operated by Hallot servo as on the Chenard-Walcker, Ballot, and Bignan. This firm made something of a speciality of the Circuit des Routes Pavées, winning it in 1923 and 1925, coming 3rd in 1926, and achieving a class win in 1927. The Lorraine-Dietrich was a good-quality $3\frac{1}{2}$-litre, and won at Le Mans in 1925 and 1926 with cars very little different from the standard models. The sports models had high-compression engines and twin carburetters, but bodywork exactly similar to the standard tourers. Delage and Hotchkiss were excellent cars, but their competition work was limited to rallies and they were not thought of as sports cars. In fact, the dividing line between sports and touring cars was difficult to draw at that time. Many fast tourers were called sports cars in England, but their French owners never considered them as such. The expression 'Type Sport' sometimes meant very little. For example the 1929 Vermorel 'Type Sport' had

lighter pistons and slightly cutaway front doors, but was only capable of 62mph, no great achievement from a 1,757cc engine.

In a class of its own was the Hispano-Suiza, the leading luxury car in France, and one of the three best in the world, yet at the same time a magnificent sports car. It was a brand-new post-war design, with 6-cylinder single-ohc engine derived from the firm's war-time aero engines. These were all V-8s, but the car's engine was one half of a projected V-12. The capacity was 6,597cc and its original output 135bhp at 3,000rpm. The seven-bearing camshaft was a superb component, machined from a solid billet of forged steel. There were four-wheel servo-operated brakes, a rare and advanced feature in 1919. The Hispano's modern design and handsome appearance made an immediate appeal and seriously threatened Rolls-Royce's claim to be the 'Best Car in the World'. It is very difficult to judge a point like this,

but certainly the Hispano made the 80bhp rear-wheel-braked Silver Ghost look old-fashioned, and one cannot imagine Rolls undertaking Hispano's sporting programme. When Rolls did adopt front-wheel brakes they used the Hispano-Pinot system as a model. The 37·2hp Hispano was primarily a luxury touring or formal town car, but it had obvious attractions for the sportsman. The apéritif millionaire André Dubonnet entered his standard four-seater in the 1921 Georges Boillot Cup, and won it. This led to a works team being entered for 1922, these cars having shorter chassis, larger engines of 7,982cc, and higher compression ratios, resulting in an output of 200bhp. About six of these works cars were made, and a whole series of victories followed during the next two years, including the Boillot Cup in 1922 and 1923 and the Spanish Touring Car Grand Prix in 1923. In the 1923 Boillot Cup the cars were said to be reaching 125mph on the straight, and their performance in these events earned the name Boulogne. This has come to be applied to all the 8-litre cars, but really only belongs to the short-chassis sports models. In 1924 the 8-litre model was put on the market as the H6C alongside the 6½-litre which was known as the H6. The works did not sponsor racing after 1923, and in the latter half of the 1920s the sporting character of the Hispano began to decline, although private owners still raced their cars. Dubonnet entered a beautiful tulip-wood bodied H6C in the 1924 Targa Florio, and finished 7th. In an effort to reduce the noise of the engine, always more obtrusive than that of the Rolls, a new cam profile was used in 1928, which reduced the power of the 8-litre car to 144bhp, not much higher than that of the 1919 6½-litre. In the late 1920s, the two cars were rechristened 46*bis* (6½-litre) and 56*bis* (8-litre). About 2,600 of the big sixes were made, production continuing in France to 1934 and in Spain to about 1939. The 6½-litre car was also made in Czechoslovakia by the Skoda works from about 1922 to 1927. The last sporting achievement of Hispano was not a works-sponsored event but the result of a wager between F. E. Moscovics of Stutz and the coachbuilder C. T. Weymann: that a straight-8 Stutz could beat an 8-litre Hispano over 24 hours at Indianapolis. The car entered was a specially prepared H6C with a light two-seater Weymann body, and it won easily, gaining $25,000 for Weymann. However, to do the Stutz justice, it subsequently won a 3½-hour race, and anyway its capacity was only 4·9 litres.

I have deliberately left Bugatti to the end of the French chapter because this was the only firm to make high performance cars in all sizes, and they need to be considered together. At the end of the war, Bugatti resumed production of the small 4-cylinder car with a slightly enlarged engine (1,368cc) and four valves per cylinder. The ultra-short chassis racing model was still called the Type 13, longer cars being the Type 22 (7ft 10½in), and Type 23 (8ft 4½in). The post-war cars were exhibited at the Paris and London Motor Shows in 1919, but the team entered for the 1920 Coupe des Voiturettes at Le Mans were the 1914 16-valve cars which had been hidden during the war. Three cars were entered, that driven by Ernest Friderich winning at 57·6mph, while another finished 5th. The third was disqualified because Ettore Bugatti touched the car while it was at a pit stop. Larger engines of 68 × 100mm (1,453cc) were used in the cars which took the first four places in the Italian Voiturette Grand Prix at Brescia in 1921, and this led to the car being called the Brescia. Generally the short-chassis racing cars are known as Brescias, or Full Brescias, while the longer chassis models are Brescias Modifiés. Engine size went up to 1,496cc in 1923, and four-wheel brakes were added in 1925, although these were often fitted earlier by private owners of tuned Brescias such as Raymond Mays' 'Cordon Bleu', which were capable of 100mph. The Brescia Modifié with a touring body could reach

20. 1925 Excelsior Albert I 5·3-litre two-seater.
(Photo: Montagu Motor Museum)

75mph, and the cars made a great impression on the sporting world of 1921, there being nothing comparable of that size. However it was by no means cheap, costing £575 for a chassis, which meant something like £700 complete. A wide variety of bodies was seen on the Brescia Modifié, mostly open two- or four-seaters, but also drophead coupés and even four-door saloons. This was the only Bugatti to be built under licence in other countries; in Italy Diatto made a few, in Germany it was known as the Rabag, being built by the Rheinische Automobilbau A.G. of Mannheim (see page 121), while in England manufacture was undertaken by Crossley. The Crossley-Bugatti was imported in component form and assembled by Crossleys. It was generally thought to be quieter than the French product, but not so sparkling in performance. It was to be made in batches of 25, as and when Crossley production allowed, but only the first batch was put through. In France, production of Brescias and Brescias Modifiés continued until 1926, about 2,000 being made in all.

In 1922, the first production 8-cylinder Bugatti had appeared, the 2-litre Type 30. This new single-ohc engine with three valves per cylinder was mounted in the Type 23 chassis. It had front-wheel brakes for the first time in a production Bugatti; hydraulic at first, but later cable-operated as at the rear. They were not very satisfactory, and altogether the Type 30 is more important as the progenitor of the immensely successful Type 35 racing cars than for its own achievements. However, Edgar Duffield, of *The Automotor Journal* liked the one he tested in 1925, and part of his report holds good for all vintage Bugattis. 'It is an outdoor car, which begins to earn nuts and/or cigars only after Esher, Staines, or Watford. It can and will trickle through Regent's Park very demurely, but to use it for that kind of motoring is rather like using a Grand National winner to haul a cart-full of mangolds.'

The Type 35 achieved practically all of its fame as a racing car, although one was fitted with flowing wings and driven by Costantini to win the 1½-litre class of the Touring Car Grand Prix in 1925. This had an engine specially reduced to 1,492cc. The Type 35A was the cheapest variant, using the Type 38 touring engine with 3-bearing crankshaft; more of these were seen on the roads than other Type 35s. In France there was no necessity to carry mudguards, so the only addition needed for road use were headlamps and horn. The same situation applied to the 4-cylinder 1½-litre Type 37. Both models of racing car were often driven to and from meetings, but would not generally be employed for ordinary road use. The Type 38 was a touring straight-8 based on the Type 35, and known as the Type 38A when supercharged. As on the Type 35, the front springs passed through the centre of the hollow axle.

When the Brescia Modifié was dropped in 1926, its place as a racing car was taken by the Type 37, and as a touring car by the Type 40. This used the same engine as the Type 37, but with heavier bodies the performance was obviously much less. Nevertheless it was good for 70–75mph, carried practical bodywork, and was much simpler to maintain than the 8-cylinder cars. Its price was not excessive at £365 complete. Considering these attractions, it is surprising that only 840 were sold in five years of production (1926 to 1930). It was probably insufficiently sporting for real Bugatti enthusiasts (who called it Ettore's Morris Cowley), while the Bugatti image of noise and difficult maintenance put other potential buyers off. It cannot be denied that the Brescia and the 8-cylinder cars had given Bugatti an unfavourable image in the eyes of many, but from 1927 onwards *le Patron* introduced a number of models which established him as a maker of high-speed touring cars as well as of sports cars. The Type 44 had a straight-8 engine of 2,991cc,

21. 1922 Marmon Model 34 speedster. Owned by J. K. Lilly III. (Photo: Spooner Studio, Falmouth, Mass.)

and was the largest post-war Bugatti to date. The use of plain bearings made for a much quieter engine than the roller-bearing Types 35 and 43, while top-gear flexibility was much better than on any previous Bugatti. Some sporting bodies were fitted, but more Type 44s carried saloon or coupé coachwork, in which form they were good for 85mph and 28mpg. A complete four-door saloon cost £850. In complete contrast was the other new model for 1927, the Type 43. This was another roller-bearing design, using the 2·3-litre Type 35B supercharged engine in the Type 38 chassis. The classic factory-supplied body was a pointed tail four-seater enabling the car to be used for long distance road work (Williams drove one in the 1928 Monte Carlo Rally), but its performance was way above cars in the Hotchkiss and Georges Irat category. As Hugh Conway has pointed out, it was comparable with a Triumph TR-3 or MGA of the early 1960s, having a top speed of 105mph and acceleration of 0–90mph in about 30 seconds. However, it was much noisier than the Type 44 and was not suitable for closed bodywork. Only 160 were sold in five years, compared with 1,095 Type 44s in four years. Of the other Bugattis announced during the 1920s, the luxury Type 41 Royale is beyond the scope of this book, while the Type 46, although announced at the end of 1929, is really a car of the next decade.

1932 Bugatti Type 43 driven by G. Bachelier at Chalfont St Peter Hill Climb. (Photo: H. G. Conway Collection)

The first two years after the Armistice saw very grim conditions in Germany. The shame of defeat coupled with acute shortages brought the country nearer to revolution than any other in Western Europe. Strikes were frequent, often accompanied by violence. On at least one occasion, the directors of the Benz company were manhandled by workers as they left their offices. Petrol was strictly rationed, and foreign currency only granted to privileged travellers. Rubber was in such short supply that practically all manufacturers sold their cars without tyres, leaving the buyer to do the best he could to get his vehicle shod. Copper and brass were virtually non-existent, so cars had a very austere appearance for several years.

In these conditions, it is surprising that any motor sport took place, and yet by 1921 Mercedes had achieved a major international victory. The pre-war shaft-driven 28/95 was put into production soon after the war, and in 1921 Max Sailer drove a short-chassis model all the way to Sicily, where he won the Coppa Florio. The journey to Sicily, the 268 miles of the race, and the journey home to Stuttgart were all made on one set of tyres, for the combined resources of Mercedes and the Continental tyre makers could not spare more than one complete set. This 28/95 was supercharged by a two-lobe Roots-type blower driven from the camshaft at 8–10,000rpm. There were two unusual features of Mercedes supercharging; the blower did not operate continuously, but could be cut in at will, and it pumped air into the carburetter instead of being placed between carburetter and engine as in most other supercharging systems. The first production blown cars were advertised in 1921, the 6/25/40PS of 1,570cc, and the 10/40/65PS of 2,600cc. However, blowers were not to be seen on any cars at the Berlin Motor Show in October 1921, and rivals claimed that supercharged engines existed only in the mind of Mercedes' advertising manager. However, Mercedes persisted with supercharging and entered three blown cars in the 1922 Targa Florio (the Targa was for out-and-out racing cars run concurrently with the Coppa Florio for stock cars). Two were 28/95s, which finished 2nd and 4th in the Coppa Florio, while the third was a small 1½-litre car. From this was developed a production sports car with the same engine and an underslung chassis. Only twenty-five of these were made, together with a further twenty-five having 2·6-litre engines; a number of well-known drivers bought them, including Rudi Caracciola and Frau Merck. By 1925, three supercharged Mercedes were available to the public, the 6/25/40PS and two new 6-cylinder cars, the 3·9-litre 15/70/100PS and the 6·2-litre 24/100/140PS. These were not necessarily sports cars, and all kinds of coachwork, including seven-seater saloons, were mounted on the supercharged chassis. The supercharger was found to be useful so long as a fairly high engine speed had already been attained, but otherwise it simply absorbed engine power and did not work fast enough to exert any useful pressure.

The new 6-cylinder cars were designed by Ferdinand Porsche, and the larger was the first of a series which led up to the SS and SSK models, perhaps the most famous of all German sports cars. In sporting form the 6·2-litre car was known as the Typ K, or 24/100/140PS in the clumsy designation by which the first figure represented the taxable horsepower, the second the

1924 Mercedes 28/95 two-seater.
(Photo: Briggs Cunningham Automotive Museum)

bhp unblown, and the third the bhp when the blower was in action. To confuse matters further, this model was known in England as the 33/180, and the touring version the 33/140. To avoid confusion it is simpler to refer to all these sporting Mercedes by their letter designations. The Typ K was announced by the old Mercedes company in 1926, but nearly all of them were sold under the name Mercedes-Benz, for the merger of the two companies took place the same year. The K was an attractive fast tourer with a maximum speed of about 100mph, and easy cruising at 60–70mph with the engine turning quite slowly. Unfortunately the brakes were very poor, and this rendered the car useless for serious competition work. At this time (1926/27) the Mercedes name was kept in the competition lists by the old 28/95, which, although out of production for three years, was still winning events, particularly hill-climbs, all over Europe. In June 1927 came the Typ S, derived from the Typ K but with larger engine of 6,789cc giving 180bhp. It had better handling and brakes than the K, although the latter were still not ideal. The bonnet was lower, and in appearance it was the most attractive of the series. Maximum speed was 110mph with four-seater body, and many racing successes were achieved. Among the more notable were first three

1927 Mercedes-Benz S sports tourer.
(Photo: Montagu Motor Museum)

places in the 1927 German Grand Prix, and first two at the same event in 1928. They also won many hill-climbs including the 21½km Klausen Pass in Austria. In 1928 came the Typ SS, with a still larger engine of 7,020cc and a chassis lighter by 65lb. The wheelbase was the same at 11ft 2in, but the short-chassis version, the SSK, had a wheelbase of 9ft 8in. The engine developed 170bhp unblown or 225bhp blown, although the SSK with larger blower developed 250bhp, and the racing SSKL with special camshaft was said to achieve 300bhp. The bonnet and radiator of the SS were higher than those of their predecessor and gave the cars a more formidable appearance. Standard coachwork on the SS was an open four-seater, or a drophead coupé. There were also many special bodies of all kinds; closed bodies were frowned on by the works, but, as with Bentley and countless other sports car makers, customers demanded them, and the special coachbuilders went to work. There were even some four-door saloons, such as the one on an S chassis by Freestone & Webb which was on the Mercedes-Benz stand at Olympia in 1928. The standard body on the SSK was a stark two-seater, although some attractive drophead coupés were also made. Both models had very successful sporting careers; Caracciola won the 1929 Tourist Trophy on an SS, and both the 1930 Irish Grand Prix and the 1931 German Grand Prix on an SSK. The 1931 Mille Miglia was the debut of the SSKL, Caracciola winning the event after an epic single-handed drive. Other victories included the 1930 Belgian 24 Hour Race (Prince Djordzadze and G. Zehender) and the Circuit of Lwow, Poland (von Stuck), both won by SSs. The SSK was particularly successful in hill-climbs, gaining the European Hill Climb Championship in 1930 and 1931, and breaking records at Mont Ventoux and Shelsley Walsh. Private owners (with the exception of Caracciola) were on the whole less successful than works entrants; some of the pitfalls for the inexperienced were using the blower when in bottom gear, keeping it applied for more than 20 seconds, using the wrong fuel, and insufficient tightening of the cylinder head. All these mistakes resulted in blown gaskets, for which the model earned a bad and undeserved reputation. The SSKL (*Super sports, kurz, leicht*) had a still lighter chassis, the frame and even the dumbirons being drilled, whereas the SSK's frame was only partially drilled. The chassis weight of the SSKL was less than 24cwt, and the car's maximum speed 147mph. With a streamlined body, Manfred von Brauchitsch achieved 156mph at the Avus Circuit in 1931. This was strictly a works car, and none

An unusual example of a 1929 Mercedes-Benz SSK carrying American coachwork by Murphy of Pasadena. (Photo: Montagu Motor Museum)

WALTER M. MURPHY COMPANY
COACH BUILDERS
PASADENA CALIFORNIA

One of the 3-litre Steigers which ran in the 1924 Targo Florio. (Photo: Neubauer Collection)

was sold new to private owners. Not more than five were built. Production figures for the other models in the series are as follows: Typ S: 146, Typ SS: 112, and Typ SSK: 33. The model was theoretically still available in 1934, but production ceased during 1933.

No other German make achieved the international fame of the Mercedes, and to many people the vintage period seems a rather barren one in Germany. However, there were a number of sporting marques which did not achieve much fame outside their country, and whose activities have been neglected by historians. One reason for this is that, for patriotic reasons, neither the British nor the French motoring press would admit that interesting cars were being made on the further side of the Rhine, and for the same reason hardly any cars were imported. This situation lasted at least until 1925.

One of the best sports cars in Germany was the Steiger. It was built in a small factory at Burgreiden whose 500 workers made practically all of the car, bodies included. Designed by Paul Henze, the 1920 10/50PS had a very long-stroke 2·6-litre 4-cylinder engine with dimensions of 72 × 160mm. The valves were actuated by a single overhead camshaft, and power output was 50bhp. Two special 80bhp 3-litre cars ran in the 1924 Targa Florio, but their chances were spoilt by poor brakes, which were only on the rear wheels. Front-wheel brakes came in 1925, but this was practically the end for Steiger. Because of the general economic situation the market for expensive cars was very small, and the little firm could not keep going until better times arrived. Production ceased in 1926, although a few cars were assembled by a former Steiger dealer in Düsseldorf for a few years. Henze had already left the firm, and Walter Steiger went to Switzerland where he designed a car for the Martini company.

When Henze left Steiger in 1923, he joined Simson & Co of Suhl, in Thuringia. This firm had produced conventional touring cars since 1911, but Henze's Simson-Supra Typ S, announced in 1924, was in complete contrast to their earlier products. It had a 4-cylinder 2-litre engine developing 60bhp at 4,000rpm. Twin-overhead camshafts actuated four inclined valves per cylinder. The only other firm in the world making a twin-ohc engine at this time was Ballot, and their 2LS model was about to be withdrawn in 1924. As the 3-litre Sunbeam did not come onto the market until 1926, for a short time the Simson-Supra Typ S could claim to be the only car in the world to use the twin-ohc layout, so widely employed in later high performance engines. The sports model had twin carburetters and a shorter wheelbase of 8ft 5in, compared with the tourer's 9ft 10in. Maximum speed of the tourer was 75mph and of the sports 85mph, no mean performance from a 2-litre engine. However, as with the Steiger, the times were against such cars (1923 was the year of galloping inflation when workers carried their wages home in sacks). Only 30 S models were made, compared with about 300 of the parallel single-ohc model and over 750 of the pushrod engined 6-cylinder Typ R. The latter had a capacity of 3·1 litres and was a fast tourer rather than a sports car. Several competed in the Monte Carlo Rally from 1928 to 1930. The last Simson-Supra design was a side valve straight-8 of 4·7 litres. Very handsome sports saloon bodies were fitted, but only 20 cars were made from 1931 to 1932.

The fact that few people could afford to buy a Steiger or a Simson-Supra did not mean that Germans were not interested in motor sport, and the makers of small utility cars soon began to produce sporting models. Their tuning techniques were similar to those of other countries: lightened

1924 Simson-Supra S tourer, seen during a Czechoslovakian rally in 1968.
(Photo: Montagu Motor Museum)

Light sports cars on the frozen Wannsee near Berlin, January 1925. Number 43 is a Bob and number 52 is a Pluto which was a German-built Amilcar. (Photo: Neubauer Collection)

Rabag two-seater with Walter Dost at the wheel. (Photo: Erwin Tragatsch Collection)

pistons, twin carburetters, higher gear ratios, raked steering columns and pointed-tail bodies were the usual recipe, although some entered cars for races with no more preparation than the removal of wings and lights. Too many firms went in for competitions to list them all; among the more successful were H.A.G., Koco, Omikron, and Ego. The latter's sports model developed 24bhp at 5,000rpm from an engine of just over a litre's capacity. On one of these Egos, Rudi Caracciola achieved his first racing victory.

Apollo continued their pre-war reputation for high-quality small cars with the Typ B, the smaller of their two 1914 models. The short-wheelbase sports model could reach 55mph in road form, and much more in its racing versions. Its valves were operated by a similar system of push/pull rods as was used in the early Salmson. Another promising small car was the Rabag, which was the Bugatti Type 22 and 23 built under licence. The engines and chassis were built in Mannheim by Union Werke who had previously made the Bravo cyclecar, while the bodies were made by Bendikt Rock of Düsseldorf. Production ran from 1923 to 1926, and both open and closed bodies were made. Some of the closed bodies were very angular and Germanic in appearance, and the radiator had a lipped top which distinguished it from its Molsheim cousin. Although the ultra short-chassis 'Full Brescia' model was never made in Germany, Rabags did well in races and trials. The original firm was taken over in 1925 by Aga of Berlin who were part of the Stinnes group, and when this group collapsed the Rabag disappeared.

The Stolle was one of the best-looking sports cars of any nationality, and would not have looked old-fashioned in 1935. The engine was a single-ohc unit with the classic dimensions of 69×100mm, giving 1,496cc, which developed 40bhp at 3,500rpm and gave a speed of 75mph. The Stolle had four-wheel brakes, Rudge wire wheels, and a beautifully smooth, low two-seater body. However, like the Simson-Supra, it was too expensive for its time, and only 30 were made in a two-year life span from 1924 to 1925.

At the other end of the scale from the light cars was the Joswin. This used the Mercedes 28/95PS engine, a 7·2-litre 6-cylinder unit developing 95bhp at a leisurely 1,400rpm. The chassis was Joswin's own and semi-automatic Soden gearboxes were used. Bodies were made to order by such firms as Szabo & Wechselmann, and varied from sporting tourers to town cars. A similar concept was the Otto, a large car built by Gustav Otto, son of Nicolaus August Otto who is generally considered to be the inventor of the 4-stroke engine. The Otto was fitted with a 27/85PS engine of about 7-litres capacity, and was often driven in competitions by Gustav Otto himself.

One of the most attractive fast tourers in Germany was the N.A.G. Typ C4. This had a 2½-litre 4-cylinder side-valve engine which developed only 45bhp, but a very light chassis enabled the car to have a reasonable performance. The C4b had a lighter body and a maximum speed of 60mph, although specially prepared team cars were capable of 84mph. They did well in long-distance trials such as the A.D.A.C. Reichs Trial, and also in track events at the Avus Circuit and at Monza. In 1924 a C4b averaged 68mph in a special 24-hour run at Monza. After 1927 company policy changed, and no further sporting N.A.G.s were made.

Apart from Mercedes, a number of other German firms offered super-charged cars. Among these was Dürkopp whose standard 2-litre 8/32PS car was fitted with a Zoller blower to raise power from 32–60bhp. The resulting model was known as the 8/40/60PS, and came in two- or four-seater form with polished aluminium exhaust pipe. One of these cars attracted a young dairy farmer named Hans Stuck who exchanged his touring Dürkopp for a

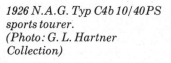

1926 N.A.G. Typ C4b 10/40PS sports tourer. (Photo: G. L. Hartner Collection)

supercharged sports model and began to enter local hill climbs. On one occasion he wagered some friends that he could climb a certain hill faster in reverse than they could do forwards. He reversed the gearbox shafts to give him four speeds in reverse, and after a week's secret practising on the hill he won the bet. Later, of course, Stuck became a champion hill-climber with Austro-Daimler and Mercedes-Benz SSKs, and a member of the Auto Union Grand Prix team.

Fafnir made a small number of 2-litre supercharged cars which developed 80bhp with blower in action, one of which was driven by Rudi Caracciola. More interesting were the small supercharged N.S.U.s. This firm managed to extract 40bhp from a 1·3-litre engine in their 5/25/40PS sports car of 1925. One of the cars driven by Alfred Momberger won the 1925 Taunus Race, defeating the 1½-litre supercharged Mercedes, and followed this with victories at the Avus and Solitude Circuits in 1926 and 1927. N.S.U. also made a supercharged small six of 1,567cc, but did not achieve any great successes with it.

Despite adverse economic circumstances Germany produced many interesting sports cars between 1920 and 1930, but towards the end of the decade the number of sporting makes shrank sharply. As in other countries, mass production was getting under way and the large firms like Opel did not consider sport a useful means of increasing their sales. In turn, the smaller manufacturers such as N.A.G. and Dürkopp abandoned their sporting programmes in order to save money and somehow keep up with the giants. Amalgamations were set up, such as the G.D.A. (Gemeinschaft Deutscher Automobilfabriken) with N.A.G., Hansa, Hansa-Lloyd and Brennabor or the more completely integrated Austrian Steyr-Daimler-Puch combine, and the directors of these groups were generally hostile to sport. An exception was the Auto Union group which sponsored a Grand Prix programme in the 1930s, albeit with substantial state aid.

6. Italy

Although many of the world's finest sports and racing cars have come from Italy, the number of manufacturers has never been very large and the variety of sporting types much smaller than in Great Britain or France. Until recently Italy was a very poor country, and in 1922 there was only one car per thousand of the population. Although car production was fairly large (45,800 in 1925), a very high proportion was exported, this figure theoretically being no less than 90 per cent (by government decree) in 1921, and fell only to 70 per cent by 1925. Italy's chief customers, Great Britain and France, expected good quality fast tourers rather than sporting voiturettes, of which the latter country made enough herself anyway, so there were virtually no light sports cars made in Italy in the 1920s. Her own car-buying population, though small in numbers, demanded the larger cars, while the less well-off young enthusiast who in France would have bought a Salmson or Amilcar had to content himself with a motorcycle at the best.

Most of the well-known Italian sports cars were in the 1½- to 3-litre category, although there were a number of larger tourers at the beginning of the period. These showed a strong Germanic influence in their appearance, with aggressive V-radiators and angular bodies. Fiat, Bianchi, Nazzaro, and S.P.A. were all making such cars for a few years after the armistice. Typical was the sporting model Fiat 510 with V-radiator, V-windscreen, separate step plates in place of a running board, and a four-seater open body. The engine was a 3½-litre side-valve unit. Like many Italian cars, it was tested in the Alps, and was excellent at hill-climbing. A small number were exported to England, and the owner of one described it as the perfect car found after a fifteen year search. The body had inlaid mahogany panelling, which the owner thought 'a shade too profiteery' (the vulgar ostentation of wartime profiteers was the subject of much comment at the time), but this may have been the special trim of a Show model. The Nazzaro was a flashy car made by a Florentine firm originally founded by the great racing driver Felice Nazzaro, although he had left in 1916. The pre-war cars had been solid, reliable machines, and Nazzaro had won the 1913 Targa Florio on one, but the new 1922 car was a more advanced design with single overhead camshaft operating three valves per cylinder, one inlet and two exhausts. One exhaust valve opened slightly in advance of the other. The car looked sporting, with a V-radiator and very low body, but performance was very disappointing, and production ceased within a year of the car's introduction.

One of the most famous sporting makes was Alfa Romeo. They began production with a heavy-looking tourer, the 20/30 with 4,084cc side-valve engine which had first been made in 1910 when the firm had simply been known as A.L.F.A. In 1920 came the revised 20/30ES with capacity increased to 4,250cc, giving 67bhp at 2,600rpm. Various bodies were fitted, mostly staid touring cars, but they included a stark two-seater, stripped models of which were entered in hill-climbs and races. In one of these, Enzo Ferrari came second in the 1920 Targa Florio. Their sporting successes continued to 1922, but meanwhile Giuseppe Merosi had designed Alfa Romeo's first new post-war model, the 2,916cc pushrod-ohv RL series. In its original form, this was a sound touring car with 56bhp and capable of 70mph. Introduced in

November 1921, the RL did not go into proper production until 1923, by which time it had been supplemented by the RLS which had many modifications. The capacity was raised to 2,994cc, there was a higher compression ratio, twin carburetters, dry sump lubrication, shorter wheelbase and V-radiator. In 1925 came the RLSS with the same size engine but more power, this now being 83bhp giving a maximum speed of 80–85mph depending on the body fitted. These were usually open two- or four-seaters on the RLSS chassis, although a few lightweight saloons were also built. Team cars, one with a larger engine of 3·1-litre capacity, came 1st and 2nd in the 1923 Targa Florio, and in 1924 two more special cars, this time of 3·6 litres, ran in the Targa, Count Giulio Masetti's car coming 2nd. Enzo Ferrari continued to drive for Alfa, and his victory at the circuit of Savio at Ravenna had a significant result. Among the spectators were the parents of the fighter ace the late Francesco Baracca, who were so impressed with Ferrari's driving that they presented him with the badge their son had carried on his plane. This was a prancing horse on a yellow background, and became the symbol first of the Scuderia Ferrari of Alfa Romeo racing cars and then of Ferrari's own cars when he became a manufacturer after World War 2.

The RL touring car was known in England as the 21/70, while the RLS and RLSS were known as the 22/90. Apart from these 6-cylinder cars, there were also some 4-cylinder cars designed by Merosi, of which the sports model was the 2-litre 44bhp RMS. Among owners of the RLSS was Benito Mussolini who said that the car had 'a magnificent engine', and another leader who tried an RLS was the Aga Khan who described his drive as 'a most interesting and enjoyable journey in one of the most excellent cars I have ever ridden in'. RLSSs continued to do well in many events up to 1927, and even as late as 1932 a Targa Florio car won its class in the Belgian 24 Hour Race. About 2,500 of the RL series were made between 1922 and 1927.

In 1925 a new designer, Vittorio Jano, had joined Alfa Romeo, and his first achievement was the highly successful P2 racing car of 1924. His first production car was the Tipo 6C, with 1½-litre single overhead camshaft engine developing 44bhp, with a maximum speed of 68mph. The engine was largely of aluminium alloy, and the crankshaft was carried on five main bearings. Two wheelbases were available, 10ft 2in for touring and saloon bodies and 9ft 6in for sporting bodies. It was an altogether lighter, more delicate-looking design than the RL series, yet very robust in practice. Introduced in 1925, the 6C did not go into serious production until 1927 and was joined in 1928 by the twin-ohc Gran Turismo which had a smaller radiator and was available only on the shorter wheelbase. Still faster was the Gran Sport with 9ft wheelbase and a Roots-type blower turning at 1½ times engine speed. This car won the Mille Miglia, the Essex Motor Club Six Hour Race at Brooklands, Belgian 24 Hour Race, the Coupe Boillot, and the Circuit des Routes Pavées, and came 2nd in the Targa Florio, all in 1928, the year of its introduction. In 1929 capacity was increased to 1,752cc, this model being the famous 1750. It was made in three forms, the single-ohc Turismo with 10ft 2in wheelbase and a maximum speed of about 70mph, the twin-ohc Gran Turismo with 9ft 6in or 9ft wheelbase and a speed of 80mph, and finally the Super Sport with blown engine giving 85bhp and 95mph. With Zagato two-seater body, the short-chassis 1750 was one of the most handsome and functional sports cars ever made, as well as being highly successful in racing. In 1929 a 1750 driven by Giuseppe Campari (of the apéritif family) and Giulio Ramponi won the Mille Miglia only three months after the car was introduced. Later that year Marinoni and Benoist won the Belgian 24 Hour Race at Spa. The 1930 model 1750 had a horizontal Roots-

22. Above: *1926 Kissel speedster. Owned by J. K. Lilly III. (Photo: Spooner Studio, Falmouth, Mass.)*

23. Below: *1930 M.G. 18/100 Tigress sports car. Owned by C. Barker. (Photo: John R. Price)*

24. Overleaf, above left: *Racing and touring versions of the Riley Imp. Left: 1934 Ulster Imp, one of the works team cars subsequently owned by the late Mike Hawthorn, and now owned by Tim Ely; right: 1934 Imp standard sports car, owned by John Roberts. (Photo: Tim Ely)*

25. Overleaf, below left: *1931 Talbot 105 3-litre sports car. Owned by Anthony Blight. (Photo: Motor Sporting Photographers)*

26. Overleaf, right: *1935 Aston Martin Mark II-S 1½-litre sports car. Owned by John J. Ullom. (Photo: William S. Jackson).*

type blower running at engine speed, whereas the 1929 model used an Alfa-made blower running at $1\frac{1}{8}$ times engine speed. From 1930 onwards the team cars were raced by the Scuderia Ferrari. Victories in their second season included the Mille Miglia, Tourist Trophy, and Belgian 24 Hour Race. Inevitably the introduction of the straight-8 2·3-litre cars in 1931 over-shadowed the 1750, but they continued to do well, coming 2nd in the Mille Miglia, Targa Florio, and at Spa. They were among the most pleasant sports cars to drive, having exceptionally positive steering and really vivid acceleration. The 1750 was made until 1934, the final development being a Gran Turismo model with capacity enlarged to 1,920cc. A total of 3,656 of the Jano-designed 6-cylinder cars were made, of which about 500 were two-seater sports cars.

Alfa Romeo was by far the most important Italian sports car in vintage times. There was no locally-made rival to the 1750, but the nearest was probably the later O.M. After making a few large Edwardian-derived 4-cylinder cars, this firm introduced a 4-cylinder side-valve engined tourer in 1920. This had a 1,352cc engine, and no sporting pretensions, and was supplemented by the Tipo 665 Superba, a 1,991cc 6-cylinder car developing 45bhp. This model was remarkable in that it was successful as a fast tourer and on the track, and yet it had a very 'touring' specification. To the end, the engine always had side valves, and usually a single carburetter, although it had the advantage of light castings. Bodies were two-seaters, four-seater tourers or saloons, and maximum speed about 70mph. The 6-cylinder O.M. came 4th and 5th at Le Mans in 1926, and took first three places in the first Mille Miglia race held in 1927. In the 1928 Mille Miglia an O.M. was 2nd, behind an Alfa Romeo 1500, a totally different type of car. In 1928 came the low chassis O.M. which had a more sporting appearance, and yet, initially, used the same 1,991cc engine. It was only available on the short 9ft 2in wheelbase and with its sloping radiator and low lines looked not unlike an Alfa Romeo. The following year a larger engine of 2·2 litres was introduced, and this could be had with a Roots supercharger in which form it developed 60bhp at 4,000rpm. For 1931 the stroke was lengthened to 110mm, giving a capacity of 2·3 litres, and although this was the fastest O.M. it was still no match for the Type 43 Bugatti or the new 2·3-litre straight-8 Alfa Romeo. The supercharged 2·3-litre cars were for works use only and not sold new to the public. For the British market L. G. Rawlence made a few overhead valve conversions, and a car so fitted ran in the 1929 T.T. The last sporting success of O.M. was 3rd place in the 1931 Mille Miglia and a victory in the 3-litre category. Production virtually ceased in 1931 in favour of commercial vehicles, but a new O.M. was announced for the 1934 season. This was the O.M. Alcyone, with a new 6-cylinder engine of 2,198cc and overhead exhaust valves. It was not a sports car, being intended as competition for the new Alfa-Romeo 6C 2300 range of saloons. In conception, and certainly in appearance, it was very similar to the Fiat Ardita, and when O.M. was absorbed by Fiat in 1933 there was no room for the Alcyone which was dropped after only a few cars had been made.

There were very few Italian cars in the 1,100cc category, but quite a number of 2-litre tourers, most of which were produced in sporting form. Among these was the Ceirano S150, with 1,460ohv engine giving 40bhp, 4-speed gearbox and four-wheel brakes. It was mostly seen as an open tourer and handled very well, but was not entered in serious competitions. In England it was sold as the Newton-Ceirano, with Newton piston-type shock-absorbers. More sporting was the Chiribiri. Named after its builder Antonio Chiribiri, it began as a dull side-valve 1½-litre car which had first appeared

27. Above: *1932 Invicta S-type 4½-litre sports car. Owned by R. C. J. Wood. (Photo: Motor Sporting Photographers)*

28. Below: *1936 Bugatti Type 57 3·3-litre drophead coupé. Owned by J. A. Veldkamp. (Photo: Guy Griffiths Moto-photo)*

A very handsome Alfa Romeo RLSS with English coachwork by H. J. Mulliner. (Photo: Montagu Motor Museum)

An Alfa Romeo 1750 driven by D. Parker at Blandford in 1949. (Photo: Guy Griffiths Motofoto)

1929 O.M. 2-litre, leading a 12/50 Alvis at Oulton Park. (Photo: Montagu Motor Museum)

in pre-war days, but in 1921 came a pushrod ohv engine of 1,453cc. This was followed by the Monza Normale and Monza Speciale sports models with 1,486cc twin-ohc engines developing over 50bhp. In supercharged form this engine could develop 72bhp, and the car reached over 100mph in racing trim. However, the racing cars were only made to special order, and even the Monza sports cars were made in very limited numbers as they cost twice as much as the ordinary pushrod cars. These continued in production until 1928. In a larger category there were several tourers such as the 1,847cc single-ohc Ansaldo which looked as staid as the O.M. but had quite a lively performance; the Aurea and Bianchi, both of which were available with flared-wing sporting coachwork; and the Itala, product of a firm who had built Grand Prix cars several years before the beginning of World War 1.

*1922 Chiribiri Monza sports car.
(Photo: Cyril Posthumus Collection)*

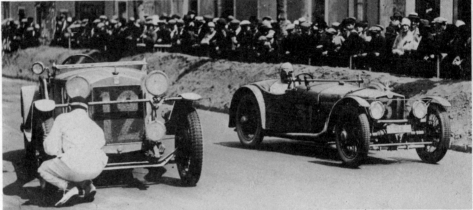

*Le Mans 1928. Dauvergne adjusts a seized front brake on his Tipo 61 Itala, while Bourcier's Tracta swings wide to clear him. The Itala eventually finished 8th.
(Photo: Autocar)*

The Tipo 61 Itala had a 6-cylinder pushrod ohv engine of 1,991cc and a 70mph top speed. In 1928 came a short-chassis twin-ohc model known as the Tipo 65, with a maximum speed of over 85mph. On this model the rear axle passed through holes the side members of the frame. Both the Tipo 61 and Tipo 65 were theoretically available until 1934, but production in the 1930s was very small. The Diatto was also a fast tourer, but more interesting as it was under the Diatto name that the first cars of the Maserati brothers appeared. In 1920 Diatto made a few Bugatti Brescias under licence, followed by a range of tourers with 4-cylinder side-valve engines. In 1922 came the 2-litre single-ohc Tipo 30 built in short-wheelbase sports form, and from this was derived the Tipo 35 with 2·6-litre engine. A Super Sports version of this was made, with pointed tail and narrow, staggered seat body, but does not seem to have played any part in competitions. Alfieri Maserati had driven a Tipo 30 in competitions including the 1922 Coppa Florio, and when he and his two brothers, Bindo and Ernesto, decided to build a car of their own they approached Diatto for financial backing. The first Maserati-designed car was a 2-litre straight-8 Grand Prix racing car built in their own works at Bologna but raced under the Diatto name. However, Diatto's finances were not strong enough to support a Grand Prix programme, so the following year the Maseratis raced the car under their own name.

Among large cars the Isotta Fraschini was pre-eminent, the Italian equivalent of the Hispano-Suiza. However, nothing like such an ambitious sporting programme was carried out, and there was no Isotta equivalent of the Boulogne Hispano. The 1919 Tipo 8 had a 5·9-litre straight-8 engine with pushrod overhead valves in place of the single ohc of the pre-war Type KM Isotta. This engine developed 80bhp at 2,200rpm, not a great deal considering its size, but it was not intended as a sporting car. The most sporting model was the Tipo 8ASS of 1926 which had the enlarged 7·4-litre engine of the Tipo 8A touring car with higher compression ratio (5·5:1 compared with

An Isotta Fraschini Tipo 8 with special sporting body. This car, driven by Anderloni, made the fastest lap in the 1923 Monza 500km Race, while a sister car driven by Vincenzo won.
(Photo: Autocar)

A Lancia Lambda on Beggars' Roost Hill, near Lynton, North Devon.
(Photo: Montagu Motor Museum)

5:1 for the standard 8A), larger valves and double valve springs. The chassis was the short-wheelbase one of 11ft 2½in. This engine developed 135bhp, or the same as the 1919 Hispano-Suiza, but was still at a disadvantage because of its extra weight. The Isotta chassis turned the scales at 30cwt compared with 22cwt for the Hispano. Nevertheless, some owners raced their Isottas, notably Duke Pio Arate di San Pietro who won the Targa Abruzzo in 1925 and 1926 with a Tipo 8ASS five-seater tourer. Another Isotta came 6th in the 1927 Mille Miglia. Another large sporting car was the S.P.A. This had a 4·4-litre 6-cylinder engine with four valves per cylinder, operated by twin overhead camshafts. An attractive four-seater sporting body with pointed tail and V-radiator was fitted, and the car had front-wheel brakes.

In a class of its own was the Lancia Lambda, a touring car which has come to be thought of as a sporting machine in Great Britain in the same way that certain French fast tourers have. The Lambda was technically very advanced with its V-4 engine, independent front suspension, and integral construction. Very successful in rallies and trials, it was hardly ever raced, except in the 1928 Mille Miglia when a tourer driven by Gismondi led the race until 300km from the finish. No less than 13,000 Lambdas were made between 1922 and 1931, which was more than any other Italian quality car, and second only to Fiat in overall production.

The peak year for car production in Belgium was 1912, and the country's motor industry never really recovered from World War 1 in which Belgium suffered proportionately more industrial damage than any other nation in Europe. The number of makes in significant production in the 1920s was not more than six. Nevertheless, several sports cars were made and the Touring Car Grand Prix at Spa attracted entries from all over Europe. It was first held in 1922 when it was a 600km (375 miles) event in which only twelve cars started and seven retired. In 1924 it became a 24 hour race, and increased in international importance.

One of the few genuine sports cars from Belgium was the Imperia-Abadal. The pre-war Spanish Abadal (see page 37) had been built under licence by Imperia at Nessonvaux. The post-war car had a single overhead camshaft engine with dimensions of 80 × 149mm, giving a capacity of 2,996cc, the same as that of the 3-litre Bentley. The car was handsome but expensive and few were sold. A team ran in the first Touring Car Grand Prix, and Baron de Tornaco won the race, ahead of a Chenard-Walcker and a Bignan. 1923 saw a complete change of Imperia policy. The Abadal types, which included a 6-litre straight-8 luxury car, were dropped in favour of small slide-valve cars. They were not especially sporting, but the 1,100cc model was made with a pointed-tail sporting body, and won its class in the 1925 Touring Car Grand Prix. There was also a sporting version of the 1,800cc Six.

The armaments firm of F.N. were the largest Belgian car manufacturers in the 1920s, and built mostly staid tourers of various sizes. However the 1923 '1300' had overhead valves and front-wheel brakes, and was made in sporting form with twin carburetters. A team of four pointed-tail four-seaters ran in the Spa Touring Car Grand Prix in 1925 and 1926, gaining class victories in both years, and the model was successful also in the 1924 Klausen Pass hill-climb, and 3rd in the 1925 Monte Carlo Rally. In 1930 F.N. launched their 8-cylinder car with 3,250cc side-valve engine. In standard form it looked very like an American sedan of the period, but a few sporting models were made.

1925 F.N. 1300 with sporting coachwork by Pritchard et Demollin.
(Photo: G. L. Hartner Collection)

Spa 24 Hour Race 1927. The winning Excelsior driven by Sénéchal and Caerels. (Photo: Autocar)

These were very handsome machines with narrow radiators and two- or four-seater bodies. F.N.s won the 2-litre class in the 1932 and 1933 Spa races, and won outright the 1933 Liège-Rome-Liège Rally.

Belgium's luxury car was the Excelsior, the new post-war model of which was the Albert 1 with 5,350cc 6-cylinder single-ohc engine. The diagonally-compensated four-wheel brakes were assisted by the Dewandre servo system. The sports model with three carburetters and a higher rear axle ratio were entered in most of the touring car races of the period. At Le Mans in 1923 they were too heavy to keep up with the smaller Chenard-Walckers, and finished no higher than 6th and 9th, but with lighter bodies and on their home ground at Spa they did progressively better. They were 3rd in 1925, 2nd in 1926, and won in 1927, when Sénéchal and Caerels won at an average speed of 57·12mph. Excelsiors also raced in the Coupe Boillot and the Circuit des Routes Pavées, winning the latter event in 1926. The sporting models came in two forms from 1927 onwards, the Super Sports at £1,250 and the dual ignition Grand Prix at £1,300, both of these being chassis prices.

There were no other truly sporting cars made in Belgium, although Métallurgique and Nagant tourers were raced in the Spa 24 Hour events, and the luxury Minerva was a fine high-speed tourer in both 6- and 8-cylinder forms.

8. Austria

The two leading Austrian makes in the vintage period were Austro-Daimler and Steyr, and both produced interesting sporting machines. Ferdinand Porsche was still in charge of design at Austro-Daimler and was responsible for the firm's first post-war design, the AD 617, with 4·4-litre 6-cylinder single ohc engine developing 60bhp. It was a good fast tourer, and a few chassis were fitted with sporting two-seater bodies. In 1923 came the ADM 1, a smaller car with 2½-litre 50bhp engine. This was much lighter than the AD 617, so performance was easily as good as the larger machine's. Two years later came the ADM 11, with twin carburetters and capacity increased to 2,994cc, developing 100bhp. In standard form this was capable of 80mph, while 100mph was not beyond the short-chassis sports model. Austria now had one of the best European sports cars, and one which achieved many successes in hill-climbs. One of the leading drivers was Hans Stuck, who won the hill-climb championship of Switzerland in 1928 and of Austria in 1929. In Great Britain a team of four ADM 11s, or 19/100s as they were called in England, won the team prize in the 1928 Tourist Trophy, while Stuck broke the Shelsley Walsh hill-climb record in 1930 with a racing version of the ADM. In 1923 Porsche left Austro-Daimler for a brief sojourn with Mercedes-Benz, and the next stage of Austro-Daimler development was in the hands of Karl Rabe, although no doubt he had discussed it with his former chief. The ADR used the same engine as the ADM, but the chassis was completely new, consisting of a tubular backbone which enclosed the propeller shaft, and which was forked at the front to carry the engine. There were swinging half axles at the rear, suspension being by transverse leaf springs. This came in

Austro-Daimler Sascha of the type driven by Alfred Neubauer in the 1922 Targa Florio. (Photo: Dr Ing F. Porsche KG)

two models, the 70bhp touring car and the 100bhp sports. In 1931 came the ADR 6 with 3·6-litre engine, known as the Bergmeister or mountain-master because of the make's hill-climbing successes, and this was followed by the ADR 8 with 4·6-litre straight-8 engine, still with the tubular chassis. A fine 100bhp touring car, it was not offered in sporting form. The Bergmeister was available to special order as late as 1937, by which time Austro-Daimler was part of the Steyr-Daimler-Puch combine, and, in theory, no longer in production.

A sideline to the larger Austro-Daimlers, and one that never received the blessing of the directors, was the Sascha, a high performance small car developed by Porsche for Count Alexander Kolowrat. The Count was a colourful character who owned a Bohemian glass firm which, among other activities, supplied Model T windscreens to Ford. He had driven a Laurin und Klement in the 1913 Alpine Trial with a pet piglet in the back, squealing away for the whole 1,500 miles. The Sascha car had a 1,090cc 4-cylinder engine, with inclined overhead valves operated by twin overhead camshafts, front-wheel brakes, and Rudge-Whitworth wire wheels. The engine developed the remarkable figure of 45bhp at 4,500rpm. Four Saschas ran in the 1922 Targa Florio, three in the touring car class, and one racing car driven by Alfred Neubauer who later became the famous team manager of Mercedes-Benz. Those entered in the touring category took 1st and 2nd places, while Neubauer finished only 5mph slower than the winning Grand Prix Mercedes of 4½-litre capacity. Saschas achieved many other victories during 1922 and 1923, but the directors were against the idea of a small car and so the Sascha was dropped, and Porsche left to spend five years with Mercedes.

The Österreichische Waffenfabriks-Gesellschaft of Steyr was an armaments firm which started car production immediately after World War 1. Their Type 11, designed by Hans Ledwinka, had a 3·3-litre single-ohc 40bhp 6-cylinder engine, increased in size in 1921 to 4 litres. This twin-carburetter unit was much more powerful, and was developed still further for the 1923 Targa Florio in which a Steyr finished 3rd. This Typ VI Sport had a longer stroke, giving 4·8-litre capacity, and led to the Klausen Sport, named after the famous hill-climb. Some very handsome bodies were fitted to this chassis, mostly open four-seaters with dual screens and pointed tails, although some streamlined saloons ran in the French Touring Car Grand Prix in 1924 and 1925. A new flat-radiatored model of the Klausen Sport appeared in 1928 and this model developed 145bhp. Only nine were made. Ferdinand Porsche returned to Austria in 1927 and joined Steyr, for whom he modernized the Typ VII 3·3-litre car, enlarging the engine to 4·1 litres and 70bhp. This model

1928 Steyr Klausen Sport 4·8 litre sports tourer. (Photo: G. L. Hartner Collection)

was cheaper than the Typ VI, and more were sold (350 of the Porsche modified cars, and 2,150 altogether). The final Porsche design for Steyr was the Typ XXX, with 2·1-litre pushrod ohv 6-cylinder engine, independent suspension by swing axles at the rear, and four-wheel hydraulic brakes. The Typ XXX occasionally carried sporting bodies, but it is more important as the ancestor of the remainder of the pre-war Steyr cars.

There were no other sports cars made in Austria at this time, although some small cars such as the Perl were occasionally fitted with sporting bodies and entered in local races and hill-climbs. The same could be said for Austria's new neighbour and former province, Czechoslovakia. The tubular frame Tatra was a very tough design which achieved remarkable performances in trials, but with only 14bhp from a 1,050cc flat twin engine it was hardly very fast. The tubular-frame design was used as the basis for larger cars, including a luxury V-12, but again these were not sports cars. The Wikov sports car began its life in the 1920s, but as most of its achievements took place after 1930 it belongs to the next section of the book.

Conditions in Spain were not conducive to the mass production of motorcars, for the roads were very bad, the bulk of the population poor, and in 1918 petrol cost the equivalent of six shillings per gallon. As in many countries which lacked a strong native industry, reasonably priced American cars were widely sold, especially Ford, Chevrolet, and Overland. The Barcelona agent for Buick was Francisco Abadal who found that there was more profit in being a retailer than a manufacturer. However, he was not content merely to sell, and he began to modify the staid-looking American cars until they were unrecognisable. Some Abadal-Buicks were town cars with Germanic V-radiators, while others were sports cars with cowled radiators and shortened chassis. They competed in a number of national events from 1919 to about 1923, when their manufacture was dropped.

Unlike Italy, Spain had quite a flourishing cyclecar industry, which had a very curious origin. In about 1909 a group of Barcelona motorists began to use steep hills near their city for races in unpowered 4-wheeled machines, not unlike the soap-box cars beloved of American boys. Steering was by cable and bobbin, and the cars were usually tandem two-seaters, although at least one tandem five-seater was built. Known as Downcars, they reached speeds of up to 40mph, and in the words of *The Cyclecar*'s Barcelona correspondent, provided 'a most agreeable sport, full of emotions and easy to practise'. To return to the top of the hill they relied on a tow from cars or a sympathetic tram-driver. In order to become more independent, the Downcarists began to fit small motorcycle engines to their vehicles. It then seemed an interesting extension to the sport to indulge in races up the hills or on the level. Larger engines were fitted, and from these home-made cyclecars came the first production car, the David. The first model, which appeared in 1914, used a V-twin J.A.P. engine, but later Davids were powered by V-twin M.A.G. or 4-cylinder engines by Ballot or Hispano-Suiza. One of the most distinguished customers was the Duque de Montpensier, and the sports David was named after him. This had an ohv engine and 4-wheel brakes. All

1919 Abadal-Buick sports, stripped for racing. (Photo: José Rodriguez– Viña Collection)

The first 4-cylinder David. (Photo: Gili de Heredia Collection)

Davids had wooden frames, belt drive, and independent front suspension by transverse leaf springs. Between 1916 and 1922 Davids did extremely well in races, hill-climbs and long-distance road trials. For example, in the 1921 Trofeo Armangué, named after José Maria de Armangué, one of the pioneer Downcarists, Davids took ten out of twelve places, including the first five. Among their rivals was the America, a 760cc 4-cylinder shaft-driven light car made in sporting form with a pointed-tail, two-seater body, and also as a racing car with ohv engine and maximum speed of 70mph. Other light cars which competed against the David were the Diaz y Grillo, with M.A.G. or their own 1,100cc engines and torsion-bar suspension, and the Ideal, with 6/8hp or 15hp engines. The most successful entrant of the latter was one of their agents, Nadal, whose tuned cars began to defeat works-entered Ideals. As a result Nadal was made manager, and the former chief engineer, Custals, had to look for another job. He formed his own company to make a car called the Nacional Custals, but achieved little success either in sales or in sport. Other less original cars which were raced included the Loryc built in Palma, Mallorca, which was a copy of the French E.H.P., and the Hisparco, which was actually made in France by A. Marguerite of Courbevoie. It used an 1,100cc Chapuis-Dornier engine. In 1926 a Hisparco won the Twelve Hour Mountain Circuit of Guaderrama, covering 449 miles of atrocious roads at an average speed of 38mph.

Among larger Spanish sports cars the most distinguished was the 3-litre Elizalde Tipo 20C. This car had a 70bhp straight-8 ohv engine with servo-assisted 4-wheel brakes, and carried a very handsome boat-tailed body and wire wheels. It was good for 80mph, and a racing version came 3rd in the 1924 Spanish Grand Prix at Sitges. Production of the Tipo 20, which was also made in touring form, continued until 1929, but few sports models were made. There was very little home market for such cars, and they do not seem to have been exported.

The Spanish Hispano-Suiza company made no truly sporting cars in the

1930 Nacional Pescara 2·8-litre roadster. (Photo: Gili de Heredia Collection)

1920s, and there was no successor to the Alfonso. Four-cylinder cars with single overhead camshafts were made until 1924, and some of these were stripped and raced. The 6-cylinder Hispanos were touring cars: the H6B, similar to the French model, and a smaller 3·7-litre car.

An interesting car which never really got into production was the Ricart. It was designed by Wilfredo Ricart, who was later with Alfa Romeo and then Pegaso, and first appeared in 1922. Originally a 1½-litre, 16-valve, 4-cylinder racing car, it appeared in 1926 as a twin-ohc six. Neither of these cars, sometimes known after their builders as Ricart y Perez, was produced commercially, but in 1928 Ricart joined forces with D. Francisco Battlo y Godo who had made a car called the España, and formed a new company to make cars under the name Ricart-España. These were mostly 2·4-litre tourers, but a few of the twin-ohc Ricarts were made in super-sports form.

In 1930 appeared the last Spanish sports car to be made for over twenty years. This was the Nacional built by a state-sponsored concern, the Fabrica Nacional de Automoviles. It had a 2·8-litre twin-ohc engine developing 100bhp at 4,800rpm, a very low chassis and hydraulic brakes. Saloons, tourers and sports two-seaters were made, all in very limited numbers. A racing version was driven by Zanelli and Tort in international hill-climbs in 1931, winning the Mountain Championship, although the cars had never competed before. In 1934 one of the racing cars driven by Sameiro came 4th in the Penya Rhin Grand Prix.

29. Above: *1936 Delahaye Type 135 3·2-litre two-seater sports car. Owned by R. R. C. Walker. (Photo: Guy Griffiths Motophoto)*

30. Below: *1935 Adler Trumpf Junior 995cc sports car. Owned by Automuseum Hillers, Tremsbüttel. (Photo- Hans-Otto Neubauer)*

10.The United States of America

The trend of car design in America was scarcely affected by the war, and production surged back in 1919 to 1,700,000 cars, three times as much as in 1914. As we have seen, this did not encourage the individual car, but nevertheless there were a number of speedsters on the market for the first five years of the 1920s, and a short but interesting final flowering of the type around 1930.

The famous Mercer and Stutz Bearcat raceabouts both survived into the 1920s, but with greatly diminished allure. Hare's Motors, the new syndicate which was running Mercer Motors Inc, expanded production into the field of luxury touring cars, and although the name Raceabout was continued until the end of production in 1925 the car itself grew progressively more staid. Up to 1922 the L-head Raceabout had staggered seating giving the driver plenty of elbow room for fast manoeuvring of the steering wheel, but this arrangement was replaced by an ordinary bench seat from 1922 onwards. Also at this time the 4-cylinder L-head engine was discontinued, being replaced by a proprietary unit, the 6-cylinder ohv Rochester. The only 4-cylinder cars made after 1922 were completed from left-over components. The so-called Raceabout was now a sedate-looking upright two-seater with dickey, no more sporting in appearance than the earlier Runabout. A new 6-cylinder line with front wheel brakes was introduced in September 1924, and included a Raceabout at $3,900, but very few were made. Production ended early in 1925. The Raceabout had lost its character, and the other Mercer models had never been very distinctive anyway. The only model for which demand always exceeded supply was the Raceabout, but profit on these cars was very low. A maximum of 150 per year were made. An attempt to revive the Mercer name was made in 1931 when the Elcar company fitted a straight-8 Continental engine into a chassis specially made by them. However the times were against such a car, and only two were built.

The Stutz Bearcat was continued until 1925, but with little change from the 1916 models except that the gearbox was moved from the rear axle to a conventional position in 1921, and as with the Mercer bodywork became more comfortable with doors and a windscreen. By 1925 the Stutz company was at a very low ebb, and a change of ownership came only just in time. Before considering the new era of Stutz, there are a number of other American speedsters from the early 1920s that are worthy of attention.

The Paige Daytona was a handsome speedster named in honour of the Paige 6–66 which had established a stock car record for the flying mile of 102·83mph at Daytona Beach in 1921. Stripped Paiges were also entered for the Pike's Peak Hill-climb in 1921, and many board track races in 1921 and 1922. The Daytona was a production model from 1922. It had the standard 5·4-litre 6-cylinder Continental engine developing 66bhp at 2,200rpm (hence the name 6–66) with striking bodywork. This was a two-seater, with a third seat which, together with its accompanying footrest, could be pulled out like a drawer from the side of the body. Wire wheels and cycle-type wings completed a sporting appearance. With a top gear ratio of 4·55:1 the Daytona was capable of 80mph for a price of $3,400. The 1923 model had better equipment which now included two side-mounted spare wheels, front and rear bumpers,

31. 1935 B.M.W. 315/1 1½-litre sports car and 1957 A.C. Ace Bristol 2-litre sports car. These represent the first and last uses of the Fiedler designed 6-cylinder engine. Cars owned and photographed by William S. Jackson.

1921 L-head Mercer driven by its owner Roswell Moore at Prescott, during the 1954 Anglo-American Vintage Car Rally. (Photo: Motor)

1920 Stutz roadster, a staid machine when compared with the classic Bearcat of 1914. (Photo: William S. Jackson)

automatic windscreen wiper, cigar lighter, eight-day clock, and rear-view mirror. The price was $1,000 less than for 1922, but, even so, there were few buyers, and as the company was making no profit at this price the Daytona was withdrawn at the end of 1923. Only 56 were made in all, but it is an interesting example of a handsome sporting car built around standard components.

Another short-lived speedster was the Daniels Submarine Speedster built by a Reading, Pa, company who had begun by making bodies only, and then progressed to expensive assembled cars powered by Herschell-Spillman V-8 engines. When the total output of these V-8 units was ordered by another company, Daniels began to make their own V-8, a side-valve 90bhp 6·4-litre unit. The Submarine Speedster was introduced in 1919, during the period when the Daniels company enjoyed its best sales. Many of these were made in the South West, to new rich oil men, including a number of Indians. The Speedster was a two-seater with cycle-type wings and step plates, its appearance rendered rather heavy by artillery wheels. The price in 1921 was $5,350 – less than that of the sedans which sold at around $6,000, and which rose to $10,000 by the time Daniels production ceased in 1924. The last cars were assembled by Levine Motors, a concern which bought up failing firms in order to be able to supply parts when the makers were no longer in busi-

1921 Noma speedster on test in England.
(Photo: Montagu Motor Museum)

ness. A feature of the Daniels was that the radiator carried no badge, the only identification being a 'D' on the hub caps. Those sufficiently interested were supposed to know what make the cars were.

The Biddle from Philadelphia was another assembled car made in speedster form. The first Biddles of 1915 had Buda engines and the ugly angular wings (military fenders) that some German cars sported, but these were dropped from 1917 onwards when the range included a Mercer-like Raceabout. The 1918 Model K was the best-known Biddle, and the only one to standardize the Duesenberg engine, although it was available to special order in other models. This 4-cylinder horizontal-valve unit had a capacity of nearly 5 litres, and developed 90bhp at 2,200rpm. From 1920 onwards it was known as the Rochester-Duesenberg, being built under licence by the Rochester Motors Corporation. Several other sporting cars used this, or similar units, including Argonne, Revere, and Richelieu. The Model K Biddle was a handsome car with Mercedes-type radiator and wire wheels, but few were sold. Speedsters such as Daniels and Biddle lacked the sporting renown of Mercer and Stutz, had no better performance, and were more expensive as well. Their exclusiveness attracted a small number of customers, but when the initial post-war boom disappeared so did the market for these cars.

There were a number of other expensive, small production speedsters at this time, such as the Duesenberg-powered Argonne whose radiator was an almost exact copy of the Prince Henry Austro-Daimler, and the Revere which had an enlarged Rochester-Duesenberg engine giving 103bhp. The Noma was a typical assembled speedster with perfectly standard Continental or Beaver 6-cylinder engines, and attractive two-seater body with cycle-type wings, step plates, and beetle back. There were plans to assemble it in England, but it would hardly have sold many units at a price of £1,050. Nevertheless, a few complete cars were imported and sold in unmodified left-hand drive form.

A higher quality car made in speedster form was the Marmon. This firm had caused a considerable sensation in 1916 with the introduction of their Type 34, with 5·6-litre ohv 6-cylinder engine whose cylinder block, body, and bonnet were all of aluminium. An unusual feature was rear suspension by double transverse springs. The tourer could reach 70mph and a speedster was available with a higher rear axle ratio and capable of 80mph. This was made in two- or four-seater form.

By 1925 the speedsters available to the American buyer were very few. The Daniels, Biddle, Richelieu, and Mercer had all gone, and the renaissance of Stutz was still ahead. However, two makers of medium-priced assembled cars kept speedsters in their catalogues, Jordan and Kissel. The Jordan began in 1916 as a typical assembled car powered by a 54bhp 6-cylinder Continental engine. However its lines were much better than average, and advertising from the start proclaimed it as a 'Smart Design for Smart Folks'. The famous Playboy speedster appeared in 1919; it had a standard engine and a two-seater body with a dickey, but an unusual feature aimed at the feminine market was a Vogue Vanity Case on the dash. With this model Ned Jordan began his celebrated advertisements which in the long run were to bring him more fame than his cars. 'A Million Miles from Dull Care', 'The Port of Missing Men', and, most famous of all, 'Somewhere West of Laramie'; they were written in romantic purple prose which stirred hidden longings. No mention was made of facts about the car, and in making this indirect appeal to desires and ambitions Jordan was inaugurating a new kind of advertising which has since become widespread for almost every kind of product. Even those who were not potential buyers of Jordan cars, or indeed of any car, looked forward to a new Jordan advertisement in the *Saturday Evening Post* or *Vanity Fair*. As late as the 1950s, Jock Ogilvy of Ogilvy and Mather made every junior copywriter learn 'Somewhere West of Laramie' by heart. The Playboy initially sold for $2,150 and was continued until 1929, by which time it was powered by a Continental straight-8 of 90bhp and cost $2,525. Other open Jordans were the Tomboy two-seater coupé, and the Blueboy touring car. Ned Jordan's marriage broke up in 1928, and he slowly lost interest in the firm, leaving it in 1929. In 1930 came the Speedway Ace, a very stylish car with 114bhp Continental engine, Woodlite headlamps, and aircraft type instruments. However the price had jumped to an exorbitant $5,000, the same as that of a Packard 734 and more than a Stutz DV-32. It is not surprising that the Speedway Ace was made to special order only. All Jordan production ceased early in 1931.

The first sporting car from the Kissel Motor Company of Hartford, Wisconsin, was a semi-racer of 1911 with the usual raked steering column and two bucket seats, but in 1917 came a much more distinctive car, the Silver Special. Conover T. Silver was the New York distributor for Kissel and Apperson cars, and designed Silver Specials for both makes. They featured very clean body lines, rounded-top radiators, and bullet headlamps, and came in three models, Speedster, Tourster, and seven-seater touring car. The former had no doors, and two-folding auxiliary seats as on the Paige-Daytona. On the 1919 models a door was added on one side for the modesty of short-skirted passengers. Silver ceased to handle Kissels in 1919, but the trend he started continued to the company's end in 1931. The 1919 show model was painted pure chrome yellow all over, and was christened the Gold Bug. This name was used for Kissel speedsters for several years, whatever their colour might be. A Lycoming straight-8 was introduced for 1925, and this chassis carried speedster bodies as well as the smaller six. The last series was known as the White Eagle, and differed considerably from earlier models. All engines were now Lycoming straight-8s, of 3-, 4-, and 4·9-litre capacity, and the radiator was almost flat-topped like a La Salle's, in place of the rounded top which had survived since the 1917 Silver Special. There was still a sporting model in the range, the White Eagle 126 speedster with the largest engine being capable of 95mph. However, like Jordan and other assembled car makers, the sands were running out for Kissel; in 1929 they made 1,071 cars, in 1930, 261, and in 1931 only 16.

In 1925 the Stutz company was acquired by Charles M. Schwab, the steel magnate, and a new team at once appointed. F. E. Moscovics came from Marmon to be president, while C. R. Greuter was appointed chief engineer. Greuter was an early designer of overhead valve engines, having designed

'Somewhere West of Laramie'. This advertisement appeared in the Saturday Evening Post *for June 23rd, 1923. (Photo: William S. Jackson Collection)*

146

Somewhere West of Laramie

SOMEWHERE west of Laramie there's a broncho-busting, steer-roping girl who knows what I'm talking about. She can tell what a sassy pony, that's a cross between greased lightning and the place where it hits, can do with eleven hundred pounds of steel and action when he's going high, wide and handsome.

The truth is—the Playboy was built for her.

Built for the lass whose face is brown with the sun when the day is done of revel and romp and race.

She loves the cross of the wild and the tame.

There's a savor of links about that car—of laughter and lilt and light—a hint of old loves—and saddle and quirt. It's a brawny thing—yet a graceful thing for the sweep o' the Avenue.

Step into the Playboy when the hour grows dull with things gone dead and stale.

Then start for the land of real living with the spirit of the lass who rides, lean and rangy, into the red horizon of a Wyoming twilight.

JORDAN

JORDAN MOTOR CAR COMPANY, Inc., Cleveland, Ohio

1930 Jordan Speedway Ace 5·3-litre roadster. (Photo: Automobile Manufacturers' Association)

the ohv Holyoke car in 1901, and later he had been responsible for all the Matheson cars. Also on the design staff was Paul Bastien, a Belgian who had designed the single-ohc Somea and 2-litre Métallurgique in his homeland before joining Stutz. This team produced the brand-new Safety Stutz, also known as the Vertical Eight because of its straight-8 engine. This was a single-ohc unit of 4·7 litres, developing 92bhp at 4,700rpm. There were two plugs per cylinder, two carburetters, a nine main bearing crankshaft, and hydraulic brakes. Worm drive gave a very low drive line, and with a double-drop frame the new Stutz was the lowest production sedan on the road. Two- and four-seater speedsters were part of the range from the start, and in 1928 were renamed the Black Hawk. They should not be confused with the Black-hawk, an altogether cheaper line of Stutz cars, mainly sedans, made from 1929 to 1931. The new speedster had 4·9-litre engines and cycle-type wings. They competed at Atlantic City speedway and Pike's Peak Hill-climb. In 1927 three Stutzes, a standard sedan, a Weymann sedan, and a Black Hawk speedster ran for 24 hours at Indianapolis, and were awarded the Stevens Challenge Trophy. The following year saw the famous Indianapolis challenge with Hispano-Suiza (see page 110) which was won by the French car al-though Stutz won a 3½-hour race held afterwards. After 1928, Stutz sponsored no more racing, but C. T. Weymann entered a four-seater tourer in the 1928 Le Mans 24 Hour Race. Driven by Bloch and Brisson, the Stutz finished 2nd behind Woolf Barnato and Bernard Rubin's 4½-litre Bentley. For much of the race, the Stutz had led the Bentley, lapping at about 2mph faster, but the wide ratio gearbox was a handicap and for the last four hours the top gear had to be held in manually. A Roots-blown car finished 5th in the 1929 Le Mans race, and two cars entered in 1930, only to retire.

The Black Hawk speedster was made until 1932. The new DV 32 was introduced in 1931, having twin overhead camshafts and four valves per cylinder in an engine now of 5·2 litres and 156bhp. The name Bearcat was revived for the long wheelbase speedster (11ft 2½in), while the new short wheelbase (9ft 8in) was known as the Super Bearcat. The latter was capable of 100mph with a drophead coupé body. The last production Stutz was prob-ably made in 1933, although they were still on sale in 1935, but it is unlikely that the Bearcat was made for the last two years. In the worst of the de-pression period, there was not much demand for a two-seater car costing $4,700. However, the Stutz had outlived its rival the Mercer by ten years,

1932 Stutz Super Bearcat with coachwork by Murray. (Photo: Briggs Cunningham Automotive Museum)

and its greatest period was that of the Greuter-designed Vertical Eight.

The Auburn had been one of the staidest of American touring cars until 1921, when the Beauty Six sports tourer was introduced. This Continental-powered car had cycle-type wings, step plates, disc wheels, and came in a wide variety of dual colour schemes. The real revolution in the Auburn image came three years later when thirty-year-old Erret Lobban Cord became general manager and hired J. M. Crawford to design a new range. The first of the new cars was the 8–88, with a 4½-litre straight-8 Lycoming engine of 68bhp. Performance was not spectacular, with a maximum speed of 62mph, but the cars looked striking, having dual colour schemes on all models. A two-seater roadster was included in the range, but in 1928 came the much more sporting Speedster, with alloy pistons and connecting rods, larger

1929 Auburn Model 8–90 Speedster. (Photo: Antique Automobile)

valves and a high lift camshaft, giving 90bhp. The boat-tail body was probably designed by Count Alex de Sakhnoffsky who also designed sporting bodies for Cord and Duesenberg. At the 1929 New York Show was shown the Cabin Speedster, with all-aluminium closed body, two wickerwork airplane-type seats, and a high compression 125bhp engine. Probably only one of these striking machines was made. Auburn speedsters competed frequently against Stutzes, enthusiasts for the latter pointing out eagerly that the Auburns were nearly always defeated. However, it should be remembered that the Auburn was much cheaper, costing between $1,895 and $2,195 up to 1930, and as little as $995 in 1931, whereas the Stutz cost at least $3,150 for the SV 16 models and considerably more for the DV 32. The Auburn was remarkably good value; even their V-12 of 1931 cost less than $1,000.

E. L. Cord had become president of Auburn in 1926, and the same year he acquired the Duesenberg company of Indianapolis. This firm had been making a fine straight-8, the 4·2-litre Model A, which was available in two-seater roadster form, but was hardly a sports car. Cord wanted to produce the finest car in the land and gave Fred Duesenberg a free hand to produce such a machine. The Model J which appeared at the 1928 New York Salon was a remarkable car. It had a 6,882cc twin-ohc engine built by Lycoming to Duesenberg's specifications. In an era when 100bhp was a respectable figure for an American luxury car, and 150bhp exceptional, the Model J gave 265bhp at 4,200rpm. In its later supercharged form this engine gave 320bhp, or more than an SSKL Mercedes, and from a slightly smaller engine. The Duesenberg Models J and SJ were made until 1937, and the rest of their story will be dealt with in Chapter 16.

The only Packard which could undoubtedly be called a sports car was the Model 734 speedster, made for one season only, 1929/1930. This used the larger of Packard's two straight-8 engines, a 6·3-litre unit which normally developed 106bhp. With different carburetter and manifolding, and a higher compression ratio, it gave 145bhp in the Model 734. A higher rear-axle ratio also contributed to the speed of over 100mph of which the car was capable. Bodies were mostly boat-tailed two-seaters but a few two-door close-coupled sedans, as well as a five-seater tourer called a phaeton, were also built on the 734 chassis. Only 150 were made in all, prices ranging from $5,000 to $5,210.

Another short-lived speedster at the end of the decade was the Dupont Model G. This used a 125bhp straight-8 engine made by Continental to Dupont's order, and was available as a two- or four-seater. The two-seater had narrow, flowing wings which made it look curiously like a scaled-up Amilcar Petit Sport, and Woodlite headlamps as used on the Jordan Speedway Ace. A four-seater was entered in the Le Mans Race in 1929, but retired after nineteen laps.

All the sporting cars so far mentioned were comparatively expensive and made by small-production firms. The only mass producer to consider making a sporting car was the Hudson Motor Company who offered the Speedabout in their Essex line in 1927. This had a boat-tailed two-seater body and used the standard 40bhp side-valve engine. Maximum speed was only 55mph, and the artillery wheels hardly gave it a sporting appearance, despite the body. Still, it only cost $850. The 1929 Speedabout was a much more attractive proposition, with 55bhp engine giving 70mph, and Biddle & Smart aluminium body with dickey seat. It had wire wheels, and the price had risen to $925, making it the most expensive Essex model. The 1930 model was more handsome still, with spare wheel at the side, but it is not certain if it was ever put on the market because of the Depression. For 1931 a Speedabout model was also offered in the Hudson line. The Hudson Speedabout had an

Below: *1930 Dupont Model G two-seater roadster.*
(Photo: Antique Automobile)

Bottom: *1930 Essex Speedabout.*
(Photo: American Motors Corporation)

87bhp straight-8 engine which gave a maximum speed of over 90mph, bringing its performance into the class of much more expensive speedsters. Unfortunately the Depression had so shaken the confidence of manufacturers that they were not willing to risk a small-production model which might eat up what meagre profits they hoped to make, and after 1931 no more Speedabouts were built. However, Hudson engines later powered the British-built Railton sports car, and Hudsons themselves were prominent in stock-car racing in the late 1940s and early 1950s.

Part Three
The Thirties

11. Great Britain

The effects of the slump were felt everywhere in the world, resulting in the elimination of many fine cars, but England continued to make a wide range of sports cars in the 1930s, and many firms which began their sporting programme a few years earlier reached the peak of their development in this generally unloved decade. In most cases this was the result of steady improvement rather than of striking innovation, so the bulk of British sports cars came into the traditional category. Before examining the quality cars, it is worth looking at a new breed of sports car, the low-price machine derived from the standard family car.

We have seen in Chapter Three how the M.G. Midget was developed with very little trouble or expense from the Morris Minor. Production of the M-type Midget continued until June 1932, by which time 3,235 had been made. An attractive little coupé was added to the range for the 1930 season; costing £245 it was a two-seater, but had limited room for children or luggage. Customers included the racing drivers Earl Howe and John Cobb. For 1931 there was the option of a four-speed gearbox, and also a supercharger at an extra cost of £65, but very few of the latter were sold. The fabric body was replaced by a metal one for 1932. In the 1930 Brooklands Double Twelve Hour Race, Midgets finished 3rd, 4th, 5th, 6th and 7th in their class, being beaten only by two Riley Nines, which were larger and more expensive cars. This led to the marketing of the Double Twelve Replica, with new camshaft as used on the team cars. Only eighteen of these were made, from August to December 1930, selling at a price of £245. The M-type also ran at Le Mans, without great success, but finished 5th in its class in the 1930 Belgian 24 Hour Race. This may not seem very impressive, but at that time it was the smallest car to complete a 24-hour race. Sir Francis Samuelson drove a coupé in the 1931 Monte Carlo Rally.

For competition in the 750cc class, the 746cc C-type was built, christened the Montlhéry as a result of successful record-breaking at the French track. With a supercharger, this engine developed 60bhp at 6,300rpm, and the car was good for 90mph. Its price was as high as £600, and in this form it was far from the original concept of a cheap 'people's sports car'. The tradition of the latter was carried on by the J-type Midget, which replaced the M-type. The J had a lower frame, four speeds as standard, twin carburetters, and cutaway doors. In appearance it started a trend of design which continued up to the TF of 1953. There were three body styles, the open four-seater and salonette, both of these being known as J-1s, and the J-2 two-seater. Special supercharged versions were known as J-3 and J-4. The J-2 two-seater was capable of 70mph. From about August 1934 they had flowing wings in place of the cycle-types previously used, this feature being continued on the 1934 PA which had a 3-bearing camshaft. For 1936 the PB was introduced, with 939cc engine, which enabled it to compete more successfully with Singer's 972cc Nine. The PB was the last of the ohc Midgets, being replaced for 1937 by the TA with pushrod-ohv 1,292cc engine developed from that of the current side valve Morris Ten-Four. This became the TB in 1939, with 1,250cc engine, which was the basis of the highly successful post-war TC series, which did as much as anything to revive sports car enthusiasm in America.

Hillman Aero Minx sports tourer taking part in the 1935 Land's End Trial. (Photo: Montagu Motor Museum)

153

The Midget was always the cheaper end of the M.G. range, but the firm made many other sports models as well. The 6-cylinder 18/80 appeared in revised form for 1930, with deeper and stronger chassis members, four speeds, and servo brakes. Known as the Mark II, this was produced alongside the Mark I for about fifteen months, prices of the improved model being at least £100 above those of the Mark I. In the summer of 1930 came the Mark III Tigresse, a genuine sports car with high compression engine theoretically developing 100bhp, and giving a maximum speed of just over 90mph. Priced at £895, it was £265 dearer than the equivalent Mark II, and only five were sold. At the end of 1931 came the Magna series, with 1,271cc 6-cylinder engine similar to that used in the Wolseley Hornet, of which a sports version was also made (see below). The F-type Magna was very low, with its frame upswept over the front axle and underslung at the rear. Capable of 70mph, it was sold as an open four-seater or close-coupled coupé. Later developments were the improved Magna, with larger brake drums, and the L-type with redesigned exhaust manifold.

After the success of the C-type Midget, Cecil Kimber decided to attack 1,100cc class racing, and in order to provide a production basis for competition activities he introduced the Magnette at the end of 1932. This had a 1,087cc 6-cylinder engine, and originally only one body style, the K-1 saloon. Within a few months this was joined by the K-2 two-seater sports car. By early 1933 the first sports-racing model appeared, the 100bhp supercharged K-3. This car's first competition event was the unlikely one of the Monte Carlo Rally; it did not shine on the road section, coming 64th out of 69 finishers, but it made fastest time of the day on the Mont des Mules hill-climb. In 1933 and 1934 the K-3s were very successful in racing, winning the team award in the 1933 Mille Miglia, and the same year's Tourist Trophy outright, with Nuvolari at the wheel. The great Italian driver's interest in the M.G. was quickened by the remarkable performance of Whitney Straight whose privately owned K-3 defeated single-seater Maseratis in the Coppa Acerbo. In 1934 the German driver Bobby Kohlrausch achieved many successes in hill-climbs. The K-3 was not a sports car for the ordinary driver, and no one who was not seriously interested in racing would have bought one. Nevertheless thirty-one were made, as well as two prototypes, and their successes must have given a tremendous boost to the sale of the more humble M.G.s. Meanwhile the K-1 and K-2 were improved, with the option of pre-selector gearboxes and triple S.U. carburetters, and for 1934 a larger engine of 1,286cc, giving a maximum speed of 80mph. The 1934 N-type was wider and more comfortable than the K, with improved handling. Open two- and four-seater bodies were available, and later an Airline Coupé was added, this style also being made on the PA Midget chassis. After 1936 the Magnette was dropped, along with all the Nuffield ohc designs. Between 1936 and the outbreak of World War 2, a range of 4- and 6-cylinder cars was made, using pushrod ohv engines of 1½-, 2·3-, and 2·6-litre capacity. The larger models were very handsome with long bonnets and flowing lines, but they were not sports cars.

The Wolseley Hornet Special was a humbler cousin of the M.G. Magnettes, having begun life in 1930 as a 6-cylinder version of the Morris Minor. The cylinders had the same bore and stroke as the Minor, while the body was almost identical, looking disproportionately small behind a considerably lengthened bonnet. It was enthusiastically hailed as the cheapest small six ever, which, at £175, it probably was. In 1932 came the Hornet Special, a sports model offered in chassis form only. With twin S.U. carburetters, special manifold, higher compression ratio, and double valve springs, the

32. *1933 Alfa Romeo 8C 2300 2·3-litre sports car.* (Photo: Montagu Motor Museum)

33. Overleaf, left: *1939 Lancia Astura 2·9-litre drophead coupé. Coachwork by Pininfarina. Owned by Michael Scott.* (Photo: Pininfarina)

34. Overleaf, right: *1932 Auburn V-12 6·8-litre speedster. Owned by Paul H. Stern.* (Photo: William S. Jackson)

engine developed 45bhp at 5,000rpm, and with reasonably light body the car was good for 70mph. A large number of coachbuilders tried their hand on the Hornet Special chassis, the most popular being Whittingham and Mitchel who made 'E.W.' bodies for Eustace Watkins, the main London distributors for Wolseley. Other bodies on the Hornet Special were by Jensen, Swallow, and Maltby. Two-seaters, two/four-seaters, saloons and coupés were all offered at prices ranging from £250 to £300. Their reasonable price encouraged many amateurs to tune and race Hornet Specials, often maintaining high revs for far too long, with consequent disastrous breakages which earned the cars a bad name. The situation was improved to some extent with the 1935 Hornet Special Fourteen, which used a 1,604cc engine giving 50bhp at 4,500rpm. Performance was really no better than that of the smaller model, but it was achieved at a lower engine speed. One of these Fourteens won its class in the 12 Hour Race at Donington in 1937. The Hornet Special was one of the most popular subjects for adorning with the trappings of the 'boy racer' – aero screens, chrome-plated stone guards, rows of badges, and so on. The owner who was more interested in performance than appearance could have a supercharger fitted by McEvoy Motors for £75. The Hornets were dropped after 1935, and the new pushrod ohv Wolseleys were not made in sporting form.

There were several other semi-sports cars based on family saloons which were aimed at the 'promenade' market, those people who entered rallies with an eye on the Concours d'Elegance rather than on the road section, or simply liked to look sporting. Such cars are often sneered at, but some, such as the Avon Standards, were very good looking. The Hillman Aero Minx first appeared for 1933 with a very streamlined two/three-seater coupé body. The only engine modifications were an aluminium cylinder head and down-draft Stromberg carburetter, but the frame was dropped giving a much lower appearance than the staid Minx saloon of the time. Cycle-type wings, sloping radiator, and a dual colour scheme gave it some distinction, and the performance was noticeably better than that of the standard saloon, with a maximum speed of 72mph compared with 57mph. Prices were £245 and £159 respectively. For 1934 two new Aero Minx body styles appeared, a foursome coupé and a four-seater tourer, while the 1935 two-seater looked as sporting as an M.G. Midget. The Cresta saloon looked not unlike the Talbot Ten, which was, in fact, derived from the Aero Minx after Rootes had gained control of Clement-Talbot. In a similar category was the Avon Standard which originally appeared as a two-seater sports car based on the Standard Nine. The body was designed by the Jensen brothers for the New Avon Body Company of Warwick, and completely transformed the Standard, with low appearance, cycle-type wings, and wire wheels. The price was £250. Later Avons were less sporting in appearance, being mostly four-seater tourers or saloons, though still highly distinctive. Designed by C. F. Beauvais, these bodies were built on Standard chassis from 9hp to 20hp. Engine and steering were sometimes modified, but Avon were unable to obtain underslung frames. The B.S.A. Scout was an attractive looking small car available as a two-seater, four-seater, or coupé. The 1,204cc side-valve engine drove the front wheels; in its final 1939 form, it gave 32bhp and 70mph.

A car which started in much the same way as those just described but went on to become one of the most famous modern sports cars was the S.S. Just as Avon had produced a sports version of the Standard Nine, so the Swallow Coachbuilding Company had made stylish sporting bodies on Austin Seven, Standard Nine and Sixteen, Fiat 509, and Swift Ten chassis. In 1931 came a development of this theme, the S.S.1, which used an untuned

35. 1948 M.G. TC sports car.
Owned by Mrs D. Bowman.
(Photo: Charles Pocklington)

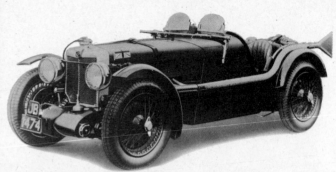

Top left: *Victoria Worsley with the M-type M.G. Midget which she drove in the 1930 Double Twelve Race at Brooklands. (Photo: British Motor Corporation)*

Top right: *1933 M.G. K-3 Magnette two-seater. (Photo: British Motor Corporation)*

Above: *An early Wolseley Hornet Special taking part in the Singer Motor Club Rushmere Hill Climb. (Photo: Montagu Motor Museum)*

2,054cc 6-cylinder Standard Sixteen engine, but had an underslung frame designed by Swallow and built for them by Standard and completely new body – a close-coupled coupé with very long bonnet and cycle-type front wings. It was only 4ft 8in high, 13in lower than the ordinary saloon. There was no other British car comparable in appearance; the bonnet might well have contained a straight-8 engine, and the whole car looked like one of the more exotic offerings at the Paris Salon. The price was only £310; in his first model William Lyons showed his remarkable capacity for building cars whose appearance suggest something two or three times as expensive. The S.S.1 was also available with the 20hp Standard engine, and in addition there was a small coupé powered by the 4-cylinder Standard Little Nine unit,

An S.S. Club Rally, about 1936. In the foreground are coupé and Airline saloon versions of the S.S.1. (Photo: Montagu Motor Museum)

1937 2½-litre S.S.100 seen during driving tests at Beaulieu in 1961. (Photo: Montagu Motor Museum)

Left: *One of the more extreme examples of promenade car was the Offord 'Vitesse' sports tourer on the Vauxhall Light Six chassis. Apart from louvres on front and rear wings its sporting amenities included a Malcolm Campbell sprung steering wheel, fold-flat windscreen and large fishtail exhaust.* *(Photo: Montagu Motor Museum)*

known as the S.S.2, priced at £210. 1933 models had improved cylinder heads, a longer wheelbase, allowing full four-seater bodies, and sweeping wings and running boards. Early in 1933 came the four-seater open tourer, a team of which ran in the Alpine Trial that year. In October 1933 the engine was increased to 2,664cc, while new bodies for 1935 included an Airline saloon and a drophead coupé. The S.S.90 two-seater sports appeared in March 1935; apart from an S.S.1 Special built for William Walmsley, Lyons' partner, in 1934, and possibly one other car, this was the first two-seater. The engine had received little attention up to now, but in 1935 William Heynes became chief engineer, and, assisted by Harry Weslake, designed an ohv head, which with twin carburetters raised power from 84bhp to 104bhp. For 1936 a new range of 4-door saloons called the S.S. Jaguar appeared, whose lines were not changed until 1948. There was also a new two-seater, the S.S. Jaguar 100, usually known as the S.S.100. It was wide and low, with flowing wings and folding windscreen, and looked every inch a sports car, although sneered at by many enthusiasts, presumably because of its pushrod engine of humble origin. For 1938 it was available with a 3½-litre engine developing 125bhp at 4,200rpm. For the first time there was an S.S. capable of 100mph, for, despite its name, the 2·7-litre S.S.100 could not better 93mph. These cars did very well in rallies, a 2·7-litre winning a Glacier Cup in the 1936 Alpine Trial, while Ian Appleyard's 3½-litre gained a Coupe des Alpes in the 1948 event, despite losing half-an-hour in aiding an injured rival. The S.S. also won the unlimited class in the 1937 and 1938 R.A.C. Rallies. It was not raced a great deal, although it won the 1937 Portuguese Sports Car Race at Villa Real, and numerous private owners were successful at Brooklands. Nearly all of the 315 S.S.100s made were sports two-seaters, although there were a few Newsome drophead coupés, and one prototype fixedhead coupé which might have gone into production had the war not intervened.

Singer had not been a sporting make in the 1920s, but the 848cc ohc Junior introduced in 1927 was a suitable basis from which to develop a sporting car. In the late 1920s, the sporting model was the Porlock two-seater, which had hardly any better performance than the normal Junior. At the 1931 Olympia Show there was a Junior Special saloon, which, apart from its styling by C. F. Beauvais, was notable for having a larger engine of 972cc. Four months later this engine was standardized in a new model called the Nine. The 1933 sports model of this had twin carburetters, a remote-control gearbox, and hydraulic brakes, costing £174 for an open four-seater. A standard model ran at Le Mans in 1933, finished 13th overall, and was the first British car of under 1,000cc to qualify for the Rudge-Whitworth Cup. Two- and four-seater Le Mans models were very successful in trials, and seriously threatened the position of M.G. They ran again at Le Mans in 1934 and 1935, and in the 1935 Tourist Trophy, but in the latter race disaster overtook the team. Three out of the four cars entered crashed at the same spot because of breakage of the steering drop-arms. Two cars, those of S. C. H. Davis and Norman Black, actually piled up on top of each other, the third crashed a short distance away, and the fourth was withdrawn immediately after the Davis/Black pile-up. Fortunately, no one was seriously hurt, but the incident did Singers a great deal of harm and the works never entered a team again. The ordinary sports Nine was continued until the 1937 season at a price of £225. It was

Singer Nine Sports in the 1935 Land's End Trial. (Photo: Montagu Motor Museum)

capable of 75mph, and its worst feature was low gearing. However this was not so much of a handicap in trials, where Singers continued to do well. There was also a 1½-litre 4-cylinder car with three-bearing crankshaft of which only twelve were made, and, from 1933 to 1936, a 1½-litre six, usually seen in four-seater form, which cost £295.

Another British firm to enter the sporting market at about the same time as Singer was Triumph. Their 832cc side-valve Super Seven appeared as a saloon in 1928, and in the following year came a two-seater sports car, available with Cozette blower at £250. It competed directly with the M.G. Midget, but did not compare very well. Its acceleration was only marginally better and maximum speed only 5mph higher (68mph compared with 63mph). The Triumph weighed over 2cwt more, and the price was £65 higher than that of the M.G. For racing, the capacity was reduced to 747cc, but this brought it up against the Austin Seven, and it fared no better. After one season it was withdrawn and for 1931 Triumph's only sporting model was the Gnat, a £185 two-seater with standard engine. In 1933 came the Southern Cross, with 1,122cc inlet-over-exhaust Coventry-Climax engine, originally available only as a four-seater sports-tourer of no great performance. Later came the Gloria Southern Cross with 1,232cc engine, and two sixes of 1,476cc and 1,991cc. The latter was quite a fast car in short-chassis two-seater form, and was more popular than the small six which was soon dropped. These Triumphs did well in the Monte Carlo Rally and Alpine Trials, but were not raced except in club events. Donald Healey was the designer from 1934 to 1936, and was mainly responsible for the Gloria. In 1937 the Coventry-Climax engine was replaced by ohv Triumph units of 4- and 6-cylinders, and no more sporting cars were made. Far more exciting than any of these was the 1934 Dolomite twin-ohc straight-8, a really high performance two-seater sports car closely copied from the Alfa-Romeo 2·3-litre. Donald Healey drove one in the 1935 Monte Carlo Rally, but hit a train en route and was lucky to escape with his life. Only six were made before pressure from Alfa-Romeo brought the project to an end. The remaining cars were sold off by an outside concern under the name H.S.M. (High Speed Motors).

During the early 1930s the Austin Seven sports was sold in very small numbers, at £185 for the unsupercharged model and at £225 with blower. In 1933 came the '65', less highly tuned than the earlier car (23bhp compared with 33bhp) and not offered with blower, but also less expensive (£152), and made in considerably larger numbers. Nearly 700 sports Sevens left the factory between 1933 and 1936, not counting chassis supplied to coachbuilders, compared with 167 from 1930 to 1932. For 1935 the '65' was renamed the Nippy, and there was a new model the '75' or Speedy with shallower doors, pointed tail, and higher gearing, priced at £172. Exact figures are not available, but fewer Speedys were made than Nippys, and the Speedy was withdrawn in the summer of 1935. There were still a number of coachbuilders, such as A.E.W. and Arrow, offering special sporting versions of the Seven, including two-seaters, four-seaters and coupés. Three Sevens ran at Le Mans in 1935 (only one finished), but Austins were doing very little racing at this period. Record breaking, however, continued. In 1936 the Nippy was offered with the standard engine at £130, or with the mildly tuned one at £142. There was also a new trials-type sports model called the Grasshopper, with different radiator. A team of three competed in most of the year's major trials with success. This was practically the end of the Seven as a sports car, for the Nippy was dropped early in 1937. A new sports car was announced, with camshaft designed by Murray Jamieson, and two-seater doorless body, but very few were made.

Not a nasty accident, but simply Donald Healey and his passenger taking a rest during the 1930 Brighton Rally. Their car is a Triumph Super Seven. (Photo: Montagu Motor Museum)

A small production car using the 832cc Triumph engine was the Vale, made at Maida Vale in London from 1932 to 1936. It was much lower than any Triumph, with chassis underslung at front and rear. Its appearance was very sporty, with cycle-type wings, bonnet straps, and quick-action filler caps. Unfortunately it was too low for trials and not powerful enough for racing. Like Triumph, Vale went over to Coventry-Climax engines for 1934, using the 1,098cc four or 1,476cc six. The company said that they would install these larger engines in existing cars, or supply complete new cars. Probably very few Vales were made after 1934, the total production for five years being 103.

Crossley made no sports cars after the sporting 20/70 described in Chapter Three, but in 1932 they introduced a low two-seater with 10hp 1,122cc Coventry-Climax engine as used in the Triumph Southern Cross. This was derived from the T.T. cars with engines linered down to 1,097cc prepared by

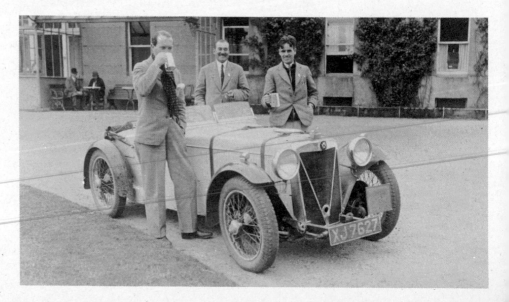

Refuelling stop for the crew of a Crossley Ten Sports. The event was the 1932 Scottish Rally. (Photo: Montagu Motor Museum)

Vernon Balls. It was unsuccessful in competitions, but was shown at Olympia in 1932, together with an extraordinary-looking 4-door sports saloon. The two-seater was priced at £350 and the saloon at £385. Neither went into production, and the only other sporting Crossley was the sports-tourer version of the Regis saloon, a promenade car if ever there was one.

In quite a different class was the Alta, a perfectionist's idea of a sports car which the builder put into small-scale production. It was the creation of Geoffrey Taylor who built the prototype in his father's stables at Surbiton, Surrey, in 1928. Most unusually for an amateur constructor, he made his own engine which was a 1,074cc unit aluminium block and head and twin ohc. He used an A.B.C. frame, but when the car went into production three years later frames were bought from Rubery Owen. Suspension was by semi-elliptic springs, and a light two-seater body was fitted with a sharply sloping radiator. The engine developed 68bhp at 6,000rpm and maximum speed was 80mph. The price in 1931 was £350, by no means high for this type of car. In 1933 a very close-coupled four-seater was offered at £365. A 2-litre engine came in 1934, developing 85bhp unblown or 160bhp blown. The latter was used almost entirely in racing cars, and indeed all Altas were more suited to racing than long-distance road work. This was possible if driver

1933 Alta 1,100cc close-coupled four-seater. (Photo: Autocar)

and passenger were prepared to put up with water and oil on their trousers, and oil in their faces, but one cannot imagine anyone buying an Alta who did not have his eye on racing of some kind. Acceleration was superb, the 2-litre model taking not much more than 20 seconds to reach 100mph, while at 30mph the wheels were still spinning on a dry road. Independent front suspension by coil was introduced in 1937. The Altas were very successful in racing, owners including Earl Howe, S. C. H. Davis and George Abecassis. The latter's 2-litre car holds the sports car record for the old Crystal Palace circuit, at 2 minutes 9 seconds, achieved exactly seven days before World War 2 broke out.

Another idealist's car, though more comfortable and far more expensive than the Alta, was the Squire. Adrian Squire had produced his first car catalogue when he was sixteen and still at school; eight years later in 1934 the first prototype was on the road, remarkably similar in many ways to the schoolboy's ideal. The 1½-litre twin ohc 4-cylinder engine was bought from Anzani, with only minor modifications being made by Squire. With a Roots blower power was 110bhp. A Wilson-type preselector gearbox made by E.N.V. was used, and the hydraulic brakes were of Squire's own design. The 15½in manganese alloy drums filled the internal diameter of the wheels, practically no daylight showing through. These were said to stop the car in 20ft from 30mph, and in some cases braking was so fierce that the front spring shackles fractured. A beautiful two-seater body made by Vanden Plas was fitted, with the later option of a four-seater on a longer chassis. Unfortunately the cost of all this was very high. The original price for a two-seater was £1,220, more than a 4½-litre Lagonda, and nearly as much as Type 55 Bugatti. Even when prices were slashed to £695 for a car with very stark and far less attractive body, Squire could still find hardly any buyers. Only seven cars were made, and most of these were bought by personal friends. A single-seater was raced at Brooklands, but on its first appearance it broke its crankshaft, and on the second the chassis fractured. Racing or some form of sporting success was the only hope for a car of the Squire's type, and without it the make had no chance. Geoffrey Taylor and Adrian Squire both built cars to their own ideals but Taylor, in going all out for speed rather than beauty, collected a number of talented drivers who brought credit to the make. This, Squire, with his much prettier and in some ways better designed car, failed to do.

After he left G.N. in 1923, H. R. Godfrey ran his own business, servicing G.N.s, and in 1935, together with E. A. Halford and Guy A. Robins, he launched a new car, the H.R.G. It was powered by a 1½-litre 4-cylinder

The prototype Squire of 1934 taking part in driving tests at Croydon in 1939. This car is now part of Harrah's Automobile Collection at Reno, Nevada.
(Photo: Klemantaski Studio)

An early 1½-litre H.R.G. during the 1937 Torquay Rally.
(Photo: Montagu Motor Museum)

Meadows 4ED engine, developing 60bhp at 4,500rpm, and had a light-alloy two-seater body. The firm suspension was by quarter elliptics at the front and semi-elliptics at the rear. The general concept and appearance was similar to the Frazer Nash, but the H.R.G. used a conventional gearbox and shaft-drive. Interestingly enough it weighed less than the contemporary Frazer Nash, and at 14cwt was among the lightest sports cars in its class. (The Frazer Nash weighed about 2,128lb depending on the model, and the Riley Sprite 2,184lb.) Maximum speed of the H.R.G. was 83mph, and the price a not unreasonable £395. In 1939 a 1½-litre ohc Singer engine replaced the Meadows, and there was also an 1,100cc car powered by the Singer Nine engine. These engines were modified by H.R.G., having stronger valve springs, high lift cams, and new manifolding. H.R.G.s were successful in trials because of a concentration of weight over the rear axle, though low ground clearance must have been a hindrance in the muddier events, and it also did well in rallies and racing. The 1½-litre cars took second place in their class at Le Mans in 1937 and 1938, and won the class in 1939. Only thirty-six cars were made up to the outbreak of war, but they built up a good reputation as functional and uncomplicated sports cars. After the war they went on to even greater successes.

Another new sports car to appear in the mid-1930s was the Morgan 4-4. The 3-wheelers were still being made, but the market for the powerful V-twin sporting machines was shrinking fast, and a range of family 3-wheelers with 4-cylinder water-cooled Ford Eight and Ten engines was introduced for 1934. Two years later came the first 4-wheeler Morgan, a light sports car powered by the 1,122cc inlet-over-exhaust Coventry-Climax engine used in the Triumph Southern Cross and Crossley Ten. It had conventional lines, but retained the traditional Morgan independent front suspension by sliding pillars. It had a maximum speed of 75mph, and in 1936 cost £180. Two- and four-seaters were available, and in 1939 came a drophead coupé powered by an ohv version of the 1,267cc Standard Ten engine which was used in all post-war 4-4s up to 1950. The 4-4 was not raced a great deal, but a so-called T.T. Replica body with cycle-type wings and Coventry-Climax engine linered to 1,104cc ran at Le Mans in 1938 and 1939, finishing 15th in the overall classification in the latter event.

A Morgan 4-4 on Fingle Hill, Devon. (Photo: Montagu Motor Museum)

A Riley Lynx sports tourer during the 1937 Torquay Rally. (Photo: Montagu Motor Museum)

The name of Riley was carried to greater successes in the early 1930s than ever before. These included 1st and 3rd places in the 1,100cc class in the 1931 Irish Grand Prix at Phoenix Park, 1st and 3rd in the 1931 T.T., outright victory in the 1932 T.T. and 2nd overall place in the 1932 Brooklands 500 Mile Race. At Le Mans in 1935 they were first in the 1½-litre class, and broke the 1,100cc class record by 9mph. These victories were achieved by the Brooklands Nine, which was continued until 1933, but a more practical road-going sports car introduced in 1932 was the Gamecock at £298. The Nine touring chassis was lowered for the 1932 season, and the Gamecock was the first sports Riley to use the same chassis as the touring car. Also in 1932 came a sports/racing version of the 14/6, with the engine reduced from 1,633cc to 1,486cc, to bring it within the 1½-litre class. Unlike the Brooklands Nine, it did not have a dropped frame, but the straight chassis members sloped from front to rear giving it a characteristic tail-down appearance. It was priced at £595 for racing only; very few were made in this form, but the engine formed a basis for the MPH Six of 1935. The Gamecock was dropped after 1933, but other sporting Nines included the Lincock fixed-head coupé (also available on the 12/6 and 14/6 chassis), Lynx open four-seater and March Special. The latter was a more rakish two/four-seater with louvres on top of the bonnet as well as the sides, prepared by Kevill-Davies & March Ltd, designed by the Earl of March, later Duke of Richmond and Gordon. For 1934 came the Imp, a sports car on a shortened Nine chassis. The prototype Imp was a two/four-seater, but production models were all two-seaters. It was a very functional, stubby-looking little car, having a speed of 75mph for £325. With a 6-cylinder engine it was known as the MPH Six; alternative sizes were 1,486cc for competitions or 1,633cc and 1,758cc for those not worried by sporting categories. It was not so popular as the Imp, only about twelve being made compared with about seventy-five of the 4-cylinder car.

In 1934 a new 12/4 engine of 1,496cc was designed by Hugh Rose. It retained the high camshaft position of the original Nine, the camshafts being driven by chains on the early models, and then by gears. A tuned version of this engine was mounted in the MPH chassis to make a new sports model known as the Sprite, introduced at the 1935 Motor Show. The Sprite had a preselector gearbox and a streamlined radiator cowl peculiar to this model. A 2-litre 6-cylinder Sprite was also made in small numbers. The 12/4 Kestrel saloon and Lynx tourer (now with four doors) were also available with the

A Riley Imp in the Lawrence Cup Trial.
(Photo: Montagu Motor Museum)

Sprite engine, main differences between the two engines being that the latter had a cross-flow head, 'hotter' camshaft, and larger valves. Freddie Dixon won the 1935 and 1936 Tourist Trophy races on a 12/4-engined car which was not very different from the standard Sprite mechanically, but had a long-tailed body and normal Riley radiator. Rileys also took the team award in the 1935 B.R.D.C. 500 Mile Race at Brooklands, and won the 1½-litre class, coming 1st, 2nd, 3rd, and 4th in the 1936 French Grand Prix, which was run as a sports car race that year. During the last season of the independent Riley company, 1937/38, the Sprite was the only sports model, and after the Nuffield Organisation took over the company in September 1938 no more sports Rileys were made.

Riley, of course, made a wide range of touring cars as well as the sporting machines described, but the two sporting specialists of the 1920s, Frazer Nash and Aston Martin, continued to make only sports cars, the former with almost no concessions to changing fashion and the demand for comfort. The principal changes in the Frazer Nashes of the 1930s were concerned with the engine. The side-valve Anzani was supplemented by the ohv Meadows 4ED of exactly the same capacity (1,496cc) in 1929, and by 1932 the last Anzani engine had been used. From 1934 a single ohc 60bhp engine, also of 1,496cc, was available. This was known as the Gough engine, after its designer Albert Gough, and was made by Frazer Nash themselves. Only twenty-six Gough-powered cars left the works between 1934 and 1938, and such a small production run meant that mistakes could never truly be ironed out. For those who wanted a smoother and more flexible unit, the 6-cylinder twin-ohc Blackburne engine was also available from 1934 to 1938. This had an unusual system of camshaft drive, one shaft being driven by chain and the other by helical gears from the first. This engine was basically the same as the single-ohc Blackburne unit which powered the 1½-litre Invicta, the twin-cams being fitted by Blackburne's to Frazer Nash's order. In theory two sizes were available: 1,498cc, as used in the Invicta, and 1,657cc; but it seems that only the larger engines were employed by Frazer Nash. Again, production was very small, only twenty-seven of the 6-cylinder cars being made. Several Frazer Nash models could be fitted with superchargers, single Cozettes on the Meadows engines, and twin-Centrics on the Gough engine. It is important to realise that all Frazer Nash production was bespoke, customers having a say at all stages, so any generalizations are likely to be wrong. Thus the Blackburne, being a 'touring' unit, was not normally supercharged, yet one Blackburne-powered car was fitted with a blower and raced at Brooklands by J. O. C. Samuel. The only other engine to be fitted to a chain-drive Frazer Nash in the 1930s was a Type 319 B.M.W. 1,911cc 6-cylinder unit. Since 1934 A.F.N. Ltd had been importing the German B.M.W. and these cars of modern design were claiming increasing attention from the firm. Chain-drive production fell off sharply after 1934, only fourteen cars being completed in 1935 and eleven in 1936. The figures for 1937, 1938 and 1939 were two, one, and one respectively. Total Frazer Nash production since 1923 had only been about 348. Apart from engine changes, the most important design alterations were the adoption of four forward speeds and a lower body without running boards in 1928, downswept chassis in 1934, and Bishop cam steering for 1935. The most popular body was the T.T. Replica two-seater, but there were also the three/four-seater Interceptor, the wide two-seater Colmore, and even a couple of saloons. Other model names resulted from the use of different engines, with or without superchargers or chassis modifications, the Shelsley having cantilevered half-elliptic springs at the front instead of the usual quarter-elliptics.

Frazer Nashes were widely entered in trials and races by their enthusiastic owners, and also in major races such as Le Mans (in 1935 only), the T.T., and the BRDC 500 Mile Race at Brooklands. However, they never achieved the success of cars such as Riley or M.G. in these events, and their greatest sporting achievements were in the Alpine Trials of 1932 to 1934, where they won four Glacier Cups for losing no marks; the 1934 team was second in the 1½-litre class (the winner of this class, interestingly enough, was their new associate, B.M.W.).

Aston Martin continued to make the International up to 1932 on two chassis, 10ft and 8ft 6in wheelbases. Bodies were a two- or two/four-seater, or sportsman's coupé on the short wheelbase and a 2- or 4-door saloon, or 4-door tourer on the long chassis. Astons came 2nd in their class in the 1931 Double Twelve Race at Brooklands, and won a Biennial Cup at Le Mans in 1931 and 1932. This led to the appearance of the Le Mans Replica model in the 1933 catalogue, in which all models had unit construction of engine and gearbox. In 1934 came a long chassis full four-seater tourer, and coupé and saloon with lower lines. These bodies were continued on the 1935 Mark II, but with the identifying feature of a chromed radiator grille. The Mark II engine was still of 1,495cc, but had a stronger, fully balanced crankshaft and improved combustion chambers. Power was now 73bhp. As a result of the marque's winning the team prize in the 1934 T.T., the new super sports model for 1935 was named the Ulster. This had twin carburetters and a higher compression ratio of 8·5:1, giving over 80bhp at 5,250rpm. The body had a long tail while cycle-type wings and outside exhaust pipe contributed to one of the most out-and-out sporting appearances of the period. Of the car exhibited at the 1935 Motor Show, *The Autocar* said that it was one of the nearest approaches to a racing car contained within the walls of Olympia. It was a source of constant complaint among enthusiasts that true racing cars were not allowed at the Motor Show, a situation which persisted until 1952. The Ulster Aston Martin had a maximum speed of 102mph, making it one of the fastest road cars of the day. It came 3rd at Le Mans in 1935 and 1937, and won its class in the 1935 Mille Miglia. In 1936 a new 2-litre engine with similar single ohc layout replaced the 1½-litre. The sports tourer and the saloon no longer used dry sump lubrication, but it was retained in the two-seater Speed Model. The latter was available with an aerodynamic body in 1939, but only six were made. Throughout the 1930s, Aston Martin production was very small, seldom exceeding 100 cars per year, but to their credit

36. 1954 Allard K3 3·6-litre sports car. Owned by J. L. Ball. (Photo: Charles Pocklington)

they were among the few British firms offering genuine sports cars in 1939.

Among the larger British cars, two makes were predominant, both developed from touring cars of the 1920s. These were Lagonda and Talbot. The former stemmed from the 1926 14/60, a 2-litre tourer whose 4-cylinder engine had hemispherical combustion chambers and overhead valves operated by high mounted, but not overhead, camshafts. It was not a sports car, and usually carried rather ponderous saloon or touring coachwork, but the engine had obvious potentialities for development. For 1928 came the 2-litre Speed Model, with twin carburetters and a higher compression ratio and lowered chassis. This car had a maximum speed of 80mph. Two ran at Le Mans in 1928, driven by Baron d'Erlanger and Sir Francis Samuelson. D'Erlanger's car crashed into the rear of his team mate's, eliminating the latter, although d'Erlanger went on to finish 11th. For 1929 Lagonda brought out a 3-litre car, with 6-cylinder pushrod ohv engine of 2,931cc (enlarged to 3,181cc in 1933). The chassis was a lengthened version of the 2-litre. For 1931 came the Continental 2-litre with sloping radiator, replaced the following year by the 16/80 powered by a 6-cylinder Crossley engine. This was withdrawn in 1934, when the line of 2-litre development came to an end. The 3-litre was made with Maybach semi-automatic gearbox in 1932, giving eight speeds forward and four in reverse; this model was known as the Selector Special. The 3-litre engine was bored out to make the 3½-litre for 1934, but few of these were made as they were overshadowed by a new model which had appeared at the end of 1933. This was the 4½-litre M45, powered by a 6-cylinder 4,467cc ohv Meadows engine similar to the one that Invicta had used since 1928. Exact output figures are uncertain, but it probably gave 115bhp at 3,800rpm, or slightly more than when used in the Invicta. The tuned M45R gave 125bhp to 130bhp. Works bodies were saloon and four-seater tourer, but there were many offerings by special coachbuilders on this and the subsequent LG45 chassis. The saloon had a speed of 90mph, and the price was a reasonable £950 – a 3½-litre Bentley cost £1,380 at this time. An M45 tourer came 4th in the 1934 T.T., its first competition appearance, and won the 1935 Le Mans race, driven by John Hindmarsh and Luis Fontes who averaged 77mph. This was a remarkable performance, and was Great Britain's only Le Mans victory between the Bentley era which ended in 1930 and the Jaguar era which did not begin until 1951. These cars had a shorter wheelbase than standard (that of the 3½-litre, in fact), but were not otherwise greatly modified.

For 1936 came the LG45 which had the M45R engine and more modern-looking bodies with valanced wings. Its design was supervised by W. O. Bentley who had joined Lagondas in 1935, but his influence was not really noticeable until a year later when the Sanction III engine with cross-flow head appeared. Power was now up to 130bhp. The sporting model of the LG45 was the Rapide, a tourer on a 10ft 3in wheelbase, 6in shorter than standard, and with a 150bhp engine. It had a striking four-seater body with pointed tail and outside exhaust pipes. Maximum speed was 108mph. The 1938 LG6 had the same engine, a new chassis with independent front suspension, and lower bodies, but was a luxury fast tourer rather than a sports car. The same applies to the 4½-litre V-12 which had the same body styles as the LG6 and an almost indistinguishable external appearance. Two tuned V-12s with higher compression ratio and four carburetters ran at Le Mans in 1939. The engines gave about 220bhp at 6,000rpm, and the cars finished 3rd and 4th behind a Type 57 Bugatti and a D.6 Delage. There was no production development from the Le Mans cars, and the war put an end to the earlier V-12.

Although smaller and cheaper than the Lagonda, the London-built Talbot

37. Above: *1955 Dellow Mark IIc 10hp sports car. Owned by P. Le Couteur.* (Photo: Charles Pocklington)

38. Below: *1948 H.R.G. 1½-litre sports car. Owned by Ian Dussek.* (Photo: Charles Pocklington)

1935 Frazer Nash T.T. Replica with Blackburne engine. (Photo: G. N. Georgano)

1935 Aston Martin Ulster seen at a V.S.C.C. Silverstone meeting in 1967. (Photo: Montagu Motor Museum)

1930 Lagonda 3-litre tourer (Photo: G. N. Georgano)

One of the Lagonda V-12s at Le Mans in 1939. (Photo: Autocar)

followed a similar pattern of development from a quality tourer through larger and faster cars to great success in sports car racing. In 1925 production of Talbots was at a very low ebb, the little 4-cylinder 8/18s and 10/23s attracting fewer buyers than before, and the larger sixes virtually no buyers at all. Georges Roesch was called in and given a free hand in the design of a new model which was to save the firm. This was the 14/45, a small ohv six of 1,665cc, giving originally 41bhp at 4,500rpm. The latter was a high speed for a touring car engine at the time. The valve rockers oscillated on wedge-shaped fulcrums, while the pushrods were as slim as knitting needles. Interestingly enough, they were made by a knitting-needle firm in Redditch. This lightness of construction was a feature of all subsequent Talbots. At the 1928 Motor Show the 10ft 14/45 chassis

A Talbot 90 with handsome drophead coupé body. The pointed tail housing the spare wheel was also a feature of the four-seater sports tourer. (Photo: Montagu Motor Museum)

appeared with new and enormously powerful brakes, and when it was joined next year by a short 9ft 3in version called the Scout the competition potential of the chassis became obvious. That same year Roesch had designed a new engine called the 18/70 with a capacity of 2,276cc, an unbreakable seven bearing crankshaft and an initial output of 60bhp. Early in 1930, at the instigation of Fox and Nicholl, this new engine was dropped in the Scout chassis and the model '90' was born, its engine being developed to give over 80bhp in sports car races and eventually 93bhp at 4,500rpm on a compression of 10:1. Two of these cars came 3rd and 4th at Le Mans in 1930, a performance often overlooked but truly remarkable. Defeated only by two Speed Six Bentleys, they finished ahead of a 7-litre Mercedes-Benz, 5-litre Stutz, and twin-cam Alfa Romeo. In addition, they were among the most silent cars that had ever competed at Le Mans. Later in 1930, they won their classes in the T.T., the Irish Grand Prix, and the B.R.D.C. 500 Mile Race at Brooklands. The production 90 carried various bodies, among the most popular being the De Luxe Sports Tourer, a four-seater with streamlined tail which housed the spare wheel. Because of the shorter wheelbase, most of the closed bodies on the 90 had two doors, the 4-door saloons being mounted on the 10ft chassis which, with the same 2,276cc engine, was called the 75 and was introduced shortly after the 90. In 1931 the 9ft 3in chassis gave way to one of 9ft 6in, the engine grew again to 2,969cc and the mating of the two produced the famous 105. With the standard compression ratio of 6·7:1 this engine gave 100bhp, but for road racing 126bhp was produced at 4,800 on a ratio of 9:1 and in some Brooklands Track events as much as 138bhp was available on 10·2:1. This 105 won its class and covered the greatest distance in the J.C.C. Double Twelve Hour Race at Brooklands and came 3rd at Le Mans in 1931 and 1932. *The Motor*'s description of the start of the Brooklands event gives a vivid impression of Talbot behaviour on the track: 'Their getaway was a wonderful and beautiful thing. Hardly had the starter dropped his flag when the cars pulled away from the pits, swinging out like half a battle squadron, forming up into line as they disappeared into the mist.' A 105 won a Glacier Cup in the 1931 Alpine Trial, and a works team won the Team Prize and Alpine Cups in the same event for 1932 and 1934. In the 1931 B.R.D.C. 500 Mile Race, the Talbot team came 1st, 2nd and 3rd in their class, the car driven by Brian Lewis and A. O. Saunders-Davis finishing 2nd overall; the latter also came 2nd in the 1937 J.C.C. 1,000 Mile Race at Brooklands, when the 105s won the Team Prize. The four team cars, GO 51, GO 52, GO 53 and GO 54 all survive, and are owned by Anthony Blight of Callington, Cornwall.

In 1932 the two lengths of 14/45 chassis were amalgamated into a single short chassis model called the 65, and later that year the 3-litre engine, detuned to give 90bhp on a compression ratio of 5·5:1, appeared in the long chassis as the Talbot 95. But by the end of 1934 the short chassis had been dropped altogether and although the 3-litre engine had by then grown to 3,377cc, the 110 model powered by it was no longer as sporting as the earlier 90s and 105s, and the former had been discontinued altogether the year before. Bodywork had become longer, lower, and very lush, including a 4-door Airline saloon with what today would be called a fastback. The same model names continued, but the image had changed with increasing size and weight; they were, in fact, transitional models, pending the arrival of a new and wholly modern range of all independently sprung cars on which Roesch was working when the rickety STD Group collapsed in 1935. All these Talbots were quiet efficient machines which achieved remarkable performance with the minimum of fuss, and when a 110 engine was fitted in one of the 1934 Alpine 105 Team in 1936 the car eventually proved itself the fastest touring car in the world, giving 50bhp per litre and lapping Brooklands at 129·7mph with a top speed of 140mph.

The Talbot company was acquired by the Rootes Group in 1935 and although the 75, 105 and 110 (renamed the $3\frac{1}{2}$-litre) were continued with little external change, in fact all but the latter were made simply to dispose of existing parts and from time to time – as these ran out – various Humber bits were grafted on. 1937 was the last season of these Roesch Talbots; the 1938 models and the 1939 Sunbeam Talbots may have looked similar, but they were Hillman Minxes, Humber Hawks and Snipes from end to end.

Another large car which reached its peak in the 1930s was the Invicta. The low-chassis S-type retained the $4\frac{1}{2}$-litre Meadows engine of the high-chassis car, but had an entirely new frame which was swept up over the front axle and carried below the rear axle. It had a maximum speed of 90mph, but the 1934 models with higher output engines of 140bhp were capable of 100mph. Nevertheless, the name '100 MPH' has often been applied to all S-type Invictas. Some of the engines were later modified to Sanction III standards as developed by W. O. Bentley in the same engine for the LG45 Lagonda, but these modifications were made on existing cars after the Invicta company ceased production. The S-type did not achieve any great success in racing, but did well in rallies. They won Alpine Cups in the Austrian and Hungarian Alpine Trials of 1930, a Glacier Cup in the International Alpine Trial of 1930, and in 1931 Donald Healey won the Monte Carlo Rally outright. For 1933 a development of the $4\frac{1}{2}$-litre engine was announced, with twin overhead camshafts and capacity raised to 4,890cc,

Pit stop for the S-type Invicta during the 1931 Double Twelve Race at Brooklands. (Photo: Montagu Motor Museum)

but the car was never completed. By 1935 production of all Invictas had practically ceased. The last few cars were assembled by the service depot in Chelsea. For 1932 a small Invicta had appeared, powered by a 1,498cc 6-cylinder Gillett & Stevens engine (1,274cc on the prototype). Output was only 45bhp and performance disappointing, with a maximum speed of only 65mph, although a supercharged version could exceed 70mph. The latter was expensive at £575, and only six were made. The unsupercharged saloon cost £399. For 1933 Invicta hoped to make a range of twin-ohc cars, and to complement the 5-litre car they announced a twin-cam 1½-litre known as the 12/100. Only one was made, and was not in fact completed until two years later when it was fitted with a supercharged 2-litre Lagonda engine and called an F.M. (Fenson-Montefiore).

Rover has never been thought of as a sporting marque, but from time to time some sports models have been made. In the vintage era the 9/20 was sold with a pointed-tail two-seater body, and from 1931 to 1934 a small number of Speed Twenty sports four-seaters was made. These had the 2,565cc pushrod ohv 6-cylinder engines used in the Meteor saloon, with higher compression ratio and downdraught carburetter (three in 1934). The engine was mounted lower and farther back in the frame, the wheelbase was shorter at 9ft 3in, and the rear axle ratio was higher. The chassis price was £495, and with four-seater close-coupled sports tourer body the complete car cost £620. Maximum speed was 83mph. They had a handsome appearance not unlike that of a 3-litre Lagonda, but they were not typical of Rover policy and were not in fact built at Coventry. The chassis were assembled at the London service depot in Seagrave Road, Fulham, and fitted with bodies made by Abbey Coachwork Ltd. Most were tourers, but at least one 4-door saloon

177

1932 Rover Speed Twenty with Abbey coachwork. (Photo: Autocar)

was also made by Abbey. After 1934 the Speed Twenty was dropped, and the most sporting Rovers were four-seater tourers on the Speed Fourteen chassis. These had slightly higher compression engines, but were otherwise like the ordinary Rovers.

Two of the great sports car makers of the 1920s, Bentley and Alvis, abandoned their traditional machines at the end of the decade, one because of change of ownership, the other through an alteration of policy. Both, however, made attractive fast tourers in the 1930s. When the new Bentley appeared in 1933, it had a tuned version of the Rolls-Royce 20/25 engine, giving 110bhp from 3,669cc. It had a low and handsome appearance with a contemporary version of the old Bentley radiator. Standard body styles were a sports tourer and a 4-door saloon, but a wide variety of special coachwork was available. It was never intended for racing, but E. R. Hall drove one with lightweight four-seater body in the Tourist Trophy races in 1934, 1935, and 1936, each time keeping the highest average speed and finishing 2nd on handicap. This car was entered for the 1936 Le Mans race which was cancelled because of political unrest. The 1936 T.T. car had a larger engine of 4,257cc and 125bhp which replaced the 3½-litre unit in all models from 1936 onwards. As so often happens the cars grew heavier with the passing of time, so performance of the new model was not much better than the previous one, though an overdrive introduced for 1939 gave more effortless cruising at 90mph, whereas the 3½-litre was just about flat out at that speed. Prices of these Derby-built Bentleys ranged from £1,380 for the 1933 sports tourer to £1,805 for a 1939 drophead coupé. With special bodies, the price was, of course, higher, though seldom exceeding £2,000. Although overshadowed by the hero-worship of the vintage Bentley, the Rolls-built cars were very popular and gave comfortable long-distance motoring to a wide range of people, old as well as young. They still commanded good prices as everyday cars well into the 1950s. About 2,440 were made up to 1940, of which slightly over half were 4¼-litre models.

After the end of the 12/50 and 12/60, Alvis turned to a range of tourers, of which the smaller were too heavy to have a sporting performance, but the larger grew in size and performance as the decade passed. The small model was developed from the 12/60, using the same 1,496cc engine together with the option of a Wilson gearbox. This was the Firefly which grew into the 1,842cc Firebird in 1935. Bodies were nearly all four-seater tourers or saloons, and the Firebird could not exceed 72mph. In 1932 a new 6-cylinder

Alvis appeared, the 2,511cc Speed Twenty. The engine was developed from that of the Silver Eagle, but had a higher compression ratio and stronger crankshaft. It gave 87bhp at 4,200rpm. The frame was dropped at the rear, giving a much lower appearance than the Silver Eagle; sports tourer and saloon bodies not unlike the 3½-litre Bentley in general appearance were offered at prices from £695. For 1934 the semi-elliptic front springs were replaced by transverse leaf independent suspension and an all-synchromesh gearbox was fitted. The engine capacity was increased to 2,762cc for 1935, but the weight had gone up, too, and performance remained about the same, with a maximum speed of 85mph. For 1936 a 3,571cc 110bhp engine was introduced for a new model known as the 3½-litre which mainly carried luxurious saloon bodywork, the Speed Twenty remaining the sporting model. However, a year later, the 3½-litre engine was put into the Speed Twenty chassis, the resulting car being called the Speed Twenty-Five. The final development of this engine was the 137bhp 4,397cc unit also introduced in 1936. Prices for this car were up to £995 for a saloon, and well into four figures for special bodied cars. The short-chassis 4·3-litre at 10ft 4in (3in shorter than standard) came in 1938. With a light Vanden Plas tourer body it was capable of 103mph, and could accelerate from 0–50mph in 7·6 seconds. It was an excellent fast tourer but the makers never offered or recommended a two-seater body, and it was not used for serious racing.

In the early 1930s a new breed of car appeared, the Anglo-American Sports Hybrid. The makers of these machines chose American engines because they produced cheap power delivered by relatively uncomplicated units at low speeds. In most cases the engines came from Detroit unmodified, alterations being made by the British manufacturer, and confined to components such as magneto, carburetter, and electrical system. The cars were purely British in appearance and sold almost entirely on the British market.

In the summer of 1933 production of the Invicta came to an end at the Cobham factory, and simultaneously Noel Macklin and L. A. Cushman of Invicta began work on the anglicised Essex Terraplane, known originally as the Railton Terraplane Eight. The modifications were the work of Reid Railton, a designer who had helped Parry Thomas with his Leyland-based racing cars, and who achieved his greatest fame in connection with the Railton-Mobil Special, the Land Speed Record car in which John Cobb reached 394mph in 1947. The first Railton was a low-built, rather angular sports four-seater with cutaway doors and the rivets down the bonnet which had characterised the Invicta. Apart from the thoroughly English body the Terraplane specification was not greatly modified. The engine was unchanged, the frame lowered, and telecontrol André shock-absorbers fitted. However the car looked English, and its performance was remarkable by any standards. The weight was 2,260lb and 50mph could be reached from rest in 7 seconds (seventeen years later, the famous XK 120 Jaguar took 7·3 seconds to reach the same speed). Maximum speed was 88mph and the car could be driven entirely on its top gear of 4·1:1. For this very reason, the Railton, like others of its breed, did not appeal to the enthusiast who enjoyed using his gears. The Vintage Sports Car Club for a long time excluded all the Anglo-Americans (Anglo-American Sports Bastards they rudely called them) and only in recent years have open Railtons been admitted to the ranks of Post Vintage Thoroughbreds. In their day, however, Railtons soon became popular on account of their acceleration. S. C. H. Davis of *The Autocar* was full of praise for them, and drove one in the 1935 Monte Carlo Rally. Changes in Railton design were relatively few throughout the make's life. During 1934 the slightly larger Hudson Eight engine (4,168cc) replaced that of the Terra-

Above: *1935 Alvis Speed Twenty taking part in driving tests at Croydon.*
(Photo: Klemantaski Studio)

Above right: *A Railton sports tourer in a 1938 Cambridge University Automobile Club Trial. At the wheel is Donald Maclean whose defection to Russia in 1951 provoked a major security crisis.*
(Photo: Montagu Motor Museum)

plane, and in 1937 an unfortunate step was the adoption of a remote control gear-change, necessitated by Hudson's change to steering column gear lever. That Railton's had to do this was one of the weaknesses of the Anglo-American Hybrids. In order to keep costs down they had to use standard American components wherever possible, and to accommodate themselves as best they could to whatever changes their suppliers, who were catering for a totally different market, chose to make. To change their suppliers, or to make more of the car themselves, would have priced them out of the market altogether, as Brough found with his beautiful V-12 saloon.

A four-door Railton saloon was introduced soon after the tourer, and within a year or two a wide range of special bodies was available. Unfortunately weight and price went up over the years; the 1938 Cobham saloon turned the scales at 3,063lb (approx 27cwt) and cost £688, compared with £525 for the 1933 tourer. However one model actually lost weight, the Light Sports Tourer introduced at the end of 1935. This was still a four-seater, but had cycle-type wings and a very light aluminium body made by E. J. Newns of Thames Ditton. This body, complete with wings, bonnet and hood, weighed only 112lb (1cwt) and the complete car weighed only 2,128lb (19cwt). Higher geared steering was fitted, together with larger brake drums and a fly-off brake lever placed outside the body. Top gear was 3·6:1. Rest to 60mph took less than 9 seconds (11 seconds for a 1954 XK 140 Jaguar), and maximum speed was over 100mph. The most dramatic demonstration of the Light Sports Tourer's powers was the ascent of the Brooklands test hill at 29·9mph, the car leaping into the air at the summit, and 'flying' for a distance of 35 feet! These Light Sports Tourers were built to special order only, and it is possible that only three were made, together with a Light Sports Saloon with a two-door aluminium body and 'fast-back' styling. After 1937 sporting Railtons were available only to special order, the standard offerings being the Cobham or Sandown four-door saloons and the Fairmile drophead coupé. Versions of the Sandown were used by the Metropolitan Police Flying Squad and by some provincial forces. The London squad cars were still in service up to 1948.

In an attempt to widen their range, in 1938 and 1939 Railton offered cars of similar appearance to the straight-8s using the smaller Hudson 6-cylinder engines of 16·9hp (2,723cc) and 21·6hp (3,455cc), but they offered nothing outstanding in performance and were pale shadows of the original Railtons. It is not generally known that Railton survived the war, but in fact fourteen cars were assembled by Hudson Motors Ltd, who had bought the manufacturing rights at the beginning of the war. They used the latest Hudson straight-8 engine, which was little changed from pre-war but had independent front suspension and steering column gear change. A drophead coupé was shown on the University Motors stand at the first post-war Motor Show at Earl's Court in October 1948. Because its American content had to be bought with devalued pounds, its price was a quite unrealistic £4,750, and no further Railtons were made. Altogether 1,425 Railtons were built, as well as about 50 'baby' Railtons using the 4-cylinder Standard Ten engines.

One other British make used the Hudson engine; this was the Brough Superior. George Brough of Nottingham was already well known as the maker of the high-quality Brough Superior motorcycle, sometimes called 'the Rolls-Royce of motorcycles'. Brough built his first experimental car in 1932, using a Dorman engine and Wilson preselector gearbox, but when the production model appeared in 1935 both engine and gearbox were by Hudson, the former being the 4,168cc unit and not the slightly smaller Terraplane 8 engine which the first Railtons had used. Power was increased from the Hudson's 113bhp to 125bhp. The body was a very handsome 2-door drophead coupé made by W. C. Atcherley of Birmingham. The price was £695, compared with £499 for the first Railton, but then the Brough was a much more 'civilised' car, with its built-in luggage boot (not all that common at the time) and fully-enclosed convertible body.

In 1936 Brough introduced a new model using the Hudson 6-cylinder engine of 3,455cc. Unlike the Eight this was available as a four-door saloon as well as a coupé, and also as a stark sports car. This Alpine Grand Sport had an open four-seater body weighing only 110lb, cycle-type wings, fold-flat windscreen, and a Centric supercharger. The makers were obviously hoping to steal some of the sports Railton's customers, but as the Brough used the smaller engine it is hardly surprising that both acceleration and speed were inferior to those of the Cobham car. But even Railtons found that the market for such a car in the mid-thirties was very small, so perhaps the Alpine Grand Sport would not have been a great success anyway, even if they had used the 8-cylinder engine, which seems the logical thing to have done. The last Brough Superior model was very different and was undoubtedly the finest quality car of all the Anglo-Americans. For power George Brough chose the 12-cylinder Lincoln-Zephyr engine, but instead of using a slightly modified American chassis he designed an underslung electrically-welded frame with boxed cross-members. The body was a beautiful four-door saloon by Charlesworth of Coventry which would not have looked out of place on a Bentley or Rolls-Royce. Unfortunately, at £1,250 its price was also similar to a Bentley's, and Brough could not make a commercial proposition of it. Three cars were laid down, but only one was actually built and sold. After the war George Brough offered to buy it back for £3,000, but the owner refused to sell it. Fortunately, this splendid car still survives today.

The most popular power unit for the Anglo-American Hybrids was the Ford V-8, used by Allard, Batten, Jensen, and Leidart. Of these, the Allard and Batten began life as virtually 'home-made' cars specially built for trials, and the Batten hardly outgrew this stage. The prototype appeared in 1935 and looked like a cut-down version of the original 1932 Ford V-8 which in many ways it was. The frame was underslung and the engine and radiator were 5in lower than in the Ford, the wheelbase, at 8ft, was 16in shorter and the track 8½in narrower. Power was boosted from 80bhp to 97bhp, and the 19cwt car had a maximum speed approaching 100mph. The price was only £325. Later Battens had more civilized four-seater sports-tourer bodies, but in 1937 a new model appeared which was the only Batten completely to break away from the Ford appearance. It still used the V-8 engine, but had a very low two-seater body, cycle-type wings, a sloping grille and headlamps faired into the bonnet sides. Maximum speed was said to be 120mph. Only one was made; the total Batten production probably did not exceed a dozen cars. Even rarer was the Leidart from Pontefract, Yorkshire. This had a Ford V-8 engine, four-seater sports body, and the general appearance of a scaled-up Morgan 4-4. It would have been suitable for trials as well as road work, but only one was made.

If the Batten and the Leidart remained obscure, the other two makes to use the Ford V-8 engine progressed from strength to strength, in their different ways. The Allard and the Jensen were about as different from each other as two Ford-based cars could be, representing the two extremes of the Anglo-American Hybrid.

Sydney Allard's first 'special' began life as a four-seater Ford which ran in the 1934 Tourist Trophy Race. Allard shortened the wheelbase and fitted the car with a body from an old Grand Prix Bugatti. The driver sat very far back, right over the rear axle, which may not have been practical or good looking but which gave excellent adhesion in the 'mud-plugging' trials which were becoming increasingly popular. Allard built his first car in 1936, and its success led to orders for other adaptations of the Ford. These followed the patterns of a greatly shortened wheelbase (8ft 6½in), a narrower chassis braced by three cross-members, and L.M.B. independent front suspension incorporating a split axle and transverse spring. Coil ignition was replaced by Scintilla Vertex magneto and the compression ratio was raised. At first these cars were built to special order, mainly for Sydney Allard's friends, but in July 1937 he announced the Allard Special as a catalogued make. Two- or four-seater bodies were available, both very stark,

Below: *A 1936 Batten Special in a post-war trial. (Photo: Motor Sport)*

Below right: *Sydney Allard's original special, 1935. (Photo: Montagu Motor Museum)*

and the price was £475. The cars were assembled in small premises in Putney, the bodies coming from Ranalah, who also built some bodies for Railton. From 1937 to the outbreak of war Allards were consistently successful in the most exacting trials, the leading drivers being Allard himself, Guy Warburton, and Ken Hutchison. The latter ordered a car powered by the Lincoln-Zephyr 4·4-litre V-12 engine, with which he was very successful, winning the Wye Cup Trial outright in February 1938. Subsequently one or two more Allards used this engine. In July 1938 a more refined car was announced, with flowing wings and running boards, and bodies suitable for touring. Two- and four-seaters were available, the former being made by Whittingham & Mitchel, the latter by Coachcraft. Prices ranged from £460 to £495, but very few cars were made before war broke out. In 1946 a new company was formed and production greatly increased, but the post-war Allard belongs to another chapter.

The brothers Richard and Alan Jensen entered the motor business as coachbuilders, being responsible for attractive bodies on inexpensive chassis such as the Austin Seven and Wolseley Hornet. In 1934 they built a sporting four-seater on a Ford V-8 chassis, and soon afterwards produced their own prototype. This used the Ford engine but had Jensen's own chassis design which was built for them by Rubery Owen. The body was an unusual four-seater with partially decked tonneau and separate windscreens for the rear seats. Unlike most sports tourers of the period, it had four doors although the rear doors were very narrow. With some modifications, this model went into production in 1936, together with a four-door saloon. An unusual feature of these Jensens was the Columbia two-speed rear axle operated by a pre-selector on the dashboard. This doubled the range of speeds available, and converted the normal top gear ratio of 4·11:1 to an exceptionally high ratio of 2·9:1. This enabled Jensen to improve considerably on the fuel consumption of the normal Ford V-8, the British car giving a figure of 22mpg compared with about 17mpg for the Ford. Coachwork was very handsome, and Jensens were regular winners in Concours d'Elegance, as well as competing in rallies. The smaller British Ford V-8 engine of $2\frac{1}{4}$ litres was fitted to some

A V-12 Allard at Poole Speed Trials in 1939. This style was also available with the Ford V-8 engine.
(Photo: Montagu Motor Museum)

cars, but more interesting was the Model H of 1938/39. This used the 4·2-litre straight-8 Nash engine, with overhead valves, developing some 120bhp. Maximum speed of the four-door saloon was 90mph, and the car came in two wheelbase lengths (10ft and 10ft 11in) enabling bodies from a sporting drop-head coupé to a seven-seater limousine to be fitted. Together with the V-12 Brough, the Model H Jensen was the most luxurious of the Anglo-Americans, but its price of £845 to £1,085 was very high and few were made. One or two 'specials' were made with the V-12 Lincoln-Zephyr engine. The first customer to order one of these was Clark Gable who had been one of the first owners of the 1934 Jensen-bodied Ford. A number of other film stars followed his example, and at least six Jensens found their way to Hollywood. This was quite an achievement for a small British firm, in the days when exports to the United States were largely confined to a few Rolls-Royces per year.

Like the Jensen, the Lammas-Graham was a handsome touring car rather than an out-and-out sports machine, despite its use of mild supercharging, inherited from its American progenitor. It used the 6-cylinder Graham engine, although the stroke was lengthened from 111mm to 114mm, giving a capacity of 3·7 litres and a power output of 128bhp. The chassis was a slightly modified Graham, but the usual anglicisations such as Luvax shock absorbers and 12-volt electrical equipment were fitted, and the bodies were typical of British practice at the time. In fact, the Lammas looked very like the 3½-litre SS Jaguar, although unfortunately it cost nearly twice as much. Bodies were by Abbott (drophead coupé), Carlton (saloon) and Bertelli (sports tourer), and prices ranged from £620 to £695. Soon after it was introduced, its sponsor, Lord Avebury, and Charles Follett, the distributor, covered 95·78 miles in an hour at Brooklands on a stripped sports tourer, but Lammas made little impact on the sporting world otherwise. Design changed little during the two years that the car was on the market, although more angular Bertelli bodies were used for the saloons for the 1938 season. Production ceased in the middle of 1938.

The last Anglo-American Hybrid to appear was also one of the most promising. Atalanta Motors Ltd of Staines, Middlesex, had entered the market with an attractive but expensive sports car with tubular chassis and independent suspension all round, powered by 1½- or 2-litre 4-cylinder engines designed by Albert Gough who had designed engines for Frazer Nash and was a director of Atalanta. Into this chassis the makers fitted a V-12 Lincoln-Zephyr engine which gave more power than the 4-cylinder engines at lower engine speed and with little increase in cost. In fact the most expensive 4-cylinder car cost £47 more than the V-12 saloon, whose price was only £740. This was a really attractive car, with low sweeping lines, excellent road holding, and a top speed of 95mph. The short chassis two-seater sports car could easily top 100mph, and achieved a number of competition successes, one of its leading drivers being Miss Margaret Wilby who was also an Atalanta director. Unfortunately this excellent car was introduced barely a year before the outbreak of war, and so never achieved the fame which it deserved.

We have dealt with the more important British sporting cars, but there were a number of other short-lived machines of interest. The Moveo from Preston was not unlike the Invicta in having a Meadows engine in a substantial dropped chassis, with close-coupled coupé body. The prototype had a 3-litre engine, but production models were to have this or a 3·2-litre or a 4½-litre engine, with the option of a supercharger, and coachwork to customer's choice. It was announced in 1931, but probably not more than one was made.

39. Above: *1949 Veritas Comet 2-litre sports car. Owned by K. Hutchinson.* (Photo: Guy Griffiths Moto-photo)

40. Below: *1954 Mercedes-Benz 300SL 3-litre sports coupé.* (Photo: Daimler-Benz AG)

41. Overleaf: *1951 Talbot-Lago 4½-litre drophead coupé.* (Photo: Musée de Rochetaillée, Rhône. Collection Henri Malatre)

The Rapier began life as a small model of Lagonda introduced at about the same time as the 4½-litre. It had a 1,104cc Lagonda engine with twin overhead camshafts developing 50bhp at 5,000rpm, and was said to be safe up to 6,000rpm. With a standard tourer body it cost £375, and several special bodies were available at prices up to £415 complete. Lord de Clifford drove one at Le Mans in 1934 and his firm Dobson & de Clifford Ltd offered a special competition Rapier with engine linered down to 1,084cc known as the de Clifford Special. When Lagonda was reformed under Alan Good in 1935 the Rapier was dropped, but a new company was formed with works at Hammersmith to continue production. All machinery and spares went to the new concern, and Rapiers were turned out in small quantities until the outbreak of war. Prices were higher, at up to £475. About 300 Rapiers were made in all.

The Marendaz was a small production sports car made first at Brixton, South London, from 1926 to 1932, and for the last five years of its life at Maidenhead, Berkshire. It originally used a side-valve Anzani engine, but by 1932 it was powered by a small sv six of 1,869cc which developed about 70bhp, assembled by Marendaz themselves. It had low lines and a Bentley-like radiator which led some people to think that they had caught a glimpse of a prototype baby Bentley. Later cars had 1,991cc inlet-over-exhaust Coventry-Climax engines (as used in the Triumph Gloria Six) or 2½-litre Marendaz engines. Both could be had with a supercharger. They did well in rallies, a notable driver being Mrs A. E. Moss, Stirling's mother. A Coventry-Climax-engined car ran in the 1935 Tourist Trophy and finished one lap short of the winning Riley.

The British Salmson was usually seen as a saloon or tourer, but from 1936 to 1939 a sports two-seater was offered with the 20/90 engine. Unlike other engines which were derived from the French Salmson S4C, the 20/90 was a purely English machine with no French counterpart. It had a twin-ohc 2,590cc 6-cylinder engine with independent front suspension by transverse leaf. The body was a simple two-seater, with a slab tank and fold-flat windscreen. It was expensive at £695, and very few were made.

Most A.C.s of the 1930s were sporting tourers and saloons, still with the 1,991cc 6-cylinder engine that had appeared in 1922 and was to survive until 1963. However, in 1935, a two-seater sports cars on a shortened chassis was introduced, and made up to 1939. Originally known as the 16/80, it became the 16/90 when fitted with a supercharger which gave it a maximum speed of over 90mph.

It will be seen that Great Britain made a wide variety of sports cars in the 1930s, certainly impressive when compared with those of other countries, and yet by 1939 there were very few still going. Too many of the great makes such as Frazer Nash, Riley, Singer, and Talbot had abandoned sports cars, while there were few new designs. Lagonda might have brought out a really advanced independently sprung V-12 sports car, but the war intervened. By contrast France, which began the period with an almost complete dearth of sports cars, by 1939 had some very promising modern machines, as did Germany and Italy. This situation, combined with the fact that the domestic family saloon was distinctly behind the better Continentals in design and handling, led many British enthusiasts to worship the foreign car. During the six years of war, when no cars were made at all, the sporting motorist in England had plenty of opportunity to lament in letters and articles about the dearth of modern sports cars in his own country, and most of them would have been very surprised by the startling renaissance which took place within a few years of the war's end.

42. 1959 B.M.W. Typ 507 3·2-litre sports car. Owned by C. W. P. Hampton. (Photo: Charles Pocklington)

189

Top: *A V-12 Atalanta seen during a 1939 J.C.C. Race at Brooklands. The start of this race is shown on page 17. (Photo: Montagu Motor Museum)*

Above: *1935 Lagonda Rapier four-seater tourer with coachwork by Abbott. (Photo: G. N. Georgano)*

Above right: *1937 A.C. 16/80 two-seater sports car. (Photo: Montagu Motor Museum)*

In the early 1930s the French enthusiast had a very meagre selection of cars to choose from. The flourishing band of light sports car makers had disappeared almost over night. Many had succumbed to the competition of Amilcar and Salmson, but even these had abandoned small sports cars by 1930. Amilcar was making a range of small 4-cylinder saloons, and a handsome but underpowered 2-litre straight-8. Some of their Delahaye- or Janvier-engined Pégase models of 1934 to 1936 were fitted with sports bodies, but very few of these were made. Salmson made touring cars with twin-cam engines throughout the period, but no sports cars. The last survivor of the 1920s breed was the Rally which continued to 1933, latterly with a Salmson engine. There was never a significant revival of the small sports car in France, and most drivers who wanted such machines bought M.G.s or Singers, or the Fiat Balilla.

One of the few native productions was the Georges Irat. This company had made medium-sized tourers in the 1920s, and after experimenting with Lycoming-engined luxury cars turned to small sports machines in 1935. These were powered by 950cc or 1,095cc 4-cylinder Ruby engines driving the front wheels. Originally with three speeds, four were provided from 1938 onwards. They were neat-looking little two-seaters, but a maximum speed of about 70mph did not recommend them to the real enthusiast. A supercharged version was shown at the 1937 Paris Salon, but it is not certain how many were made. For 1939 a new front wheel drive sports Georges Irat was announced, with the 1,911cc Citroën engine and independent suspension all round by thick strands of rubber cord. This could seat three abreast and had a maximum speed of 75mph. About 1,000 of the Ruby-engined Georges Irats were made, but there were fewer of the larger cars because of the outbreak of war. Another small French sports car was the Remi Danvignes, made from 1937 to 1939. This was also powered by the small Ruby engine, or by a 750cc vertical twin with overhead camshaft. It had independent suspension all round and a two-seater body with cutaway doors. The third small sports car was the Lambert, made at Reims by a persistent and ingenious inventor called Germain Lambert. Like a number of other French constructors such as Harris-Léon Laisne, Lambert was more interested in suspension than in engines, and he bought the latter mostly from Ruby. From 1926 to 1931 he made experimental cars at Macon, with independent front suspension and rear-wheel drive. The Reims-built cars of 1931 to 1936 were mostly front-wheel drive machines, and included a sports car powered by the 1,075cc Ruby engine known as the Sans Choc, as well as a larger-engined fwd coupé. In 1936 Lambert seems to have abandoned car manufacture after making tiny cyclecars which he called the Baby Sans Choc. However, he cropped up during the war as one of about twenty firms making battery electric cars, and after the war made a further series of small sports cars. A small number of Ruby-engined cars were turned out by Stuart Sandford in the early 1930s as a sideline from his 3-wheelers. They were 4-wheeled versions of the latter, with the same appearance and sliding pillar independent front suspension.

The only French firm to make sports cars throughout the 1930s was

Bugatti. In 1930 they offered as wide a range as they ever had, varying from the touring Type 40 through the Types 35 and 37 racing cars and the Types 44 and 46 tourers to the vast Type 41 Royale which was theoretically available at this time. The only new model was the Type 46, announced in the autumn of 1929. This was a luxury tourer rather than a sports car, and apart from the Royale of which only six were made was the largest-engined Bugatti. It had a 5,359cc straight-8 engine with single overhead camshaft operating three valves per cylinder. The three-speed gearbox was in unit with the rear axle. For 1932 a supercharged model was available known as the Type 46S; with this the maximum speed was well over 90mph. Both models were made until 1936, although by that date it seems that Bugatti had some difficulty in finding buyers, probably because of competition from his own Type 57, a more modern and cheaper car. About 400 Type 46s were made. Soon after the Type 46 appeared, Bugatti brought out another large car, the 4,972cc Type 50. This was a significant development for Bugatti, the new design incorporating two valves per cylinder, inclined at 90 degrees and operated by twin camshafts, instead of the single camshaft vertical valve layout which he had used since 1910. The Type 50 chassis and gearbox were identical with those of the Type 46, and like its predecessor it was fitted with a wide variety of luxurious bodies. Some of these had very sharply raked windscreens, bizarre-looking cars but said to be capable of 110mph. Unlike the Type 46, the Type 50 was raced occasionally; a team of four cars with four-seater tourer bodies ran at Le Mans in 1931, but after one had crashed, killing a spectator, the rest of the team was withdrawn.

The Type 43 was replaced in 1932 by the Type 55, the most sporting Bugatti of the 1930s. This used the twin-cam 2·3-litre engine of the Type 51 racing car in the chassis of another racing car, the Type 54. With 135bhp, performance was excellent; maximum speed was 112mph, and 10–80mph took only 18 seconds. Stripped for racing and with special fuel, it could exceed 120mph. The standard body was a two-seater roadster with sweeping wings and a rounded tail which carried one or, more often, two spare wheels. The

1932 Bugatti Type 55 2·3-litre sports car.
(Photo: H. G. Conway Collection)

traditional Bugatti aluminium wheels of the racing cars and the Type 43 were used. It was hard for any special coachbuilder to improve on the roadster's lines, but a few drophead coupés were made, and also fixed head coupés. The latter were handsome, but like the closed Type 43s very noisy at speed. The Type 55 was the last of the truly sporting Bugattis whose tradition stretched back through the Type 43 to the Full Brescia of 1920. Only thirty-eight were made between 1932 and 1935.

The other line of Bugatti development was the 3-litre touring car. In 1930 the Type 44 was replaced by the generally similar Type 49 whose engine was enlarged to 3,257cc. This in turn became the Type 57 in 1934 with the same capacity but a twin ohc layout. This engine developed 140bhp, and the standard saloon of 1934 had a maximum speed of 95mph. The Type 57 owed more to Ettore's son Jean than any previous Bugatti design, and was a good example of the right car at the right time. The Depression had drastically reduced the market for luxury cars, and highly tuned sports/racing cars were also less in demand. The Type 57 was a high quality fast tourer of a type which other French manufacturers such as Delage, Delahaye, and Talbot were turning out at the same time. It could easily carry 4-door saloon coachwork, although more sporting models were made as well. Six body styles were listed by the works, some being made by the nearby coach-building firm of Gangloff. These were 2- and 4-door saloons, a drophead coupé and two fixed head coupés, one a very streamlined affair known as the Atlantic. The sporting model was the Type 57S with a chassis shorter by 13in and a lower frame through which the rear axle passed. It usually carried open or coupé bodies, and nearly all the Types 57S had oval-shaped V-radiators. With a supercharger it was known as the Type 57SC and was capable of 125mph. The supercharger was also available on the Type 57, this model being known as the Type 57C. About 750 Type 57s were made, of which only about forty were S or SC models. Production continued up to the war, although the more expensive sports chassis were not made after 1938.

Although it was basically a touring car, the Type 57 was raced to a greater

1937 Bugatti Type 57SC with coachwork by Corsica. This car was originally the property of Sir Malcolm Campbell. (Photo: H. G. Conway Collection)

Earl Howe's Bugatti Type 57 leads Freddie Dixon's Riley at Newtownards during the 1935 T.T.
(Photo: Autocar)

extent than any of the other Bugattis discussed in this chapter. Two cars ran in the 1935 Tourist Trophy, Earl Howe finishing 3rd at an average speed of 79·72mph. This car had a standard appearance, but the three cars entered for the 1936 French Grand Prix had all-enveloping or 'tank' bodies. They were based on the Type 57S. The car driven by Wimille and Sommer won against competition from larger Delahayes and Talbots. Wimille won again in the Marne Grand Prix, and, with Benoist co-driving, won the 1937 Le Mans race at a record speed of 85·13mph. In 1939 a new streamlined car with 200bhp Type 57C engine won Le Mans again, driven by Wimille and Veyron. It was in this car that Jean Bugatti was killed in August 1939 while testing it near Molsheim. A successor to the Type 57 was built in prototype form in 1939. This was the Type 64 with 4½-litre twin ohc engine, the camshafts being driven by chains instead of a train of gears as on the Type 57. Only one or two were made, and it was not put into production after the war.

Two rival makes to Bugatti were Delage and Delahaye, who merged in 1935. At the beginning of the decade they were making totally different types of car, the Delage being a high-quality fast tourer, while Delahaye made a range of solid touring cars from 1½ to 2·8 litres, as well as commercial vehicles. The Delage D.8 had a 4-litre straight-8 engine developing about 120bhp, and carried some of the most handsome bodywork of any car at any time. The high, vertical radiator and long bonnet were the perfect complement to the two-door saloon or fixed head coupés by Gurney Nutting, Figoni or other high-class coachbuilders whose work was regularly seen on Delage chassis. If the D.8 did not appear on the race track or in rallies, it frequently carried off prizes at the many Concours d'Elegance held all over Europe at this time. In 1932 came the D.8S, which was considerably lower than the D.8 and less good looking. Power was up to 140bhp, and maximum speed raised from 80mph to nearly 90mph. The next model was the D.8SS whose new induction system and higher rear-axle ratio combined to raise maximum speed to over 100mph. In 1935, after the take-over of Delage by Delahaye a new range of sixes and eights was made, of which the largest was the 4·3-litre D.8.120. This was much heavier than the 'genuine' D.8, and performance lower, with a maximum speed of about 90mph. For 1939 the capacity was raised to 4·7 litres. The 6-cylinder Delages, like the D.8s, were handsome

The Delahaye 135 team for the 1938 Coronation Trophy Race at the Crystal Palace. From left to right: Count Heyden, the entrant and British concession aire for Delahayes, Louis Gerard, Jimmy Willing and J. Paul.
(Photo: Cyril Posthumus Collection)

touring cars and were not raced until after the firm came under Delahaye control. Then the 2·7-litre D.6.70 was entered for races in both open and coupé form, winning the 1938 Tourist Trophy at Donington Park. The driver was L. Gerard who also came second at Le Mans in 1939.

Considering their earlier histories, it seems strange that Delage had to wait until they were taken over by Delahaye before entering sports car racing. But the Delahaye image underwent a sudden change in 1934 with the appearance of the Superluxe, a car with a 3·2-litre 6-cylinder ohv engine based on the Type 119 truck unit. It had the more modern features of transverse leaf independent front suspension and, from 1937, Cotal electromagnetic gearbox. More important, its lines were low and handsome, a complete breakaway from the staid, upright appearance of the earlier Delahayes. It was expensive, but not unduly so, coming between the Hotchkiss and the D.8 Delage in price. Within a year two sizes of engine were available, the 110bhp 3,257cc Coupe des Alpes and the 120bhp 3,557cc Type 135. In competition form the latter gave 160bhp, and was good for 115mph. With this car Delahaye began an extensive programme of sports car racing. They came 5th at Le Mans in 1935, 2nd, 3rd, 4th, and 5th in the 1936 French Grand Prix, 2nd at Le Mans in 1937, and 1st, 3rd, and 4th in the same event in 1938. In 1939 a special race was held at Brooklands to determine the fastest car used on the roads of Great Britain. Seven cars started, including a 3-litre Delage, 4-litre Talbot-Lago, and 2·9-litre twin-cam Alfa Romeo, but the race was won by Arthur Dobson in a Type 135 Delahaye. Since he had to stop in order to extinguish a fire at one point, it was a creditable victory, although not every eligible car took part (there were no Bugattis). Incidentally, there were no British cars in the event at all.

Early in 1937 there came the 4½-litre V-12 Delahaye whose 238bhp engine had the same dimensions as the V-12 Lagonda. It was mainly used for Grand Prix racing, but a two-seater, road-equipped version came 4th in the 1938 Mille Miglia. The competition cars had a de Dion rear axle, but a very small number of cars with conventional rear axle were made for road use. They usually carried flashy roadster coachwork in which both front and rear wheels were enclosed in fairings; maximum speed was 115mph. One was bought in 1939 by W. E. Butlin, now Sir William, the holiday camp owner.

The other leading make in France's sports car renaissance was the Talbot-Lago, generally known in England as the Darracq. The old Darracq company had disappeared with the collapse of the S.T.D. group which also brought down Sunbeam and Talbot in England. The company was bought by Major Antony Lago who introduced a new range of 6-cylinder ohv cars, of which the largest was a 3,996cc machine called, in short chassis form, the Baby 4-litre. The competition version of this was called the Lago-Special and with an engine tuned to give 165bhp it was capable of over 110mph. These cars took first three places in the 1937 Sports Car Grand Prix at Montlhéry, and the car driven by Comotti won the 1937 Tourist Trophy Race at Donington Park. Another Talbot was second. The touring cars carried 2- and 4-door saloon and coupé bodies similar to those of the Delahaye, but lacked the cachet of the latter, and were not so often seen at Concours d'Elegance.

For the keen motorist who was not interested in racing, one of the most attractive French cars of the 1930s was the Hotchkiss. Their 3½-litre which appeared in 1933 was considerably cheaper than either the Delahaye or Talbot, and yet offered an almost equal performance and lines which were more conservative and therefore more attractive to many buyers. The engine was a conventional 6-cylinder ohv unit of 3,485cc developing 115bhp, and giving a maximum speed of 94mph with a roadster body, and nearly 80mph from a 4-door saloon. For 1936 there was a 'Super Sport' on a shorter chassis which normally carried 2-door coachwork. Power was up to 125bhp, this engine also being used in the Grand Sport 4-door saloon. The Super Sport roadster could reach 115mph, and the Grand Sport 95mph, a very respectable figure for such a roomy saloon. Unlike their rivals, Hotchkiss never raced their cars, perhaps remembering that one of their directors in 1905 had described racing as the curse of the automobile trade. However they were highly successful in rallies, winning the Monte Carlo Rally in 1932 (with the 3-litre AM 80), 1933, 1934, and 1939, and after the war in 1949 and 1950. They also won a Glacier Cup in the 1934 Alpine Trial, and were successful in the Paris-Nice Rally, and Rallye Feminin de St Raphael.

These four makes, Delage, Delahaye, Hotchkiss, and Talbot had brought about a remarkable revival of the French sports car, but apart from them (and Bugatti, of course) there was little else. Hispano-Suiza continued to make 6-cylinder cars as well as their superb luxury 9·4-litre V-12, but they were not sports cars. Gabriel Voisin went his individual way, making streamlined saloons with electrically opening roofs, and experimented with a 6-litre straight-12-engined car, but again these were not sports cars. Most of the other fast tourer manufacturers of the 1920s such as Cottin et Desgouttes or Chenard-Walcker had either gone out of business or were making very ordinary cars with proprietary engines.

Generally, the mass producers kept away from sport, but there were two private ventures based on mass-production designs, one of which was to lead to a new make after the war. The Simca company was set up in 1934 to manufacture Fiats in France, their main product at first being the 6CV which was the Fiat Tipo 508 Balilla. A young Italian living in France called Amedée Gordini tuned the 995cc Balilla engine to give 48bhp compared with 22bhp from the standard engine in its original form. A two-seater Gordini-tuned Simca won the Bol d'Or in 1935 and had a class victory in the Reims sports car race the same year. Later Simca-Gordinis were highly streamlined, and won the sports car class of the 1937 Bol d'Or and the Index of Performance at Le Mans in 1939. The latter car was a 1·2-litre version of the new 1,100cc engine, tuned to give 65bhp. More Simca-Gordinis were made after the war, including some single-seaters.

1939 Darracq Spécial coupé. A fine example of a pre-war Gran Turismo coupé.
(Photo: Klemantaski Studio)

Peugeot Darl'mat two-seater taking part in the 'Fastest Road Car' race at Brooklands in May 1939.
(Photo: Klemantaski Studio)

The other private developer of a well-known make was Peugeot-dealer Emile Darl'mat. He took the 2·1-litre Peugeot 402 engine and mounted it in the shorter wheelbase 302 chassis, with his own design of very low two-seater bodies, an open sports, drophead coupé, and fixedhead coupé. These Darl'mat Peugeots were assembled in Darl'mat's own works, about 200 being made between 1937 and 1939. A team of three ran at Le Mans in 1937, and of the few imported to England one took part in the 'Fastest Road Car' race at Brooklands mentioned on page 205. It finished last, which was hardly surprising in view of the competition.

Although the 1930s saw the magnificent state-aided Grand Prix racing teams of Mercedes-Benz and Auto Union, the sports car scene was much less exciting. Mercedes-Benz made a range of sporting tourers throughout the period, but they were in no way worthy successors to the SS and SSK. Obviously with such an expensive Grand Prix programme the works could hardly sponsor sports car racing as well, and this was doubtless a reason for the lack of real sports cars from Mercedes-Benz. In the large car field there were no other sports cars, but the 2-litre class contained the only really important sports car to come from Germany during the decade, the B.M.W. Typ 328. Apart from these, German sports cars of the 1930s were mostly slightly-tuned roadster versions of family cars such as Hansa, Hanomag, Opel, and Stoewer. Some of these were built originally for the 2,000km A.D.A.C. Trials of 1933 and 1934. These were curious events, though typical of the Third Reich era. The route consisted almost entirely of main roads, and there were no special sections, hill climbs, or water splashes, as an English correspondent remarked rather superciliously, thinking no doubt of events such as the London-Land's End. The crowds were strictly disciplined, and the route patrolled by 10,000 Storm Troopers. Some town and suburban roads were closed to other traffic for up to ten hours. The entry lists were enormous; in 1933 there were 176 cars taking part, including nineteen Mercedes-Benz in the 2-litre class, and 40 D.K.W.s in the 1-litre class. By 1934 the entry list had risen to 600 cars and 1,000 motorcycles. The largest car had to average 55mph which they found too high a speed, but the average for the

The start of the 1933 2000km Trial. In the foreground are two Wanderer open two-seaters, and behind them three Audi and five Horch coupés. These coupés were specially built for the event.
(Photo: Neubauer Collection)

Mercedes-Benz 540K cabriolet. (Photo: Montagu Motor Museum)

A 1937 B.M.W. 328 driven by Tony Hutchings at a wet Oulton Park meeting of the V.S.C.C. in 1966. (Photo: Montagu Motor Museum)

One of the streamlined Adlers which ran at Le Mans in 1937 and 1938. (Photo: Motor)

1-litre class was only 37mph, which the small D.K.W.s found easily within their capabilities.

The Mercedes-Benz SS and SSK were catalogued until 1934, but very few cars were made during the last two years. Parallel to the large cars was the Typ 370S Mannheim Sport, a 3,663cc 75bhp six which, despite its name, could not exceed 75mph. The larger 4·9-litre Nürburg and 7·7-litre Grosser Mercedes was not made in sporting form at all. In 1934 came the Typ 380, a 3·8-litre straight-8 with coil independent suspension all round. It developed 90bhp, or 120bhp with supercharger, but was too heavy to have a really high performance. Maximum speed was about 85mph. It was soon replaced by the 5-litre Typ 500K, which developed 100bhp unblown and 160bhp when the supercharger was working. The latter was still used for a short burst only, as on the vintage Mercedes-Benz. The larger Typ 540K came in 1936, similar in appearance to the 500K but developing 180bhp blown, giving a speed of 105mph. These large Mercedes-Benz had handsome lines, but were always too heavy, for as power went up so did weight, and their handling was not up to true sports car standards. However this tendency to put on weight was not confined to Mercedes, for the same thing happened to Alvis and Bentley at this time. Bodies of the larger Mercedes were usually 2-door styles, a roadster, an aerodynamic coupé called the Autobahn-Kurier, and drophead coupés. Some special 4-door bodies were built on the 500K and 540K, but these were rare. Except for the 2,000km Trials, these cars were not entered in competitions. Apart from these large cars, some of the smaller chassis such as the Typ 170 carried two-seater roadster bodies, but their performance was not outstanding.

The B.M.W. sports models date back to before 1930, when the Bayerische Motoren Werke made the Austin Seven under licence under the name Dixi 3/15PS. A sports version of this called the Dixi-Ihle was made in 1930. It had a lowered frame, pointed tail, cycle-type wings, and a sloping radiator grille which anticipated that of the Typ 328 of seven years later. This was the last sports car for several years, but the touring car design developed rapidly, with tubular frame and swing axles on the 1932 3/20PS, a 6-cylinder 1,173cc version in 1933 with twin tube chassis (Typ 303) and a 1,490cc six in 1934 (Typ 315). A three-carburetter version of the latter developed 40bhp and was good for 78mph. The sports model was known as the Typ 315/1. It had a neat, two-seater body with spatted rear wheels, and began the line of B.M.W. sports cars which led to the famous Typ 328. The next step was the 1,911cc Typ 319/1 with 55bhp and a maximum speed of nearly 90mph. Meanwhile the 6-cylinder engine had been increased to 1,971cc for the Typ 326 4-door saloon, and when a new sports model came out for 1937 it had this engine in the tubular frame of the Typ 319/1. However, it also had a new cylinder head, with a hemispherical combustion chamber and inclined overhead valves. Only one camshaft was used, operating the inlet valves in the usual way, while horizontal pushrods ran across the top of the cylinder head to operate the exhaust valves. In this way the advantages of a twin-ohc layout were obtained without the accompanying complexity and expense. It was also a highly efficient system, and was used on the B.M.W.-inspired Bristol cars up to 1962 and also on the 1937 V-12 Auto Union Grand Prix cars. The new sports car was known as the Typ 328, and had a maximum speed of just over 100mph. The body was a most attractive two-seater, with beetle-back into which the spare wheel was set, headlamps faired into the front wings, and twin bonnet straps. The rear wheels were enclosed in spats, but these were usually left off for competitions and even everyday road work. The standard sports body was made by the factory, but a drophead coupé built by an

43. 1956 Abarth-Fiat 750cc sports coupé. Owned by P. Stevens. (Photo: Guy Griffiths Motofoto)

outside coachbuilder could also be had. The Typ 328 came second on Index at Le Mans in 1939, but its greatest achievement came in 1940, after the war had started. In the spring of 1940 Italy was still a neutral country, and the Mille Miglia was held as usual, although on a shortened course of about 900 miles. Alfa-Romeo, Delage, and B.M.W. teams took part, the latter with specially-tuned 134bhp Typ 328 engines in aerodynamic saloons. The race was won by von Hanstein's B.M.W., with his team mate Brudes in 3rd place.

A number of light sports cars were based on the small 2-stroke D.K.W. This appeared as a unitary-construction economy car in 1928, and the customary sports car with pointed tail and cutaway doors came in 1930. It had a 584cc 18bhp engine which gave it a maximum speed of nearly 60mph. In 1931 came the first front-wheel drive D.K.W. with the 584cc engine or a smaller 498cc 15bhp engine. These engines were mounted transversely, whereas the rear-drive cars had their engines parallel to the chassis. On the later models, known as Meisterklasse, the engine capacity went up to 684cc, and a sports car remained in the catalogues up to 1939. A special sporting car using the Meisterklasse engine and drive in a tubular chassis, with all-round independent suspension, was the Tornax Rex. About 300 were made by a motorcycle firm at Wuppertal between 1934 and 1937.

The front-wheel drive Adler Trumpf saloon of 1932 became the basis of a number of attractive sports cars. The engine was a conventional 4-cylinder side-valve unit of 1,494cc, enlarged to 1,645cc in 1934. Output was 38bhp, later increased to 55bhp from the tuned models. Both this and the 995cc Trumpf Junior could be had with attractive two-seater sports bodies. Teams took part in the 2,000km Trials and also in the International Alpine Trials. A team of Trumpfs with highly streamlined coupé bodies ran in sports car races, winning the team prize at Spa in 1936, and the Biennial Cup at Le Mans in 1937/38. A streamlined coupé with a maximum speed of 80mph was offered to the public under the appropriate name of Autobahn. A stream-lined saloon was also offered on the 1938/39 2½-litre rear-drive chassis, this car having a speed of 95mph.

Several other German firms offered sports cars, but they were mostly the equivalents of the promenaders in England. Based on family saloons, the sports models were sold in very small numbers, and never achieved the renown of such machines as the M.G. Midget or Singer Le Mans. Examples were the Hansa 1700 which developed 50bhp in twin carburetter form, the 2·2-litre Hanomag Sturm streamlined saloon, the 1·8-litre Opel, the 1½-litre Rohr Junior, and 1·4-litre Stoewer R.140, all offered in two-seater form. Rather more ambitious was the Wanderer W.25K, a 2-litre car with Roots supercharger. This gave 85bhp, and 90–95mph, but the engine was not sufficiently developed to cope with blowing, and in addition gearbox and handling were disappointing. It was a handsome enough car to look at, but in no way comparable to a B.M.W.

4. 1953 Lancia Aurelia Carrera GT 2½-litre coupé. This car won the Liège-Rome-Liège Rally in 1953. Owned by Michael Scott. (Photo: Charles Pocklington)

As in the previous decade, the most successful Italian sports car in the 1930s was the Alfa Romeo. They were the only firm to make really high-performance road-going sports cars throughout the period. The twin-cam 1750 continued to be made up to 1933, but was joined in 1931 by a faster car, the 8C 2300 powered by a twin-ohc straight-8 engine of 2,336cc. With lowest compression ratio of 5·7:1, output was 130bhp at 4,900rpm, but racing versions gave up to 178bhp. Two chassis lengths were available, the Le Mans of 10ft 2in and the Mille Miglia of 9ft. The former often carried four-seater coachwork, while the latter was normally a two-seater sports car, although a few coupés were also made. In addition, there was the 8ft 8in Monza, but this was built only as a racing car, although one or two have been converted for road use. It is difficult to generalize about 8Cs, because some engines were bored out to 2·4 litres or 2·6 litres, and these might be either in the Le Mans or Mille Miglia chassis. A maximum speed of 105mph to 110mph was normal, but the fastest Mille Miglia with two-seater body was capable of 125mph, a performance not far short of that of the P.3 racing car. The 8C was very successful in competitions from the start. With drivers such as Nuvolari, Sommer, and Chinetti they virtually dominated Le Mans from 1931 to 1934, winning the event four years running, and taking the first three places in 1933. In the Mille Miglia they continued the success of the 1750, winning in 1932, 1933, and 1934. The success of Alfa Romeo in this event is truly remarkable; between 1933 and 1939, they won every year, and took first three places on every occasion but one, when L. Schell's Delahaye came into 3rd place in 1937. However the 8C was very expensive to make, and little, if any, profit was made on them. Only 188 were made in four years.

In 1934 there came a new car, the 6C 2300 with 6-cylinder twin-ohc 2,309cc engine developing 68bhp or 76bhp according to tune. It was a touring rather than a sports car, easier to maintain but lacking the fine handling of the earlier cars. The pressed-steel bodies were cheaply made, and very homely in appearance, at least on the first models. However a team of 95bhp Pescara sports saloons ran in the Targa Abruzzo 24 Hour Races, taking first three places in 1934, and 1st and 2nd in 1935. In the latter year there came the greatly improved 2300B, with all-round independent suspension and better-looking bodies. There was little change in the design of these up to the outbreak of war; the 2300 was replaced by the 2500 for 1939. This was of similar design and general appearance, with a 2,443cc engine developing 95bhp (touring) or 105bhp (sports). It was continued for several years after the war. A short-wheelbase streamlined saloon 2300B won the 1937 Mille Miglia, while a 2500 Super Sport driven by Mussolini's chauffeur Boratto won the 1939 Mille Miglia held in Libya. Farina was second in the shortened 1940 Mille Miglia behind von Hanstein's B.M.W. 107 Mille Miglia replicas were made, either sports saloons or open two-seaters.

Far more exciting than the 6C was the 8C 2900, a very high performance sports car derived from the Tipo B Grand Prix car. It had a 2,905cc straight-8 engine, with twin-ohc, of course, and twin superchargers, each feeding one block of cylinders. Maximum power was 180bhp. The 1935 Mille Miglia was won by a Tipo B with road equipment, and this was the forerunner of the 8C

2900A. Only eleven of these were made, their main achievement being a 1–2–3 victory in the 1936 Mille Miglia. The 2900B was intended as a limited production sports car, the number being restricted by the number of surplus Tipo B engines, which was thirty. When the stock of these was used up, production of the 2900B came to an end, but it is unlikely that the firm could have sold many more, anyway, for they cost nearly £2,000. They had independent suspension all round, by coil springs at the front and by transverse-leaf in conjunction with swing axles at the rear. Various bodies were made, ranging from lightweight two-seaters to drophead coupés by such firms as Pininfarina and Touring. With the highest axle ratio and light body, the 2900B was capable of 130mph, a very high speed indeed for the 1930s. One driven by Hugh Hunter came 2nd in the 'Fastest Road Car' race at

Sir Henry Birkin at the wheel of a 2·3-litre Alfa Romeo at Le Mans in 1932. (Photo: Montagu Motor Museum)

An Alfa Romeo 2900B with Superleggera coachwork, photographed in Moscow in 1962. (Photo: G. N. Georgano)

Brooklands in 1939, and they also came 1st and 2nd in the 1937 Mille Miglia, and won the Spa 24 Hour Race the same year. After 1934 there were no Alfa successes at Le Mans, although a 2900 ran in 1937 and a 2500 in 1939. The Mille Miglia entries, like most Alfa Grand Prix entries were by the Scuderia Ferrari, but the cars at Spa and Le Mans were entered by the works, often only one or two cars, whereas Ferrari ran teams of three or more.

The 2900B was the last pre-war production sports car, but in 1939 a 4½-litre V-12 car with similar body, chassis, and suspension to the 2900B appeared. Known as the Tipo 412, its engine was a slightly detuned version of the 12C-37 Grand Prix racing cars, with twin-ohc to each bank of cylinders. This was the last design by Vittorio Jano before he moved to Lancia. As used in the Tipo 412, the engine developed 220bhp at 5,500rpm. Not more than four of these cars were made, and their only sporting successes were 1st and 2nd places in the 1939 Antwerp Grand Prix. Had the war not intervened, the 412 might have had a very successful career, although it is doubtful if such a complex and expensive car would have been sold in any numbers to the general public. The Swiss driver Willy Daetwyler drove one successfully in hill-climbs until well into the 1950s.

Compared with the brilliant career of Alfa Romeo, other Italian efforts seem very tame, but Lancia made a number of sports cars, of which the most interesting was the V-8 Astura. This was introduced in 1931 as a smaller version of the Dilambda. It had a 2·6-litre narrow-angle V-8 engine whose cylinders were inclined at an included angle of 19 degrees. Because of this narrow angle, the engine could be cast as a monobloc. It developed 73bhp at 4,000rpm. It was originally a touring car with no sporting pretensions, although when capacity was increased in 1933 to 2,972cc it had a very respectable performance, the 4-door five-seater saloon being capable of 83mph. A sports model defeated an Alfa Romeo 2300B in the 1934 Coppa d'Oro, a 3,534-mile tour of Italy. Third place in this event was taken by another Astura driven by Giuseppe Farina, this being one of the first competition successes of the driver who was to become so famous at the wheel of Alfa Romeos after the war. From 1935 onwards some very attractive

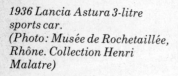

1936 Lancia Astura 3-litre sports car.
(Photo: Musée de Rochetaillée, Rhône. Collection Henri Malatre)

coachwork was built on the Astura chassis, often completely transforming the appearance of the car. Among customers of special-bodied Asturas were the racing driver Count Johnny Lurani and Bruno Mussolini, son of *il Duce*. Sports bodies were also available on the 1,954cc V-4 Artena and 1,196cc V-4 Augusta chassis. The latter was sold in England by Kevill-Davies & March Ltd with a four-seater sports tourer body known as the March Special, and mild supercharging with a boost of 3½lb–4lb psi. It had a maximum speed of 76mph, but then the standard saloon Augusta was capable of 70mph. The Aprilia saloon of 1937 was made as a drophead coupé by Pininfarina, and by Eagle in London, and there was also a two-seater sports car by the latter. However these special-bodied cars lacked the rigidity of the integral construction saloons and offered little improvement in performance.

Up to 1933 Fiat had not been thought of as sports car makers, and their 'S' suffix on cars such as the 501S mainly related to sporty-looking coachwork. However in 1933 there appeared a remarkable little car, the Tipo 508S Balilla. Derived from a mass-produced family saloon, the 995cc 22bhp Balilla, the sports model developed 30bhp and carried a completely new two-seater body with sloping radiator grille and flowing wings. It would not be too much of an exaggeration to say that its lines were a miniature version of those of the glamorous 8C Alfa Romeo, and this undoubtedly helped to sell the little Fiat, not only in Italy, but all over Europe where the Alfa was venerated. The Balilla was almost the only small continental sports car, and was sold and raced in France, Germany, Great Britain, Czechoslovakia, and Poland. The 1933 Mille Miglia cars had ohv heads and 4-speed gearboxes by Siata, a tuning firm who made cars under their own name after the war. They developed 35–40bhp, and came 3rd in the 1,100cc class behind two K3 Magnettes. Overhead-valve engines came on the production cars in 1934, giving a maximum speed of 73mph. Two types were made with the same engine, the *Spyder Normale* with flowing wings and the *Spyder Corso* with cycle-type wings. There was also the *Berlinetta Aerodinamica*, a fast-back coupé. The two-seaters sold in England had locally-built bodies with more pronounced tail fins. The Balilla sports did well in rallies, and tuned cars

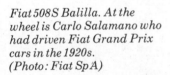

Fiat 508S Balilla. At the wheel is Carlo Salamano who had driven Fiat Grand Prix cars in the 1920s. (Photo: Fiat SpA)

were successful in Club events at Brooklands, but the greatest successes were achieved by the Gordini-tuned Simca-Fiats (see page 196). About 1,000 sports Balillas were made, out of a total Balilla production of 113,000. In the autumn of 1937 the Balilla was dropped in favour of the Tipo 508C Mille-cento with 1,089 cc 32bhp engine, giving 70mph for a four-seater saloon. There was no sports successor to the Balilla, but a few aerodynamic coupés were made, of which one was owned in England by Lord Brabazon of Tara. This had a 42bhp engine and a maximum speed of over 90mph. This model was continued after the war, with slightly modified bodywork. The only other sports model Fiat was an ohv conversion of the Tipo 500 Topolino. The 570cc engine developed 19bhp, and in England an open two-seater body with cutaway doors was made by Sydney Smith's garage in Putney.

The pre-war Maserati was almost only seen as a racing car, and the few road-going cars made were thinly disguised racing machines. In theory three models could be had in sports form, the 8C-1100, the 8C-1500, and the 8C-2500, all with straight-8 twin-ohc engines. 1100 and 2500 models ran in the 1931 Tourist Trophy, and a 2500 with four-seater bodywork took 2nd place in the Irish Grand Prix at Phoenix Park in the same year. After 1931 Maserati concentrated on racing cars. A few well-known road-going cars were developed from racing cars, notably the *Sedici Cilindri* with two 2-litre straight-8 engines mounted side-by-side, and the supercharged 2·9-litre car once driven by Sir Henry Birkin, and licensed for road use in 1948. However, these were individual machines, and it was not until after the war, when the Maserati company had been taken over by Omer Orsi, that a production sports Maserati appeared.

Apart from a few makes which survived from the 1920s, such as O.M. and Itala, described in the previous section, there were no other Italian sports cars made during the 1930s.

A Fiat Topolino with open body by Sydney Smith, competing at a J.C.C. meeting at Brooklands in March 1939. (Photo: Montagu Motor Museum)

During the 1920s the Czech motor industry had developed some very strong and advanced designs, the best-known being the Tatra with central tubular chassis. This firm never made a sports car, although some two-seater roadster bodies were mounted on the 1,690cc Typ 57 chassis from 1934 to 1939, and the rear-engined saloons of the same period had a high performance, if alarming handling. The Skoda of the 1920s was strictly a touring car, made in various sizes up to a 3·9-litre straight-8, but the Popular of 1934 formed the basis of a number of sporting coupés. It had a 995cc 4-cylinder engine mounted in a tubular backbone frame forked at the front to carry the engine as in the later Austro-Daimlers. In 1935 a streamlined aluminium coupé appeared, with 6·3:1 compression ratio, power increased from 22bhp to 34bhp, and a maximum speed of 75mph. In the 1936 Monte Carlo Rally a Skoda roadster with 1,380cc engine finished 2nd in its class and 8th overall. The following year a coupé was 4th in its class and 9th overall; enough of a success, Skoda thought, to christen their new model the Monte Carlo. This was a coupé with the 42bhp ohv Rapid engine in the Popular chassis.

The Wikov was little known outside Czechoslovakia, and yet several fine and incredibly strong sports cars were made by this small agricultural machinery firm from Prostejov. The 1½-litre single ohc model was the best-known Wikov sports car, and in the hands of its star driver A. Szcyzycki achieved many successes in hill-climbs, trials, and races. Maximum speed

1937 Skoda Monte Carlo coupé. (Photo: Motokov)

1935 Wikov 1¾-litre sports car.
(Photo: Národni Technické
Museum, Prague, courtesy
Alfred Lewerenz)

was 85mph, or over 100mph in supercharged form. The Wikovs particularly distinguished themselves in the International High Tatra Rallies of 1930 and 1931 which were remarkably punishing events involving between 5,400 and 7,900 miles, or six full circuits of the Czechoslovak republic. The 1½-litre Wikov also did well in racing, coming 4th in the 1931 Polish Grand Prix at Lwow behind an SSKL Mercedes and two Type 35 Bugattis, and 2nd in the 1932 Polish Mountain Race. Later Wikovs had larger engines of 1,750cc and 1,960cc, but were not so sporting as the 1½-litre. A few cars were made with highly streamlined Jaray bodies. Built in 1931, they would still have looked advanced twenty years later.

The Jawa began in 1934 as a 684cc D.K.W. built under licence looking exactly like the German cars except for a slightly longer wheelbase. However, within a year two-seater roadster and coupé bodies were made, the latter designed by Jaray. Teams ran in the Czechoslovak 1,000 Mile Trials, the open two-seaters having a speed of 75mph, which is more than their German equivalents the D.K.W.s ever achieved. In 1938 came a new Jawa, the 615cc Minor which was available with roadster body, but not seen much in competitions. This was the basis for the post-war Aero Minor, of which sports versions ran at Le Mans in 1949.

A handsome sports tourer of the late 1930s was the Aero. Originally a single-cylinder economy car, the Aero was gradually enlarged through 2- and 4-cylinder models to the 2-litre Typ 50 which developed 50bhp in twin-carburetter form. It was a long, low car, available as a 2-door saloon, drop-head coupé, and sports tourer with cutaway doors. Similar cars with pointed radiator grilles were made after the war until 1947.

16.The United States of America

Although one or two sports car makers such as Stutz survived into the early 1930s (see page 148), one can say that the whole American sports car story of the decade is confined to three makes, all part of the same combine and sharing designers and engineers. They were Auburn, Duesenberg, and Cord.

The Auburn speedster was re-introduced in 1932 after a year's absence. It was provided with the Columbia Dual Ratio rear axle; ratios were 5·1:1 or 3·4:1. Also in 1932 came the V-12 which was also available with a pointed-tail speedster body. The 6·8-litre Lycoming engine developed 160bhp, and the car was remarkable value, selling at only $995 for the cheapest model. This was the only 12-cylinder car ever to sell for less than $1,000. It has been suggested that Auburn would have done better to price it higher, as they would then have made a greater profit and attracted some of those snobs who, even in Depression times, thought that a cheap V-12 could not possibly be a good V-12. The twelves were continued through 1934, but for the first time for seven years there were no speedsters on either chassis. However this was not quite the end for the Auburn speedster, for in 1935 came the 851 range, all cars being lower and more modern-looking, and being available with a Schwitzer-Cummings supercharger, which boosted power from 115 to 150bhp. This supercharger was not entirely satisfactory, failing after the slightest wear in the moving parts. As with other supercharged cars including the Mercedes-Benz, many mechanics and owners did not tighten the cylinder heads sufficiently, leading to blown gaskets. The 851 range included a new speedster designed by Gordon Buehrig who was responsible for the Model 810 Cord. This had a maximum speed of 104mph. In the hands of Ab Jenkins an 851 speedster covered 12 hours at over 100mph and broke seventy records for stock cars at Bonneville. For 1936 came the 852s with only minimal changes from the 851s, but production of all Auburns ceased before 1936 was out. About 500 speedsters were made in 1935 and 1936.

The most important innovation in the Duesenberg of the period was the introduction of the SJ model in 1932. This had a centrifugal supercharger running at five times engine speed, and strengthened crankshaft and valve springs to cope with the extra power which was now 320bhp. The SJ could be distinguished externally from the J by its outside exhaust pipes, but bodies included many of the same styles as the J which remained in production alongside its more powerful sister. One of the most popular styles on the SJ chassis was the 4-door convertible sedan by Derham. A sedan by Rollston was known as the 'Twenty Grand' because its total price approached $20,000. A few special SJs cost nearly $25,000, making them the most expensive cars ever made in America. Performance of the SJ was almost incredible: a four-seater phaeton had a maximum speed of over 125mph. Most SJs were built on the shorter wheelbase of 11ft 10½in (the long wheelbase was 12ft 9½in), but in 1935 two extra short chassis two-seaters were built for the film stars Clark Gable and Gary Cooper. These were known as the SSJ. The Duesenberg factory closed early in 1937 when the Auburn-Cord-Duesenberg combine collapsed, but at least one car was assembled after the closure. About 470 Duesenbergs were made between 1929 and 1937, of which not more than 36 were SJs.

212

*1935 Auburn 851 speedster
owned by Harry Resnick.
(Photo: Harry Resnick Motor
Museum, Ellenville, New York)*

The only other American car of the period which could claim to be a sports car was the Cord Model 810. Originally intended as a small Duesenberg it was one of the most striking-looking cars ever made. The sedan was only 5ft high, compared with 5ft 8in for the average American sedan of 1935, and the wrap-around grille and retracting headlamps were quite new. Power came from a 4,729cc V-8 Lycoming engine which drove the front wheels, another unusual feature. This developed 125bhp at 3,600rpm, giving a maximum speed of 92mph. With the supercharged Model 812 of 1937 power was 190bhp at 4,200rpm, and speed rose to over 100mph. As well as the sedan, two open models were made, the four-seater Phaeton and the two-seater Convertible Coupé. Some people would dismiss the Cord as not a true sports car, but it is hard to assess its position on the American scene. It did not have handling comparable to a Bugatti or Alfa Romeo, but these characteristics are developed by and for racing. The Cord was never raced because there were no American cars for it to race against. Had events such as Le Mans or the Mille Miglia been held in America, it is more than likely that improved models of the Cord (and Auburn) would have been developed to compete in them. As it was, both cars were bought by the dwindling band of individualists who liked to motor quickly and stylishly, and were prepared to pay fairly heavily for the pleasure of doing so. The Cord could not expect a large share of the overall market considering that it cost up to $3,575, compared with $1,545 for a V-8 Cadillac. In addition, the whole group of which Cord was one make was in financial difficulties and production came to an end in 1937. Total number made of the 810 and 812 series between February 1936 and the end of 1937 was 2,320.

*One of the two Duesenberg SSJ
two-seaters built in 1935. This
was the property of Gary
Cooper.
(Photo: Briggs Cunningham
Automotive Museum)*

Part Four
Post War Recovery, 1945-1960

As in 1919, the first post-war cars to come off the production lines were essentially pre-war designs. The first sports car to appear was the M.G. TC Midget, which was in production by November 1945. It had a wider body than the 1939 TB and a number of minor improvements, but was unchanged in appearance. The 1,250cc engine developed 55bhp at 5,200rpm, and the maximum speed was 78mph. It was in no way an outstanding design, and yet it pioneered the sale of British sports cars in the United States. Its good handling and undoubtedly sporty appearance compensated for the fact that it was at least 10mph slower than the average six-passenger sedan of the time. It was certainly a crowd-gatherer, and views on its attractions varied greatly. In 1947 a correspondent wrote to the *Saturday Evening Post* complaining about the gaudiness of the new American cars, with their mouth-organ grilles, and begging manufacturers to draw some inspiration from European cars. This drew a reply from someone who said that for his money his neighbour's M.G. Midget was much flashier than any American car going, and he, for one, would be ashamed to be seen in such an ostentatious little wagon. The Midget attracted more jokes than any car in America since the Model T Ford. Stories were told of the Texas millionaire who ordered a dozen to give as Christmas presents, or of the owners who could pass a heavy truck by driving underneath it. Nevertheless, it was far more than a joke; owners soon began to race their Midgets, and many sports car clubs were set up as a result of the spread of the Midget across America. For two or three years it had virtually no rivals. Exports to the United States began in early 1946, and by the time it was replaced in January 1950 about 6,000 had been sold in North America and Canada. Total production of the TC was 10,008. The TC's successor was the TD which was a generally similar car, but brought up to date with coil independent front suspension. The wire wheels were replaced by discs, front and rear bumpers were standardized, and the body was again widened. At the time, many M.G. enthusiasts deplored the move away from a traditional appearance which dated back to the J-type of 1933, but the TD was a logical improvement of a design which could not have gone on for ever. The works approved various stages of tuning, the highest of which gave 68bhp with a 9·3:1 compression ratio. With part-Methanol fuel and a Shorrock supercharger, power could be as high as 100bhp. The TD remained in production until 1953, when it was replaced by the TF. In appearance this was a rather unsatisfactory compromise between the traditional and modern all-enveloping bodywork. The radiator sloped backwards, the headlamps were partially faired into the wings, and the fuel tank at the rear was sloped as well. Wire wheels returned as an option. Performance was slightly improved, with 3½bhp more than the TD, and the same stages of tune were available. Power was increased still further in the TF 1500 with 1,466cc engine which gave 63bhp in standard form. It was clear that M.G. would have to be completely modernized at some time. A streamlined two-seater had run at Le Mans in 1951 and when the MGA appeared in September 1955 it had a body not unlike that of the Le Mans car. The value of good aerodynamic form was shown by comparative tests made with different bodies. With 68bhp the MGA reached the same

Le Mans 1952. The winning Mercedes-Benz 300SL leading Briggs Cunningham's Cunningham which finished 4th.
(Photo: Motor)

M.G. TD Midget at an Ulster hill climb.
(Photo: W. A. C. McCandless)

An M.G. MGA takes part in driving tests during a Scottish Centre M.G. Car Club Rally.
(Photo: W. K. Henderson)

Sisters under the bonnet: Triumph TR2 and Morgan Plus Four at Silverstone in July 1955.
(Photo: Motor Sport)

speed (98mph) as a highly-tuned 97bhp unstreamlined TF. The introduction of the MGA marked the end of the name Midget (in fact the TF 1500 was never called a Midget by the works). The name was revived in 1961 for a smaller sports car which was an M.G. version of the Austin-Healey Sprite. The MGA's engine was a 1,489cc 4-cylinder ohv unit which it shared with the ZA Magnette saloon. A twin overhead camshaft version which ran in the 1955 Tourist Trophy led to a production twin-cam model in 1958. This was temperamental, but about 2,000 were made from 1958 to 1960. It was the first M.G. to have disc brakes on the front wheels, and this feature was continued on the 1,588cc MGA 1600 which replaced the smaller-engined car in 1960. Like earlier MGAs, this was available as an open two-seater or as a fixed head coupé.

The M.G. Midget's closest rival, and a very similar car in the early post-war years, was the Morgan. The 1939 10hp Standard engine was again used, Standards agreeing to produce the 40bhp 1,267cc unit for Morgan, even though they were no longer making a Ten of their own. Body styles were an open two-seater and a drophead coupé. Little change was made until 1950, when the 2,088cc Standard Vanguard engine was substituted for the Ten. Power went up to 68bhp, and speed from a modest 70mph to a very satis-factory 85mph. Brakes were hydraulic, and the traditional Morgan virtues of roadholding were as good as ever. The Plus Four, as the new car was called, was more than a match for the TD Midget, yet in two-seater form it cost only £24 more at £794. A four-seater sports tourer and two-seater drophead coupé were also available. For 1954 a curved grille modified the traditional Morgan appearance while during the year the 90bhp 1,991cc Triumph TR 2 engine became available. Maximum speed was now just over 100mph. The price was up to £869, and in order to provide a cheaper car, and also because there were doubts about the continuing supply of TR 2 engines, Morgan introduced the 4-4, powered by the 1,172cc side valve Ford Ten engine. This cost £695 and, in standard form, had a maximum speed of 75mph. With many tuning conversions available for the Ford engine, well over 80mph could be attained.

The 4-4 and Plus Four were not the only post-war Morgans, for the 3-wheelers were made in small numbers up to 1952. In 1946 a final batch of 2-cylinder sporting models with Matchless engines was turned out, all of which were exported to Australia. The other 3-wheelers used 4-cylinder Ford Eight or Ten engines, bodies being mostly four-seaters, although a few F4 Super two-seater sports models were also made. They were the last sporting 3-wheelers made anywhere in the world.

One of the most striking of early post-war British cars was the Allard. Sydney Allard was the only constructor of the pre-war Anglo-American Sports Hybrids who re-introduced such cars in 1946. The engine was the 3,622cc Ford V-8, which, as it was made at Dagenham, did not involve Allard in currency problems. Bodies were designed by Allard trials driver Godfrey Imhof and were low and streamlined, with a sharply curved radiator grille. Initially there were three models, the L four-seater tourer, the K two-seater sports, and the J1 short-chassis competition two-seater. Only about twelve of the latter were made, and nearly all were re-bodied as trials specials. Allards, suitably modified, were among the most successful trials cars until the smaller-engined machines took over in about 1950. The M drophead coupé and P1 saloon were introduced in 1947 and 1949 respectively, but far more interesting for the sportsman was the J2 of 1950. This had a very stark two-seater body and cycle-type wings. It had coil-spring independent front suspension and a de Dion rear axle derived from the Steyr-engined sprint

*The very rare two-seater
competition Allard of 1946.
Behind it are a Model L four-
seater tourer and a 1939 four-
seater.
(Photo: Autosport)*

*A J2 Allard duelling with a
Jaguar XK 120.
(Photo: Autosport)*

car which Allard had been driving in hill-climbs ever since the war. The J2 was the first Allard to use the 3,917cc Mercury V-8 engine, which gave 140bhp and 110mph in its 'mildest' form. At this time Allard was exporting some 75 per cent of his production, mostly to the United States. Many J2s were exported without engines, to be fitted in America with the more powerful engines available there. These were mostly the 160bhp 5·4-litre Cadillac ohv V-8, although Chrysler and Oldsmobile Rocket units also found their way into J2s. The most highly-tuned cars had over 300bhp, a maximum speed of 150mph, and 0–50 acceleration in 14 seconds. Sydney Allard said that sports car racing was vital to sales in America, whereas in Europe rally successes were more convincing to the buyer. In the early 1950s, Allards did well at both. A Mercury-engined J2 was 3rd at Le Mans in 1952, while Cadillac-engined cars were 1st and 3rd at Watkins Glen in 1950 and 2nd in 1953. The marque's most notable rally success was Sydney Allard's Monte Carlo Rally victory in 1952. In November 1951 the J2 was superseded by the J2X whose engine was mounted farther forward, giving a heavier appearance. In 1953 came the K3 with full-width three-seater body, and two smaller cars with similar styling, the Ford Consul and Zephyr-engined Palm Beach models. The 1956 Palm Beach had the option of the 3,442cc twin-ohc Jaguar engine. At £1,951 it was several hundred pounds more expensive than the equivalent Jaguar, and very few were sold. In fact one could say that the Allard's days were numbered as soon as the Jaguar XK 120 was introduced. The latter was at the same time cheaper and more refined, and gave more power from a smaller engine. Only in America did the Allard continue to score for a few years longer, and then because of the development potential of locally-made engines. As hot-rod enthusiast Roger Huntingdon said, 'Let's not pine for the Jaguar, but work on the stock block, and save a couple of thousand dollars.' The last development of the J series was the J2R with Palm Beach-type body and Cadillac or similar engines. About twenty of these were sold.

Two other small British firms copied the Allard theme in using Ford V-8 engines. These were the J.A.G. from Thames Ditton and the J.B.M. from Horley, Surrey. The former had a two-seater all-enveloping body, while the latter was a very stark affair with separate wings and a light alloy body on a very long wheelbase. As it was assembled from reconditioned components no purchase tax was payable, and it sold for a remarkably cheap £750. However, it was too uncomfortable for general use, and its long wheelbase hindered it in trials.

Mention of trials brings us to the very small class of cars which were built commercially for trials purposes. The 'mud-plugging' trial grew out of the earlier road event in which a few poorly-surfaced hills were interspersed to make the event a little more challenging. The famous long-distance trials such as the London-Exeter and London-Land's End continued, but alongside them there grew up in the 1930s more specialized trials such as the Wye Cup and Colmore in which the cross-country section became more important than the road section. Organisers vied with each other to find fiendishly difficult slopes of about one in three gradient, whose surfaces were compounded of mud and leaf mould. The road sections became relatively unimportant, and the extreme was reached in some post-war trials when the cars were taken from one hill to another on a truck. Success in these events called for a powerful short-wheelbase car, with as much weight as possible over the rear axle. Up to about 1950 Ford V-8-based cars such as the Allard were the most successful, but then the smaller car with Ford Ten engine took over. With these the drivers skilfully and delicately picked their way to the top of the hill, instead of storming up with full power as the V-8s had done. Most trials cars were home-built, but at least three makes went in for limited production, Dellow, Ausfod, and Cannon.

The Dellow was the most famous, and did well in rallies after lighter, more spartan specials had surpassed it as a trials car. It was powered by the 1,172cc Ford Ten engine, favoured by most trials car constructors, and had a light two-seater aluminium body. The chassis was a tubular A-shaped structure. The original Dellow had cutaway sides with no doors, but in the Mark II models doors were optional. Other optional extras were a twin-carburetter layout for £13 or a supercharger for £80. Later improvements included the Mark III with longer wheelbase and four-seater body, the Mark IV with 1,508cc Ford Consul engine in the Mark III chassis (prototypes only), and the Mark V lightweight trials car with coil springs all round. In 1956 a new company introduced the Mark VI, which used the fashionable all-enveloping fibre-glass body, still with Ford Ten engine. Very few of these were sold. The Dellow was normally used for sport, but one large firm of agricultural implement makers bought a small fleet of Mark IIs for their representatives who had to cover really rough country.

The Manchester-built Ausfod was a short-lived trials car which used the Ford Ten engine in an Austin Seven chassis, hence its name. The firm's chief engineer, R. H. Dyson, drove a blown version in a number of trials in 1948. An aerodynamic two-seater was advertised, but it is not certain if it was ever built. The other commercially-made trials special was the work of Mike Cannon, a Tasmanian farmer from Tonbridge, Kent. His first car, built for his own use, was so successful that he began to turn out a few for customers. Working almost single-handed, he built about 120 cars between 1953 and 1966 when he turned to the manufacture of lightweight trailers. Cannons were strictly trials machines and not suitable for road work. He normally used Ford Ten engines in a space frame clad in thin aluminium alloy sheet. Front axle was a Ford Eight beam-type with transverse leaf suspension, while suspension at the rear was by vertical coil springs with telescopic shock absorbers. Cannons were so successful that by the early 1960s nearly all trials cars were on Cannon lines. When the Ford 98E engine was replaced by the 100E, Cannon preferred the lighter earlier unit, and advised customers to find second-hand examples if they could. When good 98Es became hard to find, Cannon turned to the BMC A-type engine in 1,098cc or 1,275cc form.

Despite the brief appearance of a three-seater roadster on the 2½-litre chassis, the post-war Riley was not a sports car. However the 2½-litre Big Four engine was the basis of an interesting new make, the Healey. Designed and produced by Donald Healey (see page 163), it was a well-streamlined car available as a four-seater roadster or a 2-door sports saloon. The latter was Britain's fastest production saloon in 1946, with a maximum speed of 104·7mph. These early Healeys ran in the 1947 and 1948 Alpine Trials where they won their class; they also won the touring car class in the 1949 Mille Miglia. In 1949 came the Silverstone, the first two-seater sports car from Healey, and considerably cheaper than the others at £1,260 compared with over £2,000. However, it was only £20 cheaper than a Jaguar XK 120. It had a narrow two-seater body, separate wings, and a spare wheel which projected beyond the tail so that it acted as a bumper. Maximum speed was well over 100mph, and the Silverstone became very popular in club racing in Great Britain and in the United States. No fewer than eight competed in the 1950 Production Car Race at Silverstone, Duncan Hamilton winning his class at 79mph. Also in 1950 Briggs Cunningham drove one into 2nd place in the Watkins Glen sports car race. Some Silverstones raced in America were

Above: *1950 Healey Silverstone.*
(Photo: Michael Ware)

Above right: *Dellow Mark II*
with passenger energetically
aiding traction.
(Photo: Motor Sport)

powered by Cadillac engines. The car was in production for a little over one year, with a total production figure of 105, when it was crowded out by a new international car.

In June 1950, as a result of a shipboard meeting between Donald Healey and George W. Mason, president of Nash-Kelvinator, a Nash-engined Silverstone ran at Le Mans and finished in 4th place. This led to a production car known as the Nash-Healey. Built for export only, this car had a 125bhp 3·8-litre 6-cylinder Nash Ambassador engine with non-standard aluminium head, and an all-enveloping three-seater body made by Panelcraft of Birmingham. 104 of these were made between December 1950 and March 1951, when production was suspended. In the following January a new Nash-Healey appeared with body designed and built by Pininfarina. The chassis was shipped from Warwick to Turin, and the completed cars thence to America. The first few Farina-bodied cars had the 3·8-litre engine, but most had the new 4·1-litre unit. Hard-tops as well as open three-seaters were made, and when production ended in 1954 a total of 506 Nash-Healeys had been made, more than any other single Healey model.

At the 1952 London Motor Show a new Healey appeared which was to extend the make's renown far beyond what it had been previously. This was a two-seater sports called the Healey Hundred, powered by a 2·6-litre 4-cylinder Austin A90 engine. It had a new chassis with underslung frame and leaf springs at the rear, and coil-and-wishbone independent front suspension. At only £1,063 it attracted so much attention that barriers had to be put round the car on the stand. Before the show ended arrangements were made for it to be built by the Austin Motor Company, and its name was changed to Austin-Healey. Only twenty cars were made at Warwick before production at Longbridge began. It had a maximum speed of 102mph, but lowering the hood and folding back the windscreen increased speed to about 107mph. A special model averaged 104mph for 24 hours, and covered the flying mile at Bonneville at 142·6mph. From this model came a production version, the Austin-Healey 100S. This had a completely new Weslake-designed cylinder head, while valves, crankshaft, and almost every part of the engine were modified, raising power from 90bhp to 132bhp. All special modifications were

221

An early Austin-Healey 100 at Silverstone in 1955. Behind it is a Buckler DD-1.
(Photo: Motor Sport)

carried out at Warwick, so mechanically the 100S was much more of a 'genuine Healey' than the standard 100. Less than 100 were made, compared with 15,700 of the 100 and 100M. The latter had slight modifications available from the factory or as a conversion kit for private owners. A high porportion of all Austin-Healeys were exported; the 100S came 3rd at Sebring in 1954, 6th in 1955 and 11th in 1956. With the end of Nash-Healey production in August 1954, the marque Healey came to an end, but the Austin-Healey went from strength to strength. In 1956 came a 2·6-litre 6-cylinder car known as the 100-6. Similar in styling to the 100, it had room for two children in the rear seats, but was 4cwt (448lb) heavier. It was more of a roadster than a sports car, and was raced much less than its predecessors. However, it was very successful in rallies, especially the Alpine Rally. This it won outright in 1961 and 1962, winning also the Liège-Rome-Liège and the Austrian Alpine Rally in 1964. Capacity was increased to 2,912cc in 1959, and gradual improvements were made over the next seven years. By 1964, power was up to 150bhp. Production continued until February 1968, by which time total production of the larger Austin-Healeys was over 50,000. Vast though these figures were, they were to be overshadowed by those of the smaller Austin-Healey, the Sprite.

This was announced in 1958, and was a classic example of a popular small sports car derived from a mass-production saloon. The engine was the 948cc BMC A-type, as used in the current Austin A35 saloon. This was mounted in

Austin-Healey 3000 driven by Timo Makinen and Paul Easter in action on a special stage in the Scottish Highlands during the 1965 R.A.C. Rally of Great Britain.
(Photo: B.M.C. Competitions Press Office)

a welded platform frame, with a light two-seater body. The engine, which was specially fitted with twin S.U. carburetters, developed 45bhp at 5,500rpm, giving the Sprite a maximum speed of 81mph. Numerous conversion kits for improving performance soon became available, among the most popular being those offered by Speedwell Conversions of London. Body modifications included a streamlined nose-piece and fast-back coupé top, while engine tuning raised power to 60bhp. In 1960 a Speedwell coupé driven by Graham Hill reached 110mph on a Belgian motorway. Another modification was by Paddy Gaston. It had a detachable hard-top by Ashley Laminates and engine bored out to give a capacity of 994cc. With larger valves and other engine improvements, power went up from the standard 45bhp to 70bhp at 6,500rpm. Maximum speed was 101mph. Thus the Sprite owner, like that of the Austin Seven in the 1920s, could buy a wide variety of modifications to give increased performance and altered appearance. The latter was something of a joke, with the characteristic 'bug-eyed' headlamps projecting from the bonnet, and many kits modified the front end in some way. The 'bug-eyed' Sprite was replaced in 1961 by a more conventional Mark II, but now, only nine years later, Mark Is command higher prices than early Mark IIs because of their distinctive appearance. Although made in large numbers (49,000), the 'bug-eyed' Sprite seems set to become a collector's piece. The later Sprites will be described in the next part.

An interesting attempt to build a sports car in the smallest category was the Berkeley, made by a firm of caravan manufacturers from Biggleswade, Bedfordshire. It was designed by Laurie Bond who was also responsible for the Bond 3-wheelers and the later Bond Equipe coupés. The Berkeley sports appeared in 1956, having a 322cc 2-cylinder Anzani engine driving the front wheels via chains, all-round independent suspension, and a two-seater fibreglass body. Maximum speed was 60mph. Later Berkeleys had the 492cc 3-cylinder Excelsior or 692cc 2-cylinder Royal Enfield engine. The latter developed 40bhp and was good for 90mph. Berkeleys had a remarkable run of success in Italian events in 1959. The 492cc car defeated several streamlined Fiat-Abarths to win its class in the Monza 12 Hour Race, and they also won their class in the Mille Miglia and several smaller Italian events. The Berkeley's popularity was short-lived, however, as they were eclipsed by the appearance of the Austin-Healey Sprite in 1959. This was cheaper than the bigger Berkeleys, and had the advantage of a 4-cylinder engine. Berkeley turned to four cylinders themselves with the Ford-engined Bandit of 1961, but this was more expensive still. Berkeley production ceased that year.

The classic H.R.G. was revived in 1946 with little change. There were two

A 692cc Berkeley in action at Mallory Park. (Photo: Autosport)

models, the 1100 and the 1500, both with Singer engines. The 1500 was also available with a striking aerodynamic two-seater body, at £1,246 compared with £882 for the ordinary 1500. The body was mounted on outriggers from the chassis; the flexibility of the latter soon caused the body to deteriorate and fall to pieces after hard use. Only thirty aerodynamic cars were made, and production ceased in 1947. H.R.G. did not run a works team after the war, but private entrants were very successful in rallies and races. They won the 1,100cc and 1,500cc classes in the 1948 Alpine Rally, and gained a Coupe des Alpes in 1951. In the 1949 Spa 24 Hour Race they took the first four places in their class, while a lightweight model won the 1½-litre class at Le Mans in the same year. Three of these lightweights were made, of which two were rebodied aerodynamic cars. They were prepared at the Monaco Engineering Works at Watford. Another lightweight version was made in Australia, having a streamlined body but exposed wheels. Named the Woodside, it had a top speed of 100mph, but a very hard ride made it too uncomfortable for general use. The traditional H.R.G. was made with little change until 1955, but in decreasing numbers each year. Production figures declined from forty in 1948, their best year, to eleven in 1950, nine in 1951, and six in 1952. Total production from 1936 to 1955 was 231. In 1955 a completely new H.R.G. was announced, with a twin-cam version of the Singer SM 1500 engine, tubular frame and disc brakes. The price was to be £1,867, much too high for a 1½-litre car, and only three prototypes were made. Yet another prototype H.R.G. appeared in 1965, powered this time by a Vauxhall VX 4/90 engine, but the firm closed down completely the following year.

Frazer Nash was another famous make which had a distinguished career for several years after the war. The chain-driven models were not revived, and all post-war Frazer Nashes were derived from the B.M.W. The 1947 prototype two-seater had a body with flowing wings, closely copied from that of one of the 1940 Mille Miglia B.M.W.s. It was put into production in 1948

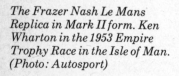

The Frazer Nash Le Mans Replica in Mark II form. Ken Wharton in the 1953 Empire Trophy Race in the Isle of Man. (Photo: Autosport)

with a much simpler body and cycle-type wings. This model gained 3rd place in the 1949 Le Mans race, being known thereafter as the Le Mans Replica. This was the most successful post-war Frazer Nash. Among its victories was Franco Cortese's win in the 1951 Targa Florio, the only time a British car has won this taxing Sicilian event. The Le Mans Replica also won the 1951 British Empire Trophy with Stirling Moss at the wheel, and the Sebring 12 Hour Race in the same year, drivers being Harry Grey and Larry Kulok. Other successes were 3rd place in the 1951 Tourist Trophy and 2nd in the 1952 Jersey Road Race. It was exported to many countries including the United States, Italy, Portugal, and Sweden, while one of the first 1948 cars (before it was called the Le Mans Replica) went to Czechoslovakia. It was quite suitable for rally driving as well as for racing, and won a Coupe des Alpes in the 1951 Alpine Rally. In order to keep up with new types of sports car such as the Cooper-Bristol, which were designed for racing rather than road use, a new Mark II Le Mans Replica appeared in 1952. It had a 140bhp engine and a lighter and lower body. It was with this car that Ken Wharton came 2nd in the 1952 Jersey Road Race behind a C-type Jaguar. However, the basic design had reached the limit of its development, and in the face of increasing competition from the 'racing-type' sports cars Frazer Nash withdrew from active support of sports car racing in 1955.

Apart from the Le Mans Replica, a confusing variety of other Frazer Nashes were made. Unlike the Le Mans car, they mostly had all-enveloping coachwork. Some were touring models, such as the exotic-looking 1950 Cabriolet with partially spatted front and rear wheels. These were made in very small numbers, hardly surprising considering the price of over £3,000 for a car of less than 2-litre capacity. The Targa Florio Turismo was an all-enveloping open two-seater with similar grille to that of the Le Mans Replica. There were plans to offer this with the Austin A90 engine, but the Healey Hundred stole its thunder, and it was never put into production. Another all-enveloping two-seater was the Sebring of 1954; at £3,657 this was the most expensive Frazer Nash yet, and only three were made. In 1953 came the Le Mans coupé with de Dion rear axle, one of the few closed cars ever catalogued by Frazer Nash. Just as in 'chain-gang' days, Frazer Nashes were bespoke cars, made largely to special order with customer's choice of seat type and shape, instrument layout, and control positions. For this reason, it is difficult to give finishing dates for the various models, as one that had been in abeyance for several years would be put together if a customer asked for it. However there was a change of engine in 1956 when the new 2,580cc 120bhp B.M.W. V-8 was introduced to the range, and very few 6-cylinder cars were made after that date. The new car was called the Continental; it had a similar chassis to the Le Mans, with de Dion axle and a two-seater coupé body. However, it was hardly competitive, at a price of £3,751. Since 1954 A.F.N. Ltd had been importing Porsches, and just as in the 1930s they found that importing was more profitable than manufacture, so they did twenty years later. The Frazer Nash last appeared at the London Motor Show in 1959, by which time a 3·2-litre V-8 engine was fitted. Production ceased soon afterwards.

The 6-cylinder B.M.W. engine was the heart of two other British makes, the Bristol, and from 1956 to 1962 the A.C. The Bristol was the first motorcar venture of an aircraft firm which had been in business since 1910. They chose the B.M.W. 328 engine as a suitable basis for their new high performance touring car, and went into production with a modified version giving 80bhp with single carburetter, or 85bhp with twin carburetters. The body of this first model, the 400, was a handsome two/four-seater coupé, with radiator grille and body lines that one would have expected from a post-war B.M.W. While no production Bristol has been a sports car, they have all been attractive high speed tourers and done well in rallies. The 400 was supplemented by the Italian-styled 401 in 1948, and this in turn by a more powerful version, the 100bhp 403 in 1953. The 404 was a short-chassis two-seater coupé, while the 405 was Bristol's first, and so far only, 4-door saloon. In 1953 a sports two-seater was built to be sold on the American market under the name Arnolt-Bristol. The chassis was that of the 404 with 125bhp engine. This was shipped to Italy, where a light two-seater body was built onto it by Bertone of Turin, and the complete car sent on to the U.S.A. There they were sold by S. H. Arnolt of Chicago who was able to sell them for less than the price of a 404, despite all the peregrinations from Bristol to Turin, and thence to Chicago. In addition, the Arnolt was suitable for racing. In 1955 they came 1st, 2nd, 4th and 5th in the 2-litre class of the Sebring 12 Hour Race, and continued to do well for several years afterwards, although outclassed by the Ferrari Testa Rossa. A fixed-head coupé version appeared in 1955, and production of Arnolt-Bristols continued until 1964. Total production was 340. The other competition Bristol was the Type 450. This had the same engine as the production cars, tuned to give 155bhp, a tubular chassis based on that of the G-type E.R.A. racing car, and an aerodynamic coupé body with twin stabilising fins. They ran at Le Mans in 1953 and 1954, taking first three places in their class in the latter event, and also winning their class in the 1953 Reims 12 Hour Race. Open versions were 1st, 2nd, and 3rd in their class at Le Mans in 1955. The 450 was never considered as a production car, and seems to have had little influence on the development of Bristol touring cars.

A.C. began post-war production with saloons and tourers powered by the well-tried 6-cylinder 1,991cc engine which now developed 74bhp. In October 1953 an 85bhp version of this was employed in an otherwise completely new two-seater sports car called the Ace. This had all-independent suspension by transverse leaf springs and wishbones. The frame was a tubular structure designed by John Tojeiro who had used this layout in M.G. and Bristol-engined sports cars made at his small works at Royston, Herts. The body and grille were very reminiscent of the contemporary Ferrari. The Ace had excellent road holding, and a maximum speed of 103mph allied to fuel consumption of 25–30mpg. A fixed head coupé called the Aceca was added in 1954. Early in 1956 both the Ace and the Aceca became available with the Bristol engine in 105bhp or 120bhp form, although the A.C. engine continued to be made until 1963. The 2·6-litre Ford Zodiac engine was also used in the Ace from 1961 to 1963. A new body style for 1960 was the Greyhound, a 2-door, four-seater saloon.

Lea-Francis returned to the sports car field for 1948 with a semi-stream-lined two-seater powered by the 1½-litre 4-cylinder engine used in the firm's saloon, but with power increased from 50–64bhp. This engine had twin camshafts mounted high in the block, a Hugh Rose design originated for Lea-Francis in 1938, and similar to the contemporary Rileys with which Rose had been associated. The 1½-litre engine was soon supplemented by the 87bhp 1,767cc Fourteen, and later by the 2,496cc Eighteen unit developing 105bhp in standard form and 125bhp with higher compression ratio. This model had similar styling, with the addition of two occasional seats. The 1,767cc engine was used in a small-production sports car. the Connaught. This had a light two-seater body, and semi-elliptic suspension at front and rear. The body was poor, with few of the comforts of the average road-going sports car, but the car handled very well. At least one journalist was

45. Above: *1952 Ferrari Tipo 225 Export Competition coupé. Coachwork by Vignale. Owned by George L. Sterner. (Photo: William S. Jackson)*

46. Below: *1952 Fiat 8 V 1,996cc two-seater coupé. (Photo: Fiat SA)*

prompted to wonder if all the fuss about independent suspension was justified, after driving a Connaught for 200 miles. With high-compression pistons and four Amal carburetters, 140bhp was available. Connaughts were successful in club racing in 1949 and 1950, but made little impact on the international scene. The firm entered Formula 2 racing in 1950, and their limited resources were largely concentrated in developing their racing cars. This programme resulted in Tony Brooks' victory in the 1955 Syracuse Grand Prix, Britain's first Grand Prix victory since Segrave's in 1923. In 1951 a new sports car was introduced, the L3SR. It had the same engine, with independent front suspension by double wishbones and torsion bar, a light-weight body by Abbott, and cycle-type wings. Twelve were laid down, but possibly fewer completed. A car entered for Le Mans in 1955 had an all-enveloping body and engine linered down to 1,484cc, so that it could compete in the 1½-litre class, but it was unsuccessful.

A newcomer to the ranks of 1½-litre sports cars was the Jowett Jupiter, the first serious entry into sport by this old-established Yorkshire firm. It used the 1,486cc flat-four engine of the firm's Javelin saloon in a tubular frame designed by Professor Eberan von Eberhorst of E.R.A. The body was a rather bulky-looking two-seater with wind-up side windows. With 60bhp and 86mph it was a pleasant road car, but hardly a serious sports car for competitions. However, an almost standard car won its class at Le Mans in 1950, averaging 75mph. In 1951 a special sports/racing model called the R.1 was built, with narrow body and cycle-type wings. This 65bhp car won its class at Le Mans in 1951 and 1952. It was not sold to the public, and only three were made. Other Jupiter successes in this period included class victories in the 1951 Tourist Trophy and Sebring 12 Hour Race, and 1st and 2nd places in their class in the 1951 Monte Carlo Rally. The final development of the Jupiter was the R.4 with completely new all-enveloping body. On the prototype this was of aluminium, but production bodies were to be in fibreglass. The wheelbase was 9in shorter than the earlier Jupiter, and weight was down by 5cwt (560lb). The chassis was that of the new 2-cylinder range of cars and vans that Jowetts were planning in 1953. It had the same engine as its predecessor, but an optional overdrive gave a maximum speed of 100mph. However its introduction coincided with Jowett's problems over the supply of Javelin bodies. Only three R.4s were made, the aluminium prototype and two 'production' fibreglass cars. A total of 1,200 Jupiters were made.

As we saw in Chapter Eleven the famous sporting firms of Sunbeam and Talbot together gave their name to a series of Rootes Group cars in the immediate pre-war years, of which the smaller was derived from the Hillman Minx and the larger from Humbers. The post-war Sunbeam-Talbot range consisted of the Minx-based Ten and Humber Hawk-based 2-litre. They were not sports cars, but made in handsome saloon and sports tourer forms. New bodies came in 1949, and a two-seater version in 1953 was called the Sunbeam Alpine. For 1955 the Talbot suffix disappeared from all models. The Alpine had a tuned version of the 2,267cc Rootes engine also used in the Humber Hawk and in the smaller Commer and Karrier commercial vehicles. The Alpine was a 100mph car, and did well in the Alpine Rallies of 1953 and 1954. In the latter event, Stirling Moss won a Gold Cup and Sheila Van Damm a Coupe des Dames. The original Alpine was dropped in October 1955, but the name was revived for 1960 on a low, integral-construction two-seater sports car with 1,494cc engine. This developed 78bhp and gave a speed of 98·4mph. Further developments of this Alpine will be described in the next part.

One of the most successful post-war British sports cars was the Triumph TR series. This was intended to fill the gap which existed in 1952 between

47. 1948 Cisitalia 1,090cc coupé. Coachwork by Pininfarina. Owned by Museo dell' Automobile, Turin. (Photo: Josip Ciganovic)

229

Above left: *Connaught L3
winning its class in the
Nottingham Sports Car Club
meeting at Gamerton, in July
1951.*
(Photo: Autosport)

Above right: *Jowett Jupiter on
the starting line at Prescott,
September 1952.*
(Photo: Guy Griffiths Motofoto)

the 1,250cc M.G., and the 3,442cc Jaguar. It was originally planned to use a
traditional body of the Morgan type, but to reach 100mph from 70bhp a
more aerodynamic body was called for. When introduced at the 1952 Motor
Show, the car was called the 20 TS. It had a 1,991cc version of the Vanguard
engine, Triumph Mayflower front suspension and rear axle, and a chassis
frame based on that of the old Standard Eight. The body was a very simple
open two-seater. With a basic price of £555 it attracted much attention,
although a great deal of development work was obviously needed. The
production car, now rechristened TR 2, appeared in March 1953. It had a
more powerful engine of 90bhp, while a longer tail gave the luggage accommodation that was noticeably lacking in the prototype. Actual production
did not start until August 1953. With overdrive the maximum speed was
108mph, and at its total price of £871 it was the cheapest 100mph car on the
British market. As well as performance, it was renowned for its economy;
40mpg at a constant 60mph and an overall consumption of 34mpg. TR 2s did

very well in club racing, and in rallies, finishing 1st, 2nd, and 5th in the 1954 R.A.C. Rally. In 1956 came the TR 3 with 100bhp engine, new radiator grille, and an optional bench seat at the rear for children. In 1957 disc brakes for the front wheels became available, the Triumph being the first British car in substantial production to offer discs. Many other items of equipment were offered by the works or by accessory makers. These included wire wheels, an undershield, and an adjustable steering column. The TR 3 was one of the most successful British sports cars, 75,000 having been made when it was replaced in 1962 by the TR 4.

Two semi-sporting cars which used the TR engine were the Swallow Doretti and the Peerless. The Doretti was intended to meet the demand for a car of TR character but with the comforts of a drophead coupé. It used the same engine, gearbox, transmission, and front axle, in conjunction with a tubular frame, and new body designed and built by the Swallow Coachbuilding Company. It was well equipped and finished, but had little luggage space, and cost £230 more than the TR 2. Production ceased in March 1955 after only a year, not through any fault of the car but owing to a change of policy by the controlling company. The Slough-built Peerless was a 2-door saloon using the TR 3 engine, gearbox, and front axle. It had a de Dion rear axle and a 2-door fibreglass body by Whitson of West Drayton on a tubular frame. Maximum speed was about 100mph, but the car was expensive at £1,498. An almost standard saloon ran at Le Mans in 1958, finishing 16th. Production ended in 1960 after about 250 had been made. The following year the design was revived under the name Warwick, but few of these were made.

It will be noticed that apart from the foreign-engined Allard, all the British sports cars described in this chapter have had capacities of under 3 litres, and most under 2 litres. During this period, only two firms made cars in the larger-engined class, both being highly successful. These were Jaguar and Aston Martin. Jaguar represents one of the greatest success stories of motoring history. In 1946 it was a respected but not especially famous car, while fifteen years later it was a household word in two continents. This success was due to two cars, both using similar twin ohc engines; the XK series sports cars and the Mark VII saloon and its descendants. Ever since the war enthusiasts had been waiting for a new two-seater sports Jaguar. Their appetite was sharpened by a streamlined Belgian body on a pre-war S.S. 100 chassis which was shown at the 1948 Brussels Salon. The XK series arrived at the London Show later the same year. Two models were announced, the 4-cylinder 2-litre XK 100 and the 6-cylinder 3·4-litre XK 120,

but only the latter went into production. It had a 3,442cc engine developing 160bhp at 5,200rpm, with a seven bearing crankshaft and chain-driven twin overhead camshafts. Front suspension was by torsion bar and wishbones. The body was a most beautiful slender, lithe shape with flowing wings and spatted rear wheels. Originally a production run of only 200 was planned, to whet public appetite for the following year's Mark VII saloon with the same engine, but so great was the interest that full production was started. As they had to tool up for a much larger run than anticipated, production was slow to begin. Export deliveries, which naturally took priority, did not start until mid-1949, and very few came onto the home market until 1951. During a road test by *The Motor*, the XK 120 recorded a speed of 125mph, while a model fitted with an undershield reached 132·6mph on the Jabbeke motorway in Belgium. The firm's racing programme began in 1949 with the Silverstone Production Car Race, in which they finished in first three places. Later that year Ian Appleyard won the Alpine Rally and Stirling Moss the Tourist Trophy. 1950 also saw the first Le Mans appearance of the XK. Three were entered, Johnson and Hadley maintaining 3rd place for twenty-one hours. At first, only the two-seater was made, but in 1951 an equally handsome fixed-head coupé was added, joined in 1953 by a drophead coupé.

Meanwhile the competition programme was developing. For Le Mans in 1951 the works prepared a team of special cars, the XK 120C, usually known as the C-type. This had a completely new tubular frame, and new rear suspension by single transverse torsion bar anchored at the centre. The engine had different camshaft timing, but was generally similar to the XK 120. It developed 200bhp or 210bhp, according to the compression ratio. Three C-types ran at Le Mans, the car driven by Peter Walker and Peter Whitehead winning at a record speed of 93·8mph. They were 1st, 2nd, and 4th in that year's Tourist Trophy. For 1952 a new body with longer nose and tail was prepared for Le Mans, but all retired with overheating. Later C-types reverted to the 'short-nose' body. 1952 saw the foundation of the Scottish team Ecurie Ecosse, which played a very important part in Jaguar racing history over the next few years. The C-type's victories included Le Mans in 1951 and 1953, and the Watkins Glen Grand Prix and Jersey Road

Below: *Stirling Moss at the wheel of a C-type Jaguar at the* Daily Express *Silverstone Meeting in 1952.*
(Photo: Guy Griffiths Motofoto)

Below right: *1950 Aston Martin DB2 coupé.*
(Photo: Autosport)

Race in 1952, as well as the sports car records at Prescott and Shelsley Walsh. The C-type was built for sale to private owners from August 1952 to 1954, 54 cars being made in all. Disc brakes came in 1953. It was replaced by the D-type, which was shorter, lighter, and more powerful, with 250bhp. The integral construction body had more rounded lines than the C-type, with the option of a stabilising fin behind the cockpit. It was less of a road car than the C-type, but very successful in racing. D-types won at Le Mans three years running, in 1955, 1956 and 1957, thereby enabling the marque to equal Bentley's record of five victories in seven years. They also won the Sebring 12 Hour Race in 1955 and Watkins Glen in 1955, 1956, and 1957. The road-going version of the D-type was the XK-SS, similar to the road-racing car, but with hood, windscreen, and side-screens. It had a maximum speed of 144mph. Only 16 were made before the disastrous fire in February 1957 which destroyed nearly one-third of the factory. After rebuilding, it was decided not to continue with the SS, which was inevitably a very small seller, but to begin work on a completely new volume production sports car. This emerged in 1961 as the E-type.

Meanwhile the XK 120 was replaced in 1954 by the generally similar XK 140 with 8:1 compression ratio engine giving 190bhp. A Special Equipment model was available with the 210bhp C-type engine and wire wheels. When its replacement, the XK 150, appeared in 1957, only the two coupés were listed. The makers probably intended the ill-fated XK-SS to be the two-seater of their range. However, the omission was rectified in 1958 with the XK 150S. This was a two-seater with 250bhp 3·8-litre engine and disc brakes all round. It was the final development of the XK series, and remained in production until the E-type appeared in the spring of 1961.

Aston Martin were acquired by the David Brown Organisation in 1947, but the first post-war cars had been designed by Claude Hill while the company was still independent. However, as production only began after the David Brown takeover, the car was known as the DB 1. It had a 4-cylinder pushrod ohv engine of 1,970cc developing 90bhp and independent front suspension. Bodies were a drophead coupé and a sports tourer. A special sports/racing two-seater won the 1948 Spa 24 Hour Race in the hands of St John Horsfall and Leslie Johnson. In 1949 a 2,580cc twin-ohc 6-cylinder Lagonda engine was fitted experimentally into a DB 1 chassis; in April 1950 this went into production as the DB 2. It has an all-enveloping 2-door saloon body which seated two, or three at a squeeze. For 1954 came the DB 2/4 with two additional rear seats 'for children or dwarfs' as journalists said about this, and many subsequent Gran Turismo cars. The engine was available in two stages of tune; the standard with 6·5:1 compression ratio and 105bhp, and the Vantage with 8·16:1 compression ratio and 125bhp. The DB 2 did well at Le Mans in 1950 and 1951, and won its class in the 1951 Mille Miglia. The DB 3 was an open competition version, with 160bhp engine, de Dion rear axle, and tubular frame designed by Eberan von Eberhorst. This car won the 1952 Goodwood Nine Hours Race, an event which, most unusually for England, included several hours of darkness as it ran from 3pm to midnight. Late in 1952 the DB 3's capacity was increased to 2,912cc, this engine being later used in an improved DB 2/4 which had a speed of 120mph. In 1953 the DB 3 was replaced by the DB 3S with more rounded lines and torsion-bar suspension. This car won the 1953 Goodwood Nine Hours Race. It was offered for sale as a 150mph road-going sports car for 1955, at a price of £3,684. A fixedhead coupé was also made. In 1956 came the first of the DBR series of sports/racing cars with space frames, de Dion rear axles, and disc brakes. This was the DBR 1/250 with 2½-litre engine, which was followed by the 2·9-litre DBR 1/300 and the 3·7-litre DBR 2. These did very well in racing in the years 1956 to 1959, victories including the 1,000km race at Nürburgring, in 1957, 1958, and 1959, the Tourist Trophy in 1958, and 1st and 2nd places at Le Mans in 1959. In the latter year, Aston Martin won the Sports Car Constructors Championship, the first and only time that a British manufacturer has achieved this title. A detuned (240bhp) version of the 3·7-litre engine was used in a new disc-braked coupé, the DB 4 of 1959. This was the first British car to enter the new class of high quality Gran Turismo coupés, typified by Ferrari and Maserati in Italy. It had a top speed of 140mph, and gave really comfortable high speed touring for four people. In 1960 an even higher performance version became available, the DB 4GT, with shorter wheelbase and 302bhp engine.

There were no other large-engined sports cars made in England, although several fine fast tourers made their appearance. The R-type Bentley Continental coupé introduced in 1952 had the distinction of being the most expensive British car at the time (£7,326), and also one of the most beautiful cars ever made. It had a gently-sloping fast-back body by H. J. Mulliner; in overall length it was 7in longer than the standard saloon, but thanks to light alloy construction it was 4½cwt lighter. Maximum speed was 117mph. A total of 193 Mulliner Continentals were made, exactly 100 being sold on the home market. The name Continental was carried by later Bentleys of the S series, but they were heavier cars without the outstanding grace of the R-type. Despite larger engines, their performance was inferior as well. A 1960 S.2 Continental with 6·2-litre V-8 engine was nearly three miles per hour slower than the 4½-litre R-type of 1953.

After making saloons and drophead coupés since 1946, Jensen introduced a Gran Turismo car for 1954. This was the 541 powered by a 130bhp Austin 4-litre engine. It had a fibreglass four-seater body and a maximum speed with overdrive of 116mph. Disc brakes were fitted in 1956, but little major change was made until 1963 when the Austin engine was replaced by a Chrysler V-8. It was not a sports car, but an interesting entry into the new high perform-ance Gran Turismo category.

Apart from the better-known sports cars so far described, the 1950s saw a host of small makes in two categories not previously seen in England – or indeed anywhere else. These categories, which often overlapped, were the kit car which could be assembled at home by a reasonably competent amateur mechanic, and the sports/racing car not intended for ordinary road use. Some of these makes died quickly, while others went on to become well-known cars of the 1960s. Engines were generally by Ford, or Coventry-Climax. The latter firm was as invaluable to the small British sports car maker of the 1950s as the Ruby had been to their French equivalents thirty years before. One make which began as a humble home-made special and has become a household word is Lotus. This appeared in 1949 as an Austin Seven-engined trials special; re-engined with a Ford Ten, it was entered successfully for hill-climbs and speed trials. 1951 saw the Mark 3 with tuned Austin Seven engine, independent front suspension, and ultra-lightweight aluminium body. This was entered in club events by Colin Chapman, its designer, builder, and driver. All work on it was done in spare time, and Chapman did not give up his job with the British Aluminium Company until 1955, by which time he had made over thirty cars. The Mark 3's performance was infinitely better than one would have suspected from its crude appear-ance, and observers soon realised that here was evidence of a 'special' builder quite out of the ordinary. Another trials car followed, and in 1952 Chapman went into production with the Mark 6. This was a two-seater

Aston Martin DBR1/300 which won the 1,000km Race at the Nürburgring 1958. (Photo: Montagu Motor Museum)

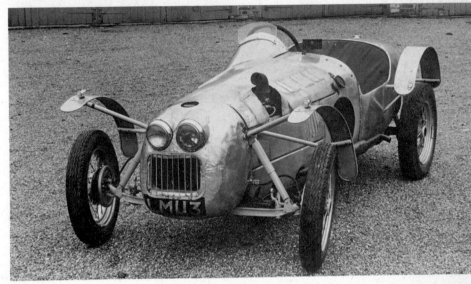

A far cry from the sleek Elan and Europa: the 1951 Lotus Mark 3 with tuned Austin Seven engine. (Photo: C. Crossthwaite)

sports car with multi-tube frame, simple aluminium body and i.f.s. The original engine was a Ford Consul with stroke shortened to give a capacity of under 1,500cc. It was sold in kit form, so any reasonable engine could be fitted. Among these were the Ford Ten, 1,098cc Coventry-Climax, and various M.G. units from the 746cc J 4 to a 1½-litre. The Mark 6 was very successful in Club racing, and about 100 were made by 1957 when it was replaced by the Mark 7. This was a similar functional car with simple doorless two-seater body suitable for racing or road work, so long as the occupants were not too fussy about rain and draughts. Engines were Ford Ten or Coventry Climax. Meanwhile Chapman's ambitions extended beyond such simple machinery, and in 1954 he built his first aerodynamic sports car, the Mark 8. In this he was aided by a de Havilland's employee Frank Costin, who was later responsible for the Marcos (see page 279). The Mark 8 had a low, wide, all-enveloping body on a complex space frame. Maintenance had to be carried out through small gaps in the frame. Engines were either 1,497cc M.G. or 1,098cc Coventry-Climax. Later cars in the series were the Mark 9 with de Dion axle, made in two forms, the Climax-engined Le Mans, and the Ford-engined Club, the Bristol-engined Mark 10, and the improved Ford or Climax-engined Mark 11. A Climax-engined Mark 11 had a maximum speed of 115mph, but it is difficult to generalize about speeds as so many modifications to engines were carried out by owners. The Mark 9s and 11s were very successful when running well, but inclined to be temperamental. The simpler Mark 6 was more reliable, and more profitable for the firm.

235

1957 saw the first closed Lotus, and one of the prettiest cars ever made by the firm. This was the Mark 14 Elite, a fibreglass monocoque coupé with 1,216cc single ohc Coventry-Climax engine specially made for Lotus. This developed 75bhp, giving a maximum speed of 112mph. The Elite had all-round independent suspension and disc brakes on all wheels. It was the first Lotus intended primarily for road use, but was not entirely satisfactory because of maintenance problems and the high noise level in the closed body. However, it achieved many racing successes, including a class win at Nürburgring in 1959 and at Le Mans every year from 1959 to 1964. It was also widely used in club racing, one of the drivers who gained experience in Elites being Jim Clark. 988 Elites were made up to 1963, when the model was replaced by the Ford-engined open two-seater Elan. Meanwhile the sports-racing Mark 11 had been replaced by the Mark 15 with canted engine and 5-speed gearbox on the rear axle. Engines were usually 1,475cc Coventry-Climaxes, although 2-litre units were also offered. In 1960 the company was divided into two groups: Lotus Cars Ltd who made complete cars and supervised the racing programme and Lotus Components Ltd who made the kits. Both were located in a new factory at Cheshunt, Hertfordshire.

Lotus' Grand Prix rival, Cooper, also made sports cars, although these never played such a large part in the firm's programme as did Lotus sports cars, and there was never a Cooper equivalent to the popular Elite and Elan. The first Cooper sports was a 1947 prototype with a rear-mounted 500cc J.A.P. engine, followed by front-engined cars powered by Vauxhall Wyvern or M.G. units. Very few of these were made, and the most significant sports Cooper was the rear-engined Climax car of 1955. This was strictly a sports/racing car, with central driving position which gave no place for a passenger. Its low front and squared-off Kamm-profile tail set a fashion for such cars which has lasted into the 1960s. In 1958 this car was called the Monaco, a catalogued sports car for 1½- or 2-litre Coventry-Climax engines. About thirty were made.

Another sports car with centre steering was the M.G.-engined Kieft of 1953. The driver sat between the main frame members and a nominal passenger's seat was outrigged from the main frame at one side. Later Kiefts had conventional seating, and engines by Coventry-Climax, Bristol, and de Soto.

1954 Kieft with Coventry-Climax engine.
(Photo: Charles Dunn)

An 1,100cc Climax-engined car with all-round independent suspension ran at Le Mans in 1954, and won its class in that year's Tourist Trophy. It was catalogued at £1,560 and shown at Earl's Court, but fewer than six cars were sold.

There were numerous small firms offering kit cars. One of the most popular among amateur builders was Buckler of Reading. The first Buckler was a 'special' built in 1947 with Ford 10 engine, tubular frame, and independent front suspension. Most were two-seaters, although the long wheelbase Mark VI could carry four-seater bodywork. Bodies were either narrow, with cycle-type wings, or all-enveloping, made of light alloy or fibreglass. It is hard to generalize as Buckler components were supplied to customer's requirements, but all had tubular frames and independent front suspension, and the majority used Ford engines. Later Bucklers had B.M.C. engines and components, while the most powerful, the DD-2, had all-round independent suspension with de Dion rear axle and was intended to take any engine up to 2 litres. Throughout the 1950s, Bucklers competed in races, trials, sprints, and hill-climbs, being among the best-regarded kit cars. About 500 chassis were built, including a few complete cars.

The Fairthorpe Electron of 1956 was a simple fibreglass two-seater powered by a 1,098cc Coventry-Climax engine. At £1,050 it was one of the cheapest cars to use this unit, but a year later there came an even cheaper Fairthorpe, the Electron Minor, powered by the 948cc Standard Ten engine. Later Fairthorpes included the Ford Zephyr-powered Zeta, and the Rockette with 6-cylinder Triumph Vitesse engine. All were available in kit form, or fully-assembled. Other kit cars included the Ashley with open or saloon fibreglass bodies, and Ford or B.M.C. engines, and the Falcon with Ford, M.G.A., or Coventry-Climax engines. Both these firms made fibreglass body shells for sale separately, and supplemented their business by such activities as making hard tops for Austin-Healey Sprites. Turner of Wolverhampton made a wide variety of sports cars, some to special order, with Ford, Lea-Francis, Vauxhall, or Coventry-Climax engines. The Turner made in the largest numbers was the light two-seater powered by the 948cc B.M.C. 'A' engine, in production from 1957 to 1965. A tuned version was made by Alexander Engineering of Haddenham, Buckinghamshire, with cross-flow light alloy

A supercharged Buckler driven by Derek Buckler at Brunton Hill Climb in September 1952.
(Photo: Charles Dunn)

A 948cc Turner at Mallory Park.
(Photo: Autosport)

A Lister with Chevrolet Corvette engine at Lime Rock, Connecticut, in June 1958.
(Photo: Autosport)

cylinder head giving 60bhp compared with 45bhp from the standard engine. An Alexander-Turner won the 1959 *Autosport* Championship. T.V.R. became more famous in the 1960s, but the familiar squat shape appeared in 1957 with the Grantura fibreglass coupé. It had Coventry-Climax or Ford 100E engines, and was sold in the United States under the name Jomar.

There were a few other interesting small-production cars not made in kit form such as the Lister and the Tojeiro. The former was the product of a small engineering works at Cambridge. The first Listers had simple tubular frames with coil independent suspension and M.G. or Bristol engines. The one-armed driver Archie Scott-Brown achieved many successes with these cars. From 1957 to 1959 Jaguar engines of 3·4 or 3·8 litres were used, Stirling Moss and Ivor Bueb being among the drivers. In May 1959 a highly stream-lined space-frame designed by Frank Costin and intended to use Jaguar or Chevrolet Corvette engines appeared, but only one or two were made. Listers were never on general sale, being made only to the special order of racing drivers. In 1959 the company gave up motorcars for general engineering, after about fifty machines had been made. Tojeiro of Royston, Hertfordshire, also made use of Jaguar engines in their most powerful ver-sion, although earlier cars used M.G., Bristol, or Coventry-Climax units. The Tojeiro design formed the basis of the 1953 A.C. Ace (see page 226). The last Tojeiros were rear-engined coupés powered by 2,495cc Coventry-Climax engines, and built for Ecurie Ecosse. One ran at Le Mans in 1962, but retired.

The existence of all these small firms was an indication of the widespread enthusiasm for motor sport in Britain in the 1950s. Many club meetings were held every summer weekend all over the country. Few of the drivers were particularly rich, nor indeed were the companies whose cars they drove, yet they all had a great deal of fun. These small firms had no parallel in other countries, the nearest being Italy with her many Fiat-derived sports car makes.

For the enthusiast, either for sporting or luxury cars, the post-war French story is a very sad one. In 1946 many of the firms which had been making such cars before the war announced plans for resumed production, and some succeeded for a while, but by 1960 none of the great names survived, and all French sporting cars were derivations of the mass-produced Panhard or Renaults. This sad state of affairs is usually blamed on crippling taxation, by which any car with a rating of over 15CV paid a tax equivalent to nearly £100 per year. Also, an expensive car was one of the chief visible signs of wealth by which the owner's income tax was assessed. Another factor was the rigid National Plan imposed on French manufacturers by the Government. By this, a firm's range was decided by bureaucrats, and many interesting designs were stifled at birth because they did not fit in with the National Plan. For example, Hotchkiss had a promising prototype with a roomy five-seater body and 1,100cc ohv engine, as a successor to the Amilcar-Compound which they had made before the war. With this they might have reached a large market, and thus made enough profit to keep their more expensive cars going as well, rather as Rolls-Royce maintained car production only because of their much more significant aero engine activities. However, the French government decided that there were enough cheap family cars made by other firms, and that Hotchkiss must make expensive cars only. This they did for several years, but dwindling markets eventually forced them to abandon cars altogether. Another interesting small car lost to French motorists in this manner was the Mathis 3-wheeled aerodynamic saloon.

Four firms resumed production of expensive cars in France after the war, Delahaye and its sister marque Delage, Talbot, and Hotchkiss. Delahaye re-introduced the 6-cylinder 3½-litre Type 135, as well as the smaller 4-cylinder 134. Power of the former was up to 130bhp, and a wide variety of coachwork was fitted by *carrossiers* such as Chapron, Saoutchik, and Figoni et Falaschi. However they were *concours d'elegance* cars rather than sports cars, and there was no return to the stark sports-racing Type 135s of pre-war days.

The only new Delahaye was the 4½-litre Type 175, introduced in 1948. Output was 185bhp, giving a speed of over 100mph, and the cars were equipped with hydraulic brakes. However, they were very expensive and found few buyers. For their final model, the Type 235, Delahaye returned to the 3½-litre engine, but clothed the car with new all-enveloping coachwork. This model was made from 1951 to 1954 when car production ceased altogether. The associated firm of Delage also re-introduced a pre-war design, the 3-litre D.6. This was simply a smaller Delahaye, with the same range of bodies to which a seven-seater limousine was added. No sports model was catalogued, although one ran at Le Mans in 1949, coming 2nd behind a 2-litre Ferrari. Hotchkiss re-introduced the 686 6-cylinder 3½-litre sports saloon, supplemented by a smaller four of 2·3 litres. The 686 finally acquired i.f.s. in 1948, and a more modern body with faired-in headlamps came in 1950, but otherwise there was little change in the design. With this model, Hotchkiss won the Monte Carlo Rally in 1949 and 1950, making a total of six victories in this event. Although Hotchkiss made a larger number of cars than the other French luxury manufacturers, they did not survive beyond 1954.

The Talbot-Lago story was more sporting than that of its rivals. The $4\frac{1}{2}$-litre 6-cylinder engine was used in a Formula 1 racing car which had the advantage over the $1\frac{1}{2}$-litre supercharged cars of being able to complete a race without refuelling. These competed regularly from 1947 to 1951, while a two-seater version with sketchy road equipment won the 1950 Le Mans 24 Hour Race, with Louis Rosier at the wheel. This was the last time that a French car won this classic event, although Levegh's Talbot very nearly did so in 1952, after an heroic single-handed drive in which he was finally eliminated by a broken con-rod. The production Talbot-Lagos had 170bhp engines, and carried handsome saloon and drophead coupé bodies in the pre-war style. Some very exotic coupés were built by Saoutchik and other coachbuilders. In 1949 the name Baby was revived for a 2·7-litre four with similar styling to the larger cars. This came in several body styles, but in 1954, with sales dwindling, production was concentrated on one model, a 4-cylinder $2\frac{1}{2}$-litre Gran Turismo coupé. This was a handsome, up-to-date car, with 115bhp engine, and a maximum speed of 120mph. However, the home market was very small, and on the international market it had to compete with such makes as Jaguar, Aston Martin, and Ferrari. About seventy were made before Tony Lago took the sad step of buying a proprietary engine for cheaper and greater power, as he lacked the resources to develop such an engine himself. The unit he chose was the 2·6-litre V-8 B.M.W. By 1957 production was down to two cars per week, and two workshops were let out to other firms. In 1958 Lago sold out to Simca, and the last Talbots used the old side-valve Ford V-8 engine from the Simca Vedette, in the same body shell as the Talbot- and B.M.W.-engined cars had used. Production ended in 1960.

A smaller quality car was the Salmson. This was a fairly staid touring car until 1953 when the G.72 appeared. It was a two/four-seater GT coupé powered by a tuned version of the 2·3-litre twin-cam engine used in the saloons. Maximum speed was over 100mph. Although made in small numbers, it was quite successful in competition, coming 2nd overall in the 1955 Liège-Rome-Liège Rally. Open versions ran at Le Mans in 1955 and 1957, while the 1956 Le Mans car was a standard coupé with full upholstery and even a radio. Production ended in 1957, after Renault had acquired the Salmson company.

The post-war Bugatti story is a sad one, although the hopes of Bugattistes were kept alive for several years. Before Ettore died in August 1947, he planned the production of two new cars, a 370cc minicar powered by a minute 4-cylinder twin-ohc engine and a $1\frac{1}{2}$-litre sports and racing car with a single overhead camshaft. Only one prototype of the minicar and possibly two of the larger machine were built. The nearest to a production car that Bugatti came after the war was the Type 101, a modified Type 57 with all-enveloping coachwork and chain-driven camshafts, as on the 1939 prototype Type 64. It appeared four years after Ettore's death, under the direction of Pierre Marco who was to guide the Bugatti firm for what remained of its lifetime. The Type 101 was made as a saloon and as a drophead coupé, and there was also a supercharged version, the 101C. It was very expensive, costing three million francs, or over £3,000. Not more than twenty were sold. Apart from an unsuccessful Grand Prix racing car, the Type 101 was the last Bugatti made, although rumours of new models persisted up to 1960. These were finally dispelled when the Bugatti factory was taken over by Hispano-Suiza, themselves no longer car makers, in July 1963.

Just as the old luxury cars were disappearing, a new make arrived briefly to enliven the French motoring scene. This was the Facel Vega, the first of the post-war generation of Euro-American hybrids. With a $4\frac{1}{2}$-litre 180bhp

Chrysler V-8 engine, the 1954 Facel Vega had a maximum speed of 115mph, and carried very handsome coupé bodywork by Facel-Métallon, S.A. They were never entered in competitions, but were interesting examples of the really fast, luxurious 'businessman's express' exemplified in the next decade by the Jensen Interceptor, Iso Rivolta, and Monteverdi. By 1962 the Facel had a 390bhp 6·3-litre Chrysler engine, giving a maximum speed of 135mph. Alongside the larger cars was made the Facellia, with similar styling and a 1·6-litre twin-ohc 4-cylinder engine of Facel's own design and manufacture. This gave 118bhp, and 106mph, but was unreliable. Later Facellias, known as Facel IIIs, used Volvo or Austin-Healey 3000 engines, but production of all models ceased in 1964.

A curious survival from pre-war dàys, and even from the 1920s, was the Lambert. Although the pre-war cars of Germain Lambert had been largely experimental, the post-war 1,100cc sports cars with almost vintage lines were made for sale in small numbers. The engine was a 4-cylinder ohv unit, described as a Lambert-Ruby for Ruby themselves were no longer in business, but of similar dimensions to the classic engine. The frame was tubular, and suspension was non-independent by semi-elliptic springs. Three models were made, the Grand Sport with very simple aluminium body and cycle-type wings, the Sport Luxe with greater comfort and more flowing lines, and the Modèle Course with twin carburetters and racing body. All these models could be supplied with a supercharger if desired. Speeds varied from 75–100mph according to model. Germain Lambert competed regularly in the Bol d'Or from 1947 to 1951, winning his class in the latter year. Succumbing to fashion, the 1952 Lambert had an all-enveloping coupé body by Schmitt, but very few were made. With more resources behind him, Lambert could have provided young Frenchmen with a popular sports car similar to the M.G. or Morgan 4-4.

Apart from the cars mentioned, French sports cars were confined to derivatives of small saloons. This is not to disparage them, for some remarkable little machines were made. Two cars formed the basis for these: Panhard and Renault. The flat-twin front-wheel-drive Dyna-Panhard saloon appeared in 1946, with a 610cc 28bhp engine. This was replaced by a 750cc 32bhp unit in 1950, of which a sports version, the 38bhp Junior, appeared in 1953. Special Panhards ran regularly at Le Mans in the 1950s, winning the Index of Performance in 1950, 1951, 1952, and 1953. These Le Mans cars were actually called Monopoles, as they were entered by the Ecurie Monopole. They had streamlined bodies quite unlike any production Dyna-Panhards, and highly-tuned engines. Several other firms came to fame with Dyna-powered cars. The most successful of these was D.B., a small sports car made by Charles Deutsch and René Bonnet. This appeared in 1948 with a 610cc engine, but production did not get seriously under way until the early 1950s, by which time 750cc engines were used. Bodies were alloy until 1955 when a new and more bulbous fibreglass design appeared. This model had a 48bhp 850cc engine, and a maximum speed of 96mph. A belt-driven supercharger was available. Most production D.B.s were coupés, but open models were also made, and these were very successful in racing. One of these, driven by G. Laureau, won the 1954 Tourist Trophy outright, and D.B.s have won the Index of Performance at Le Mans in 1954, 1956, 1959, 1960, and 1961. In 1961 the partnership was dissolved, Deutsch joining Panhard as a technical adviser, while Bonnet continued under his own name, making Renault-based sports cars. Several other makes used Dyna-Panhard engines, including the Marathon coupé which had its engine at the rear, the Arista, and the Moroccan-built R.E.A.C. The engine was also used by the German Veritas company (see page 249).

50. *1967 Shelby Cobra 427 CS hardtop coupé. This is one of the thirty-six Competition Street Cobras built. Owned by Michael B. Clark. (Photo: William S. Jackson)*

Left, above: Louis Rosier's victorious Talbot-Lago at Le Mans in 1950. (Photo: Autocar)

Left, below: The Salmson G.72 coupé which ran at Le Mans in 1956 complete with radio. (Photo: Motor)

Right: 1950 Lambert Grand Sport. (Photo: Lucien Loreille Collection)

Below: 750cc D.B. Coupé at Le Mans in 1957. (Photo: Motor)

1954 Alpine A 106 Mille Miles coupé. This prototype was similar to the first production models of 1955. (Photo: Anthony Pritchard Collection)

The most famous make based on the rear-engined Renault was the Alpine. This used the 750cc 4-cylinder engine and transmission, with a fibreglass two-seater coupé body. Driven by its designer/builder Jean Rédéle, it first appeared in the 1955 Mille Miglia, and won its class in this event the following year. In 1957 open and closed models were offered, while engine options included 845cc and 904cc units, the latter giving a speed of 103mph. The Alpine went on to greater successes in the 1960s. Other Renault-based cars included the Ferry, V.P., and B.G., but these were prototypes built for Le Mans, without any production outcome. There were also some non-sporting convertibles using Renault components, of which the best known was the Autobleu with Chapron coachwork.

From 1949 onwards Simca included a so-called sports coupé in their range, but it was a promenader rather than a sports car. Carrying names such as Week-End and Coupé de Ville, it was, as *The Motor* said, 'A car which seems to enjoy a certain vogue with the elegant young ladies of Paris.' Such styles were still to be found at the top end of the Aronde range in 1961. More serious were the Simca-Gordinis, derived by Amédée Gordini. The 1·4-litre engine had hemispherical combustion chambers, and a 5-bearing crankshaft, and developed 84bhp. With lightweight open bodies, these Simca-Gordinis won their class at Spa in 1948, and open cars and coupés ran at Le Mans. In 1951 Gordini set up as a manufacturer on his own, but although he struggled on for seven years very few cars left his factory. He made a wide range of racing and sports cars; among the latter was a twin-ohc 2·3-litre 6-cylinder car which developed 175bhp. It had all-round independent suspension by torsion bars and wishbones. This car was followed by a 3-litre straight-8 with 5-speed gearbox, but neither progressed beyond the prototype stage. In 1957 Gordini joined Renault to work on a high-performance version of the Dauphine saloon.

At the end of the war in 1945 the German motor industry had virtually nothing to show but rubble and wrecked machinery. Within a year, production of some touring cars had started, and a few sporting events were held. The only German car to compete in these early events, mostly hill-climbs, was the B.M.W. Typ 328, and when new competition cars appeared they were, at first, all based on this remarkable car. Racing cars included the A.F.M. and the Monopol, but the best-known B.M.W.-based sports car was the Veritas. Designed by Ernst Loof, this had the 1,971cc 6-cylinder engine installed in a tubular frame, with light metal bodywork. Three bodies were available, the Scorpion convertible, the Saturn fixed head coupé, and the Comet sports/racing car, the latter with engine tuned to give 140bhp, and 135mph. All Veritas had twin-wishbone independent front suspension and de Dion rear axles. In 1950 came a new engine with single overhead camshaft and 1,988cc capacity, built for Veritas by the Heinkel aircraft company. This again was available in various stages of tune, from 100bhp to 140bhp. Five-speed gearboxes were used, controlled from the steering column on the coupés, but with a floor change on the sports cars. From 1948 to 1951 Veritas entered sports and racing cars in many German meetings at circuits such as the Nürburgring, Hockenheim, the Grenzlandring, and Solitude. They had no international competition at that time, and did very well. Political feeling prevented German cars from competing abroad until the early 1950s, so Veritas had little chance to pit their cars against foreign competition. Sales were strictly limited, only forty cars being made in five years of production, which saw two reformations of the company and changes of address. Another car made from 1950 to 1952 was the Dyna-Veritas. This had a tuned Dyna-Panhard 745cc flat-twin engine giving 55bhp and Veritas-styled bodies built by Baur of Stuttgart.

The other German sports car to use B.M.W. engines came from East Germany. This was the E.M.W. (Eisenacher Motoren Werke), made at the

1950 Veritas Saturn coupé.
(Photo: Autocar)

1957 Borgward Rennsport at Salzburg–Gaisberg Hill Climb. (Photo: Autocar)

former B.M.W. works at Eisenach, Thuringia. Although they made a few cabriolets similar to the pre-war B.M.W. 327, their first sports car had the same cylinder head design as fitted to the improved Veritas and a Hirth roller-bearing crankshaft. These engines were mostly fitted to Formula 2 racing cars, and later E.M.W. sports cars had newly-designed 1½-litre 6-cylinder engines with twin overhead camshafts. These gave 130bhp at 7,000rpm in 1954, and 155bhp by 1956 when E.M.W.'s sporting programme came to an end. The cars were strictly for competitions, and none was made for sale. Indeed, there were few buyers for cars of any kind in the German Democratic Republic at that time. E.M.W. operated a State-aided racing programme with highly-streamlined cars, their fastest models reaching 155mph at the AVUS circuit in 1955. The later cars were called A.W.E.s (Automobil Werke Eisenach). Their leading driver was Edgar Barth, who was five times East German champion, although he achieved most of his success at the wheel of Formula 2 racing cars.

B.M.W. themselves did not re-enter car production until 1952, as their car plant at Eisenach was behind the Iron Curtain, and their Munich plant had been confined to motorcycle production. When new cars emerged from Munich, they used the well-tried 1,971cc engine with new saloon bodies. A new 2·6-litre V-8 engine supplemented the six in 1954, and the first sports car was the Type 507 with 140bhp 3·2-litre V-8 engine, introduced in 1955. The 507 had a short wheelbase of 8ft 1in, light two-seater body, and, with the highest axle ratio, a top speed of 130mph. However, it was very expensive and never became a serious rival to the Mercedes Benz 300SL. Production from 1956 to 1960 was 250 cars. In the late 1950s, B.M.W. were concentrating mainly on small 2-cylinder cars, and there were no more sports cars until the 1800 series was introduced in 1962.

Baron von Hanstein's Porsche 356 at Silverstone in 1953. (Photo: Guy Griffiths Motofoto)

Borgward made a number of sports/racing cars derived from their family saloons. The standard 1949 Hansa had a 1½-litre 52bhp ohv engine whose power was increased to 66bhp in a special car built for record breaking at Montlhéry in 1950. This was the basis of the Rennsport coupés and open two-seaters which Borgward fielded in German events from 1952 to 1955. For 1956 the Rennsport had a twin-cam engine giving 130bhp, tubular frame, and de Dion rear axle. They achieved no striking victories, but came 2nd in the German Sports Car Championship and German Hill Climb Championship in 1958, being defeated by Porsche in each case. No Borgward sports cars were sold to the public, but the lessons of racing were applied in the 75bhp TS version of the Isabella saloon, and there was an attractively-styled three-seater sports coupé in the range for a while.

The name of Ferdinand Porsche has been connected with motor cars since 1898, but it was not until 1948 that a production car appeared bearing the famous name. In its final conception, this was the work of Ferry Porsche, the celebrated designer's son, who worked on the car in Austria while his father was in a French prison camp just after the war. The new car was given the number 356, as it was the 356th design study since Porsche set up his studio at Stuttgart in 1931. It was initially a roadster version of the Volkswagen, with the same 1,131cc engine, placed ahead of the rear axle for better road-holding, and light metal two-seater body. Later cars had the engine behind the axle as on the Volkswagen; ideal road-holding had to be sacrificed for reasonable luggage accommodation. Fifty coupés were made at Gmünd, Austria, before Porsche moved to Stuttgart where they have been ever since. The capacity was reduced to 1,086cc to bring them within the 1,100cc competition class. International competition began with the 1951 Le Mans race, when two coupés with spats on all four wheels won their class,

1956 Porsche RS Le Mans coupé.
(Photo: Motor)

repeating the performance in 1952. New models for 1951 included the 1300 with 1,286cc 44bhp engine, and the 1500 with 1,488cc and 60bhp. All these were variants of the basic Type 356 which remained in production until 1965. Like its cousin the Volkswagen, it was gradually improved over the years, so that the last models had scarcely a component that had not been modified, but the overall appearance was little changed. Most cars were the familiar coupés, although a number of convertibles were made as well. The final Type 356S/C of 1965 gave 95bhp from a 1,582cc engine, and had a maximum speed of 112mph. In 1953 a sports/racing version was developed, with four overhead camshafts and roller-bearing crankshaft. Known as the 550RS, this engine developed 100bhp. Porsche built 100 of the open Spyder model in order to achieve homologation, and then installed the 550RS engine in the 356 coupé body, this model being known as the Carrera. Maximum speed was approximately 125mph.

The post-war sporting story of Mercedes-Benz began in 1951 when they introduced the Typ 300. This had a single ohc 2,996cc 130bhp engine, and was originally a 4-door saloon or cabriolet. Less than a year later came an attractive short wheelbase coupé, the 300S. For the 1952 Le Mans race, Mercedes produced three striking coupés called the 300SL. These used the 300S engine tuned to give 215bhp, and canted at an angle to allow for a low bonnet. They had lightweight streamlined bodies with gull-wing doors. In the race the cars of H. Lang/F. Riess and L. Helfrich/H. Niedermayer finished 1st and 2nd. Production versions of the 300SL came onto the market early in 1954, with modified styling, but still using the gull-wing doors. The production cars had 240bhp engines, with fuel injection in place of carburetters. With a maximum speed of 150mph, they were the fastest road cars of the time. The gull-wings were dropped in 1956, but production of the 300SL continued until 1963, by which time 3,250 had been made.

For the 1954 season Mercedes-Benz returned to Formula 1 racing, building the 2½-litre straight-8 W196. A 3-litre version of this engine was used in sports car racing in 1955, the car being known as the 300SLR. Despite its name, this had nothing in common with the production 300SL except its capacity, and even this was slightly smaller at 2,979cc. It developed 300bhp, and gave the car a speed of 180mph. This remarkable machine won nearly all the major sports car events in 1955, including the Mille Miglia (Stirling Moss), the Nürburgring 1,000km (Fangio), Tourist Trophy (Moss), and Targa Florio (Moss). It would almost certainly have won at Le Mans as well, but the team was withdrawn after Levegh's car had crashed into the crowd, killing the driver and a large number of spectators. A total of nine 300SLRs were made, including two gull-wing coupés. One of these was used as a road car by chief engineer Rudi Uhlenhaut. Since 1955 Mercedes-Benz have not sponsored a works team of sports or racing cars, and apart from the occasional privately-entered 300SL the great name did not figure in sporting results after the 300SLR's one glorious year.

There were no other German sports cars to compare with those mentioned so far. Sporting versions of the Goliath and Gutbrod 2-cylinder light cars were made, the latter reaching 75mph from a 600cc fuel-injection engine. A vehicle not normally thought of as a sports car, but with remarkable performance, was the Messerschmitt Tiger. Most Messerschmitts were tandem two-seater 3-wheelers, with 175cc or 200cc engines, and very limited performance, but in 1958 Messerschmitt added another wheel at the rear and gave the car a 500cc 25bhp engine. With this, a speed of over 80mph was attainable. One of these Tigers won the London Motor Club Cats' Eyes Rally in 1958.

After the paucity of Italian sports cars made in the 1930s, the post-war period saw a remarkable renaissance. On the one hand, the great makes of Alfa Romeo and Lancia were joined by a remarkable newcomer, Ferrari, while on the other there was a proliferation of small makers whose cars were derived from the Fiat 1100.

For their first post-war car, Alfa Romeo revived the 6-cylinder 2500, now with steering column gearchange and more modern body styling. Three versions were made, the Touring, Sport, and Super Sport, with outputs varying from 90bhp to 105bhp. In addition, there was a special competition coupé, the 2500 Competizione, with short wheelbase, and engine tuned to give 145bhp. This had a maximum speed of 130mph. Only three were built, of which two ran in the 1950 Mille Miglia. The 2500 was made until 1953, but was supplemented in 1950 by a completely new car, the 1900. This had a 1,884cc twin ohc engine developing 80bhp. Not only was this a new design, but it marked a great change in Alfa Romeo policy, being an integral construction saloon aimed at a mass market and produced in really large numbers. Whereas production of few earlier Alfa models reached four figures, nearly 20,000 1900s were made between 1950 and 1958. Most were 4-door saloons, but there were several sporting variants. The TI (Turismo Internazionale) used the same body, but had an engine tuned to give 99bhp. Maximum speed was 105mph, but some special cars were further tuned to give 120bhp at 6,000rpm, and a speed of 115mph. As so often happens, this extra power had to be paid for in uncertain temperament, and only 650 TIs were made. A parallel model was the 1900 Sprint with the same engine and 2-door coupé body. The 1900 Super was a more reliable car with larger engine (1,975cc) and a lower speed. Although the standard 1900 had integral construction, a separate chassis model was available for the many special coachbuilders who tried out their art on the 1900.

In 1954 a new small Alfa appeared, the 1,290cc Giulietta. In its original form this was a 2-door coupé, but this was joined by a 4-door saloon and, later, by an open sports model, the Spider Veloce. The saloon bodies were made by Alfa Romeo, the open cars by Pininfarina, and the coupés by Bertone, together with a few special sports coupés by Zagato. The first Giulietta engine developed 60bhp at 5,500rpm, but in later form it was giving over 100bhp. The 1962 Spider Veloce had a maximum speed of 120mph, while the SZ with lightweight Zagato body could reach 130mph. When it was finally withdrawn in 1962, the Giulietta had sold over 157,000 units.

Besides these mass-produced sports cars, Alfa Romeo built a number of special competition cars in the 1950s. Among these were the Dischi Volanti (Flying Saucers), so called because of their flat, all-enveloping body shape. They were originally powered by a 6-cylinder 2,995cc version of the 1900 engine, intended as a design study for a 3-litre saloon which was never built. In 1953 four Disco Volante coupés were entered for the Mille Miglia, one with a 4-cylinder 2-litre engine, and the others with the 6-cylinder engine enlarged to 3,576cc. Each of these three, driven by Sanesi, Fangio, and Kling, led the race at one time or another, but Marzotto's Ferrari eventually won, Fangio coming 2nd. Later in 1953 the three 3½-litre cars ran at Le

Alfa Romeo 1900C Super Sprint coupé.
(Photo: Alfa Romeo SpA)

Mans, Spa, and the Nürburgring, but, although fast, they proved unreliable. Unless a great deal more money had been spent on them, they would have damaged Alfa's prestige, and so they were raced no more after the 1953 season. Nine Dischi Volanti were made in all, although the later ones had bodies considerably modified from the original 'saucer' shape. Another interesting prototype was the 2000 Sportiva of 1954. It was powered by the enlarged 1900 engine used in the smaller Disco Volante, which gave 138bhp at 6,500rpm. A maximum speed of 137mph was claimed, and it was made in open two-seater and GT coupé forms. Had it been produced, it would have provided interesting competition for the 2-litre Ferrari and Maserati A6GCS, as well as being a very desirable 'business man's express'. *The Motor* described it as 'something like every Italian's ambition at the moment'. However Alfa Romeo were just getting into stride with the mass-produced Giulietta, and were not interested in an expensive, small-production car. Only four Sportivas were made.

Up to 1950 Lancia built cars of pre-war design, the Ardea and Aprilia saloons. In that year the Aurelia saloon was announced, in many ways a similar concept to the Aprilia, being a roomy 4-door pillarless saloon of integral construction. The engine was a narrow-angle V-6 of 1,754cc, developing 56bhp. A standard saloon won the 2-litre touring car class in the 1950 Mille Miglia. The following year there appeared a G.T. coupé version of the Aurelia, known as the Aurelia B.20. This had a 2-door two/four-seater body, and was powered by a 1,991cc engine also used in the 1951 saloons. In the B.20 this developed 75bhp, giving the car a maximum speed of 112mph. The B.20 became a most successful competition car. For the first three years of its career it had a distinguished racing record, and when superseded on the track by more modern cars it continued to do well in rallies. Bracco and Maglioli came 2nd in the 1951 Mille Miglia, behind Villoresi's Ferrari, and ahead of another Ferrari. Lancia won the 2-litre class at Le Mans the same year, and in 1952 came 1st, 2nd, and 3rd in the Targa Florio. A supercharged B.20 was 4th in the 1952 Carrera Panamericana in Mexico. In 1953 B.20, known as the 3rd Series, had its capacity enlarged to 2,451cc, giving 118bhp. This model won the 1953 Liège-Rome-Liège and 1954 Monte Carlo Rallies, drivers being Johnny Claes and Louis Chiron respectively. An open two-seater with body by Pininfarina was available in 1954, but the coupé was better looking and remained more popular. The 1954 4th series had a de Dion rear axle, but otherwise there was little change in the B.20 design until it was dropped in 1959. It was a much respected car, and one of the last which could win its class at Le Mans and still be a practical machine for everyday use.

The other Lancia sports cars of the 1950s were specialized competition machines with no commercial equivalents. The D.20 coupé of 1953 was powered by a 2,983cc V-6 engine derived from the Aurelia design, but with twin-ohc. It had a completely new tubular frame and all-independent suspension by transverse leaf springs. Both front and rear brakes were mounted inboard. With one of these cars Maglioli won the 1953 Targa Florio. Four cars ran at Le Mans in 1953, with capacities reduced to 2,693cc and Roots-type superchargers. They were unsuccessful, their best lap speeds being over 15mph slower than those of the winning C-type Jaguars. After the D.23 open 3-litre model came the D.24, also an open two-seater which achieved remarkable success in the 1953 Carrera Panamericana. Lancia had already had experience of this event with the blown B.20 in 1952, and they were the only company to field a team for 1953. Three D.24s ran with engines enlarged to 3·3 litres, and developing 240bhp. The fourth car, driven by Castellotti, was a D.23. Bonetto's car crashed, killing its driver, but the others, driven by Fangio, Taruffi, and Castellotti, finished 1st, 2nd, and 3rd. 1954 victories included the Tour of Sicily, Mille Miglia, and Targa Florio, a remarkable trio for a firm which had only entered serious racing with specialised cars the year before. The Lancias were not entered for Le Mans, and the 3·7-litre D.25s were outperformed on handicap in the Tourist Trophy, which was won by a 745cc D.B. Even so, they came second in the Sports Car Constructors' Championship in 1954. Concentration on Grand Prix cars led Lancia to discontinue sports car racing after 1954. Not until the mid-1960s did the name Lancia figure significantly in sporting results, and then it was with the Flavia and Fulvia coupés in rallies.

One of the most famous names in post-war motor sport is Ferrari. Enzo Ferrari had managed the highly successful, unofficial works team for Alfa Romeo from 1929 to 1938 when Alfas resumed control of their racing activities. The first Ferrari car ran in the 1940 Mille Miglia under the name Auto Avio Costruzione because Enzo Ferrari had undertaken not to use his name in competitions for four years after leaving Alfas. Known as the Tipo 815, the car had a 1½-litre straight-8 engine made up of two Fiat Tipo 508 heads on a specially-cast light alloy block. Frames and suspension were largely Fiat, and the cars carried aerodynamic bodies by Touring. Only two were built, both ran in the Mille Miglia, and both retired. The first post-war Ferrari sports car appeared at the end of 1946, and was powered by a 118bhp 1½-litre V-12 engine later used in Ferrari Grand Prix cars. Designed by Giaochino Colombo, the cars had 5-speed gearboxes, tubular frames and independent front suspension. The body was a simple all-enveloping two-seater. This 1½-litre car was known as the Tipo 125; few were made, some were modified to Tipo 159, and some later converted to Tipo 166, with capacity enlarged to 1,992cc. This was made in three models, the 89bhp sport, 110bhp Inter, both usually carrying coupé coachwork, and the 140bhp Mille Miglia which was the competition model, and had a maximum speed of 136mph. With this model Ferrari won the 1948 Mille Miglia and Tour of Sicily, and the first post-war Le Mans race in 1949. Many lesser victories also fell to the 166; with this as with most other Ferrari models, it is possible to list only the major sporting achievements of an incredibly successful make. Develop-

51. Above: *1964 Lotus Elan 1·6-litre hardtop coupé (special off-white paint finish). Originally owned by the late Jim Clark. (Photo: Charles Pocklington)*

52. Below: *1965 Elva Courier 1·6-litre coupé. Owned and photographed by P. D. Filsell.*

ments of the 166 included the heavier and less successful 2·3-litre Tipo 195, the 2·6-litre Tipo 212, and the 2·7-litre Tipo 225. The next phase of Ferrari development was really a continuation of this theme, although design was now under the direction of Aurelio Lampredi. Capacity went up to 3,322cc and power to 270bhp on the 1950 Mille Miglia cars, but both retired in the race. Still pursuing power (to compete on the American market with the Cadillac-Allard) Ferrari took the 4·1-litre engine used in the 1950 Grand Prix car and put it in a new, sturdier frame, the new car receiving the type number 340. This was raced in both open and coupé form. These 340s won the 1951 and 1952 Mille Miglia races, but did not do especially well in other races, and acquired a reputation for dangerous handling. Tom Cole was killed in one at Le Mans in 1952, and at least two other private entrants died in these cars. Capacity was enlarged to 4,522cc in the Tipo 375, and finally to 4,954cc in the Tipo 410. This was the largest-engined Ferrari made, and achieved a number of successes, including Le Mans in 1953 and 1954 and the Carrera Panamericana in 1954. Production versions of these large cars were made under the designations 342 America and 375 America. They carried a wide variety of open and closed coachwork by all the leading Italian coach-builders. Probably the best-selling coachbuilder was Pininfarina. After 1955 Ferrari did not build large-capacity competition cars, but the big V-12 remained in production until 1966. Disc brakes were added in 1959.

Meanwhile Ferrari had been working on two other lines of development, 4- and 6-cylinder sports cars and a series of smaller V-12s. The 4-cylinder cars were developments of the Formula 2 racing cars, and were made in 2-litre (Mondial and Testa Rossa) forms as well as larger 2½-litre, 3-litre and 3·4-litre sizes. They were not notably successful in competitions, although a 3·4-litre Tipo 860 driven by Fangio won the 1956 Sebring 12 Hour Race. Although some competition cars were sold to private owners, they were not suitable for ordinary road use. No touring versions were made. The same applies to the 6-cylinder cars which were raced during the 1955 season only, without adding any lustre to the name of Ferrari. For 1956 Ferrari returned to V-12s, building a 2·9-litre 350bhp car for the Mille Miglia. Castellotti won at 85mph. A development of this car with 4,022cc engine and two camshafts per bank of cylinders ran in the 1957 Mille Miglia, Taruffi and von Trips coming 1st and 2nd. Another of these cars, driven by the Marquis de Portago crashed, killing the driver, passenger, and about twelve spectators. The furore resulting from this incident led to the end of the Mille Miglia in its traditional form as a road race from town to town. Among those who urged its abolition was Pope Pius XII, and since 1957 it has been merely a rally.

For 1958 the capacity of the V-12 was reduced to under 3 litres (2,953cc) as the Sports Car Constructors' Championship was limited to that capacity. The new model was known as the Testa Rossa (like the 2-litre 4-cylinder car, because the cylinder heads were painted red) and was one of the most successful of all Ferraris. With it, the firm easily gained the 1958 Championship, winning at Buenos Aires, Sebring, Le Mans, and in the Targa Florio. The touring version of the Testa Rossa was the 250 GT, which could be driven on the road and raced by private owners. The engine developed 220bhp at 7,000rpm, and the maximum speed of a Pininfarina 2 + 2 coupé was 143mph. The 250 GT was built in larger numbers than any Ferrari hitherto, and was the first to be homologated by the F.I.A. as a Grand Touring car. For this, 100 had to be built, but this figure was exceeded several times over by the 250 GT. It has been gradually developed from 1958 onwards, and its descendants are the mainstay of Ferrari road car production in 1969. The rest of its career will be dealt with in Chapter 26.

53. 1967 Matra M530A 1·7-litre coupé.
(Photo: Charles Pocklington)

Above: Ferrari Tipo 340.
(Photo: Guy Griffiths Motofoto)

Above right: Ferrari Testa Rossa at Le Mans 1959. This is the Gendebien/Hill car which retired.
(Photo: Autosport)

Ferrari's greatest Italian rival in the 1950s was Maserati. As far as road-going sports cars are concerned, this was virtually as new a make as Ferrari, for their few pre-war sports cars had been racing cars in disguise. In 1947 the Maserati factory came under the control of Omer Orsi, who developed a new engine suitable for sports car or Formula 2 racing. The A6 was a 6-cylinder single-ohc unit of 1,488cc capacity, developing a modest 65bhp. With a Pininfarina two-seater coupé body, the A6 was capable of 95mph, but a sports/racing version with cycle-type wings was much faster. In 1948 a 2-litre 125bhp car with twin ohc appeared, known as the A6GCS, but Orsi did not develop these, preferring to concentrate on the 4CLT Grand Prix cars. Between 1950 and 1953 no sports cars left the Maserati works, but in the latter year appeared the A6GCS 2000. This was a sports/racing version of the Formula 2 car, and was therefore a descendant of the old A6 but with a considerably developed engine. For the Formula 2 cars the head had been re-

Far left: Lancia D25 3·7-litre driven by Alberto Ascari in the 1954 T.T. (Photo: Klemantaski Studio)

Left: Ferrari Tipo 166 at Silverstone, Alberto Ascari at the wheel. (Photo: Motor Sport)

designed with valves inclined at 90 degrees, and twin camshafts were, of course, employed. As used in the A6GCS 2000, the engine gave 165bhp. This engine was also used in Cooper and Lister cars, the latter being very successful with Archie Scott-Brown at the wheel. Touring versions were also made, with coachwork by Allemano, Frua, and Zagato. However, very few were sold. Maseratis were not seen at all frequently on the roads until the introduction of the 3500 series in 1957.

Maserati's sports/racing programme continued with the 300S, introduced for the 1955 season. This had a 2,991cc 6-cylinder engine derived from that of the Colombo-designed 250F Grand Prix car, with 5-speed gearbox and tubular frame. In its first season it was unlucky in having to compete against the highly-successful Mercedes-Benz 300SLR, but in 1956, after Mercedes had retired from racing, the 300S was more successful. With Stirling Moss at the wheel, they won the Buenos Aires and Nürburgring 1,000km races, while Taruffi came second in the Targa Florio. A 3½-litre engine was used in some races, such as the Mille Miglia and Rheims 12 Hours, but the cars so fitted were very difficult to handle and either crashed or were withdrawn. These handling problems also bedevilled the next Maserati sports car, the 4,477cc Tipo 450S. This had a brand new V-8 engine developing 420bhp at 6,800rpm,

Above: Roy Salvadori's well-known Maserati A6GCS 2000. (Photo: Autosport)

Above right: Maserati 450S coupé at Le Mans in 1957. Driven by Stirling Moss and Harry Schell, the car retired after three hours. (Photo: Motor)

installed in a strengthened 300S chassis. Maximum speed was about 190mph when using the upper ratio of a supplementary two-speed gearbox with which some of these cars were fitted. An aerodynamic coupé was driven by Stirling Moss in the 1957 Le Mans race, but retired, as did Fangio's open version. The only important victories of the 450S were the Sebring 12 Hours and Swedish Grand Prix. At the end of 1957 Maserati retired from sports car racing. However, they continued to build cars for private owners to race, and for this purpose a new design was prepared. This Tipo 60 had a 2-litre 4-cylinder engine developing 195bhp, canted at an angle of 45 degrees. The chassis was a true space frame, being built up of a large number of small diameter tubes. This gave rise to the nickname 'Birdcage' applied to this car and its successor, the 3-litre Tipo 61. Disc brakes were fitted all round, a long overdue factor in Maserati sports cars. The Birdcage's racing career began in 1959, but is mostly part of the 1960s, so will be dealt with in Chapter 26.

1957 saw a new range of production sports Maseratis, powered by a 3,485cc 6-cylinder engine derived from that of the 300S. They carried very handsome open or coupé coachwork by Vignale or Touring, in which two people could travel at up to 135mph in comfort. This 3500 at last gave Maserati a Gran Turismo car competitive with the Ferrari V-12s.

Apart from Alfa-Romeo, Lancia, Ferrari, and Maserati, there were no large-engined Italian sports cars until the coming of the Italo-American hybrids such as the Iso Rivolta in 1962. However, there were many makes of small sports car, almost all of them using Fiat engines and components. Fiat themselves produced a number of sports cars, beginning with the 1100S coupé, a development of the pre-war 1100S. One of these took 4th place in the 1949 Mille Miglia. In 1952 there appeared the 8V, a two-seater coupé powered by a 1,996cc ohv V-8 engine developing 110bhp. This engine was developed for Fiat by Siata, a tuning firm who had done a lot of work on Fiats since the 1930s, and also built cars under their own name. The 8V was a specialised venture quite out of step with the main line of Fiat development, and only remained in production for two years. It had a maximum speed of 120mph, and was raced by private owners, but without great success. After the demise of the 8V the only sports Fiat was a two-seater version of the 1100, a pleasant little sports car with a top speed of about 85mph. In 1959 an Osca-designed twin-ohc 1,491cc unit powered the 1500 Sport, a model progressively developed during the 1960s.

Of the many Fiat derivatives, probably the best-known is the Abarth. This was the work of Carlo Abarth, an Austrian who had worked on the Cisitalia Grand Prix project. His first car was a coupé with tuned Fiat 1100 engine in a chassis using many Cisitalia components. This came 6th overall in the 1950

Mille Miglia. A number of other Fiat 1100-based cars were made, including some with very advanced coachwork, but Abarth did not become a well-known name until 1955 when the rear-engined Fiat 600 appeared. The Abarth version used an engine bored out to 748cc developing 47bhp, compared with 21·5bhp for the ordinary 600, and had an attractive Zagato two-seater coupé body. Maximum speed was nearly 100mph. Later an 850cc engine with twin-ohc head was made, developing 70bhp at 6,800rpm. The latter was known as the Bialbero, which simply means twin camshaft. Apart from these special cars, Abarth has modified the standard Fiat 500 and 600 saloons in a variety of tunes. Alterations include stiffer crankshafts and lowered suspensions.

Cisitalia began in 1946 by making 1,100cc racing cars which sold at the low price of £1,000, and followed these by sports versions, one of which Nuvolari drove into 2nd place in the 1947 Mille Miglia. The 1947 coupé had most attractive coachwork by Pininfarina, being one of the first Gran Turismo cars for which Italy has become so famous. Its clean lines have hardly dated in twenty-two years, and it remains one of the classics of coachwork design. When the New York Museum of Modern Art chose eight cars according to their 'excellence as works of art', the Cisitalia was among them. Mechanically it was not outstanding, having a standard Fiat 1100 engine available in 50bhp or 60bhp forms. Thanks to light weight (8cwt) and aerodynamic form, maximum speed was 105mph. Unfortunately the Cisitalia company wasted a great deal of money on an unsuccessful flat-12 Formula Grand Prix car, and in 1949 all operations were transferred to Argentina where the cars' constructor Piero Dusio hoped to gain government backing. Nothing came of this, but it marked the end of the beautiful little Pininfarina coupés. A re-organised company produced a larger coupé powered by a 2·8-litre B.P.M. marine engine in 1952, and a new 1100 with less attractive lines than its predecessor appeared in 1954. This was made in small numbers up to 1958, when Cisitalia ceased car production. A new Cisitalia appeared in 1961, this time a rear-engine coupé based on the Fiat 750.

The Osca (Officine Spezialitata Costruzione Automobili) was founded by the Maserati brothers after they left their own firm in 1947. Their first product was a 1,100cc sports car with single-ohc engine with which Villoresi won the 1948 Naples Grand Prix, followed by twin-ohc machines in three sizes for the 750cc, 1,100cc, and 1,500cc classes. They achieved class victories at Le Mans and in the Mille Miglia, but their greatest success was the outright victory in the 1954 Sebring 12 Hour Race. A 1,500cc car, driven by Stirling Moss and Bill Lloyd, and entered by Briggs Cunningham, won at 73·65mph, defeating much larger Lancia and Austin-Healey cars. In 1959 Osca produced a twin-ohc version of the Fiat 1500 engine for use in a Fiat sports model, and from then on their attention was turned to *ameliorazioni* of Fiats. These included sports coupés with special bodies which they sold under their own name, but mechanically they were Fiats.

Moretti was another small firm who made cars of their own design before succumbing to the more profitable but less adventurous trade of modifying Fiats. The first Moretti of 1947 was a 350cc minicar. Called La Cita, it was more sporting than most of its breed, with a maximum speed of 60mph. It was followed by a 4-cylinder 750cc sports car with twin-ohc engine developing 55bhp at 6,500rpm. Later Morettis had single or twin-cam engines in sizes up to 1·2 litres. The firm demanded fifty per cent of the purchase price before an order was accepted. Production seldom exceeded 100 per year in the 1950s, and from 1960 onwards Moretti concentrated on modified Fiat 750s and 2300s, which they sold under the Moretti name.

Battle of the 1100s: Stanguellini No. 44 and Lotus No. 42 at Le Mans in 1957. (Photo: Autocar)

There were several other Fiat-derived marques, including Bandini, Ermini, Giaur, Siata, and Stanguellini. The first three were very small production sports/racing cars. Bandini began in 1947 with a tuned Fiat 500 engine in a tubular chassis, but by 1952 he was building a beautiful little car with capacity increased to 750cc, a twin-cam head and twin carburetters. This gave 45bhp at 6,500rpm, and a speed of 100mph. The Giaur, named after its builders Giannini and Urania, was a similar 750cc car which won its class in the Mille Miglia four times between 1950 and 1954. Siata used a wide variety of Fiat engines, including the 500, 1400, 1500, and 8V. The Rallye tourer of 1951 was most unusual for an Italian car in having deliberately pre-war lines with separate wings and headlamps, and cutaway doors like an M.G. TD. Interestingly enough, when a fashion for 1930s-style 'fun cars' developed in the mid-1960s, Siata was among the first in the field with their 'Spring' roadster. More serious sporting Siatas had 725cc Crosley engines, and one or two cars were powered by the big V-8 Chrysler unit. Stanguellini was another small firm making sports cars with twin-cam versions of Fiat 750 and 1100 engines. These had speeds of 110mph and 120mph respectively. After 1959 Stanguellini became more interested in Formula Junior racing cars.

21.Other European Countries

The smaller European car manufacturing countries did not produce many sports cars in the post-war period. The most interesting was undoubtedly the Spanish Pegaso, a beautiful, complicated, and expensive machine which never really fulfilled its promise. It was built in the former Hispano-Suiza factory at Barcelona by a government-owned firm who were, and still are, Spain's largest producers of heavy trucks and buses. Designed by Wilfredo Ricart, the Pegaso engine was a 2½-litre V-8 with two camshafts per bank of cylinders, dry sump lubrication, and 5-speed gearbox on the rear axle. Power developed was 165bhp to 225bhp, and maximum speed in the region of 125mph. Later developments had 2·8-litre and 3·2-litre engines, and the final pushrod ohv Z.103 series had engines as large as 4·7 litres, giving 300bhp.

Pegaso Z.102B two-seater. (Photo: Studios Miarnau, Barcelona)

The Pegaso made little impression in international racing, largely because the brakes were inadequate for the car's weight and performance. Prices were extremely high; 375,000 pesetas ($9,500) for early models, and up to 600,000 pesetas ($15,000) for the 1957 Z.103 which had Italian bodies. About 125 Pegasos were made from 1951 to 1957, of which not more than four were Z.103s.

Austria produced one sports car, the Denzel, which was a Volkswagen-based two/three-seater, not unlike a Porsche in appearance. The engines were Volkswagen units, bored out to 1,281cc or 1,488cc, the latter giving 85bhp. This was 10bhp more than the output of the contemporary Porsche Type 356B. Denzels were made in small numbers from 1948 to about 1960, and were successful in national events, winning the 1954 Austrian Alpine Rally. Another Volkswagen-based sports car was the Enzmann from Switzerland. This had a doorless two-seater body of fibreglass. With the largest engine option of 1,295cc, it had a maximum speed of 100mph. Production was very limited, not more than 100 Enzmanns being made between 1957 and the end of 1966. At the time of writing a new model is in preparation.

Development of sports cars in Czechoslovakia was practically extinguished by the communist take-over in February 1948, after which production was limited to utilitarian cars. However, two two-seater versions of the 744cc Aero Minor ran at Le Mans in 1949, entered by Jacques Poch, the Paris agent for Czech cars. They won the 750cc class, and repeated this performance at Spa the same year. In the early 1950s, sports cars based on the Skoda 1100 and the rear-engined Tatraplan appeared at shows, but none went into production. The nearest to a Czech sports car since then has been the twin-carburetter two-seater convertible Skoda Felicia, a mildly-tuned version of the stock sedan.

A Denzel on the Col du Ste Baume during the 1956 Alpine Rally. (Photo: Motor)

22. The United States of America

The Cunningham team at Le Mans in 1952. From left to right: the Briggs Cunningham/Bill Spear open car which finished 4th; the Phil Walters coupé which retired and the John Fitch open car which also retired.
(Photo: Autosport)

In 1944 the Sports Car Club of America had fifty-two members, most of whom owned lovingly-preserved Mercers and Stutzes over twenty years old. Sports cars were not status symbols because they were scattered so widely and sparsely that many people had never seen one. To the average American, motor sport meant Indianapolis or stock car racing. Within a few years this situation was to change completely, and the renaissance of the sports car in America was as striking as the spread of jazz music thirty years earlier. It was brought into being by foreign cars, especially M.G., Allard, and Jaguar, but before long American makers began to join in. One of the earliest and most dedicated sports car constructors was millionaire yachtsman Briggs Cunningham, who built cars with the primary aim of giving America a victory at Le Mans. Although he never quite succeeded, he produced some very interesting sports cars while he was trying. The first Cunningham entries at Le Mans were two Cadillacs in 1950. One had an enormous, all-enveloping two-seater body, while the other was a stock sedan with tuned engine. The latter finished 10th, competing against the world's best sports cars. For 1951 a specially-built sports car powered by a Chrysler V-8 engine, modified to give 220bhp, with tubular frame and all-independent suspension, was made. In the race it held 2nd place for nine hours before being eliminated by valve failure. Later in the year, Cunninghams came 1st and 2nd at

Watkins Glen. In 1952 a coupé and two open cars ran at Le Mans, Cunningham himself finishing 4th with one of the latter. By 1953 the Chrysler engine was giving 310bhp, and the Cunningham C5R was the fastest car on the Mulsanne straight at 154mph. That year they finished 3rd, 6th, and 9th. The last Cunningham was the C6R with 2,942cc Meyer-Drake engine as used in many Indianapolis racing cars. It developed 272bhp, and with a much smaller and lighter car performance should have been very good, but the car retired through transmission failure. Even the vast fortune of Briggs Cunningham was not up to continuing a racing programme which was as lavishly organised as the works team of a big factory, and no more Cunninghams appeared after 1955. A small number of production cars were also made, beautiful coupés and convertibles with Vignale bodies and Chrysler engines. Maximum speeds were about 145mph, and prices ranged from $10,000 to $15,000.

Another pioneer post-war sports car builder was Frank Kurtis of Glendale, California. He had been building track racing cars for Indianapolis and elsewhere for many years when his first sports car appeared in 1949. This had a 3·9-litre Mercury V-8 engine and two-seater body partially of fibreglass. Thirty-four were made before the design was taken over by television set manufacturer Earl Muntz who transferred production to Evansville, Indiana, and later to Chicago. The Mercury engine was replaced by more powerful Cadillac or Lincoln units of over 5 litres, giving a speed of 112mph. Muntz lengthened the wheelbase to allow for a four-seater body, but the race-bred Kurtis handling suffered in consequence. Not many Muntz cars were sold, at a price of $5,500. Meanwhile Kurtis turned to much faster competition machinery. The 500K of 1953 was similar to an Indianapolis racing car, with two-seater body, cycle-type wings, and headlamps. Engines were to customer's choice, usually being Mercury or Cadillac. The 500K could accelerate from 0–100mph in 11·1 seconds, and they regularly defeated Jaguars, Ferraris and Cadillac-Allards in West Coast racing. A more aerodynamic model, the 500M, followed in 1954, but Frank Kurtis soon turned to other fields, including the development of rocket-propelled sleds for Cook Electric Research Laboratories. About thirty 500Ks and eighteen 500Ms were built, as well as less than half a dozen of the 500X, a highly-specialized machine with Indianapolis-derived tubular chassis.

Most American sports car makers, not unnaturally, chose their power units from among the big V-8s, but at least two firms used the 2·6-litre 4-cylinder side-valve Willys engine used by Kaiser for their Henry J compact car. These were the Excalibur J and Woodill Wildfire. The former was sponsored by Brooks Stevens of Milwaukee. It was a lightweight sports car with aluminium body and cycle-type wings. Three prototypes were raced very successfully in the 1952 season, scoring twenty-six victories in SCCA events, but production plans were hit by the demise of Kaiser. The Woodill was a fibreglass sports car available in open or coupé forms, made from 1952 to 1958 at Tustin, California. They used Willys transmissions and, originally, Willys engines, although later options were Cadillac or Ford V-8. An interesting junior version of the Wildfire was the Brushfire, a perfectly scaled-down model of the larger car, on a 5ft 3in wheelbase, for children up to 12 years old. It had a 3hp engine, one gear, and top speed of 35mph.

Kaiser themselves built the Kaiser-Darrin 161, a stylish two-seater designed by Howard Darrin, and powered by a Continental 6-cylinder engine. The body was of fibreglass and a feature was that the doors slid forward into the wings to give easy access to the car in confined spaces. With a maximum speed of only 95mph it was not particularly suited to competitions. Only 240

1958 Kurtis 500K with Frank Kurtis at the wheel. This particular example had a Hudson engine but other power units available included Cadillac, Chrysler, De Soto, Dodge, Lincoln and Mercury. (Photo: Associated Press Ltd)

1952 Excalibur J. (Photo: Autosport)

*1958 Chevrolet Corvette hard-top coupé. Sir Gawain Baillie at the wheel.
(Photo: Patrick Benjafield)*

were built before Kaiser abandoned car production in 1955, but Darrin marketed a few similar-looking cars under his own name from 1956 to 1957. For power he chose the 305bhp Cadillac engine, which must have given the good-looking car the performance it sadly lacked with the smaller engine.

One of the most powerful sports cars in America, made in small numbers only, was the Bocar from Denver, Colorado. Builder Bob Carnes began producing Chevrolet-powered sports cars in 1958. They came in various forms, the nearest to a production car being the XP-5, with 245bhp Corvette engine, complex space frame, and fibreglass body. About ten of these were made, but Carnes' pride and joy was the XP-6 with longer wheelbase, and the same engine fitted with a powerful G.M.C. supercharger. With this, power was 400bhp at 6,200rpm. The XP-6 had a maximum speed of 170mph, and 0–100mph took only 12 seconds. Alas, the price of $11,700 was too much for buyers who could get a Ferrari for $10,000. Only the prototype XP-6 was made. The last Bocar was the Stiletto with fuel-injection supercharged Corvette engine developing a claimed 510bhp. This was Carnes' own car, but a few other less powerful Stilettos were sold to private owners.

There were several other American sports car makers in the 1950s, mostly using fibreglass bodies and a choice of engines. They included the Chicagoan from Blue Island, Illinois, the Yank from San Diego, California, and the Panther from Bedford Hills, N.Y. In a class of its own was the Crosley Hotshot. The Crosley engine was a remarkable little unit, with single overhead camshaft, five main bearings and a capacity of only 726cc. It was originally developed for a small sedan, but had obvious sporting possibilities. In 1949 the Hotshot was announced, a small two-seater sports car. It was no beauty, the body being sometimes likened to a bathtub on wheels, but it could reach 75mph. A Hotshot won the 1950 Sebring 12 Hour Race, on handicap, and Briggs Cunningham entered one at Le Mans in 1951. It failed to finish, but lapped at 74mph, which was the speed of the winning car

1956 Ford Thunderbird in London with Houses of Parliament and Big Ben (undergoing repair) in the background. (Photo: Autocar)

at Le Mans seventeen years earlier. Crosley Hotshots were raced in SCCA events all over America, and continued to do so for several years after production ended in 1952.

All the American cars so far described have been the products of comparatively small manufacturers, but they and the European imports were sufficiently popular to arouse the interest of the automotive giants of Detroit. The first result of this interest was the Chevrolet Corvette which appeared at the end of 1953. This used the stock 6-cylinder Chevrolet engine of the period, a 3·7-litre side-valve unit, but with three carburetters and tuned to give 160bhp. The two-seater body had very attractive simple lines which were gradually spoilt over the years by over-decoration. Neither the performance nor the handling of the Corvette were remarkable at first, but the former was improved for 1956 with the new 4·3-litre ohv V-8 engine which gave 180bhp in the Corvette. Handling was greatly improved in 1960, by which time the 'hottest' production Corvette had 290bhp, and a fuel-injection engine. They were successful in SCCA events, while an experimental Corvette SS was built in 1957. It ran at Sebring, without success, and was entered for Le Mans but was withdrawn because of a change of Chevrolet policy.

Ford's answer to the Corvette was the Thunderbird which was introduced for 1955. This again was a handsome, functional machine in its original form, but the sporting character was lost after three years. It was larger and more powerful than the Corvette, the 4·8-litre engine giving 200bhp and 115mph. Handling was not up to the standards of the later Corvette, and it was not especially suitable for racing. Had the Thunderbird been developed as the Corvette was, it would no doubt have been a worthy rival to the General Motors car, but, instead, Ford gave it four seats in 1958, and so the Thunderbird sports car was lost. Sales from the end of 1954 to the end of 1957 were slightly under 50,000.

Part Five
The Sports Car
Today, 1961-1969

In the 1960s the gap between the road-going sports cars and some of those seen on the race track grew to proportions that would have been unbelievable ten years earlier. The process was already evident with such cars as the C-type, and even more with the D-type Jaguars, and the Aston Martin DBR 1 series. The background to this situation is given in the introduction. In Great Britain none of the famous sports car makers of the 1950s directly supports racing, and with good reason. The cars they make for sale to the public would stand no chance in top-class racing, and to produce special machines would be too costly. However, a new breed of sports / racing car has grown up, all with rear or mid-engine mounting, using highly-tuned large American engines in the biggest cars, and British units lower down the scale.

Because of the separation of the road-going sports car from active competition (although many still compete in club racing) the former have tended to become Grand Tourers, rather than sports cars in the traditional sense. The development of motorways has encouraged the fast, comfortable 'businessman's express', always a closed car, and not a sports car according to some people's definitions. With the demise of the A.C. Cobra in 1968, the only large, open two-seater made in Britain is the E-type Jaguar, and its days are clearly numbered. The E-type appeared in the spring of 1961, replacing the XK series which had been made since 1948. The new car used the 3,781cc engine fitted to the XK 150, giving 265bhp. It broke with Jaguar tradition in having independent suspension all round and disc brakes. Bodies were highly streamlined, owing much to the D-type and XK-SS in their design. Styles were open two-seater, with or without hardtop, and fixed head coupé. The latter was the fastest, with a speed of 151mph. The E-type cost only £2,196, a remarkable figure for such a fast car, but for young drivers, at any rate, the attractions of low cost were offset by extremely high insurance rates. The E-type sold very well, both at home and abroad, with little basic change from its introduction to the time of writing. Capacity was increased to 4,235cc and an all-synchromesh box introduced in 1965, while the following year came the 2 + 2 coupé, which gives accommodation for four people without in any way spoiling the car's handsome lines.

Jaguar's rival, Aston Martin, have developed their DB 4 GT coupé progressively during the 1960s, and, save for a short-lived association with Lola, have also kept well clear of racing. The 3·7-litre DB 4 became the 4-litre DB 5 in 1964, and this in turn was developed into the DB 6 for 1966. The 4-litre engine developed 282bhp, and for those who wanted still more performance there was the option of the 325bhp Vantage engine. Body styles were open and coupé four-seaters, and a two seater coupé by Touring of Italy, to special order only. For 1968 Aston Martin brought out the DB S with a two-seater coupé body lower and sleeker than that of the DB 6 and de Dion rear axle. This cost £5,718, or £1,489 more than the DB 6. British firms have built several other large cars in the Grand Touring category including the Chevrolet-engined Gordon-Keeble (1964–67) and the Chrysler-engined Bristol (1962 to date). More unusual is the Chrysler-engined Jensen FF with Ferguson-type drive to all four wheels and disc brakes incorporating the Dunlop Maxaret anti-skid system.

Ferrari driven by Willy Mairesse in the Targa Florio of 1963. This was an election year as shown by the streamer above the road.
(Photo: Geoffrey Goddard)

*1966 Jaguar E-type 2 + 2
coupé.
(Photo: Autocar)*

A short-lived sports car of the early 1960s was the Daimler SP 250, a totally new venture for this old-established firm, and one that set them on a new course of development. The engine was a 2½-litre pushrod ohv V-8 designed by Edward Turner, who had recently joined Daimler from the Triumph motorcycle firm. It was an excellent engine giving 140bhp at 6,000rpm, and generally thought to be too good for the chassis which was lightly braced and too flexible. The SP 250 had a fibreglass two/four-seater body, and a speed of over 120mph. It was raced successfully for several seasons, both in Great Britain and in the United States where it was twice raised into a higher class by the SCCA because it so dominated its equals. It was made from 1959 to 1964, and the engine was later used in a Daimler saloon which had the Mark 2 Jaguar hull, Jaguar having taken over Daimler in 1960.

One of the last of the old-style large front-engined sports cars was the A.C. Cobra. At the suggestion of former American racing driver Carroll Shelby, A.C. installed a 4·2-litre Ford V-8 engine in the Ace chassis. As testing revealed shortcomings in the latter, numerous improvements were made, notably in strengthening the frame, and also in improved cooling. After 75 cars had been made, the engine was replaced by the 195bhp 4,736cc Ford engine in 1963. From mid-1965 the much larger Ford engine of 6,989cc and 345bhp was used in Shelby Cobras sold by Shelby American Inc. It was very much an Anglo-American car, those sold in the United States being known as Shelby Cobras, and then as Ford Cobras, with no mention of A.C. at all. In England the smaller car was known as the A.C. 289, and the larger as the A.C. 427 (from their respective engine capacities in cubic inches). The larger-engined car was only available through Shelby American, so very few were seen in England. The Cobra had no luxury or frills, but a staggering performance, especially as regards acceleration. Even with the smaller engine, it could reach 60mph from standstill in 5·5 seconds, and had a maximum speed of 138mph. Carroll Shelby entered teams in all the major European sports car races in 1964 and 1965. They were often dogged by misfortune, but won the GT Championship in both years. The team cars were open two-seaters or the special Daytona coupé. This car, not sold to the public, had a tuned 4·7-litre engine giving 380bhp, and a speed of 195mph. In 1965 Carroll Shelby began to enter the Ford GT in races, and from 1966 onwards did not officially race the Cobras any longer. Production of Cobras was discontinued in 1968, Shelby now concentrating on special versions of the Ford Mustang. A luxurious development of the Cobra is the A.C. 428, with 7,016cc 345bhp engine, still by Ford, of course, and with convertible or GT coupé coachwork by Frua of Italy. The 428 has a maximum speed of 140mph.

The traditional sports car lived on in the popular British machines of the 1960s, most of which were improvements of earlier models. The Austin-

The Daytona Coupé version of the A.C. Cobra in the 1965 T.T. at Goodwood. (Photo: Peter Burn)

1969 Austin-Healey Sprite with Le Mans Coupé body shell by the Lenham Motor Company. (Photo: Lenham Motor Company)

Healey Sprite received a new body shell in 1961, and the 948cc engine was replaced by a 1,075cc 55bhp unit in 1962, when disc brakes were fitted on the front wheels. In 1966 capacity went up to 1,275cc, and power to 65bhp. At the time of its introduction, this Mark IV Sprite cost £671, or £7 less than the original 1958 model. This was a remarkable achievement, to hold the price down over an eight-year period of general inflation. Maximum speed was 95mph. As with the earlier Sprites, many engine and body modifications are available, some of the latter completely transforming the appearance of the car. A variant of the Sprite was the new M.G. Midget introduced in 1962. It was almost identical to the Sprite, but had more luxurious equipment and cost £28 more. The larger MGA was replaced in 1962 by the MGB, an entirely new car with integral construction and 95bhp 1,795cc engine. Like the MGA it was available as an open two-seater, or as a GT coupé. It was still being made in the spring of 1969, but was supplemented by the MGC, a more powerful machine with seven main bearing version of the 6-cylinder Austin-Healey engine. This had a capacity of 2,912cc and 145bhp, giving a top speed of 120mph, compared with 100mph for the MGB.

Triumph widened their range of sports cars in the 1960s, beginning with the Spitfire in 1963. This was a popular sports car powered by the 1,147cc Herald engine, and was an obvious competitor for B.M.C. Sprite and Midget. It had the Herald's frame and all-round independent suspension, with disc brakes at the front. The engine gave 63bhp, and the maximum speed was 92mph. The current model has a 1,296cc engine, and 75bhp. In 1967 a new Spitfire derivative appeared, known as the Triumph GT 6. This was a fast-back coupé using the 2-litre 6-cylinder Vitesse engine in the Spitfire frame. The trusty TR 3 was replaced in 1962 by a new car, the TR 4. This had a restyled body and 2·1-litre engine. Independent rear suspension came on the TR 4A of 1965, and the next major change came in the 1968 TR 5. This had a new 6-cylinder 2½-litre fuel-injection engine, the first quantity-produced engine of this kind to be made in England. The latest of the series is the TR 6, with TR 5 engine and chassis, and a new body styled by Karmann of Germany.

Morgan continued their 4-4 and Plus 4 range, with few changes except those made by their engine suppliers. The Plus 4 had a 120bhp Triumph TR 4 engine which Morgan continued to use after Triumph dropped it. When supplies of this obsolete engine became uncertain, Morgan took the dramatic step of turning to a V-8 power unit. This was the Buick-designed, Rover-built 3½-litre 160bhp engine that Rover used in their 3500 saloons. The new model, known as the Plus Eight, came out in the autumn of 1968. It retained the traditional Morgan appearance, but performance was a great advance on earlier standards, with a maximum speed of 124mph. Morgans were raced a great deal by private owners during the 1960s and competed in a few international events. Credit for this must go to Christopher Lawrence who prepared most of the faster Morgans, and ran a four-year-old Plus 4 at Le Mans in 1962. With this, he finished 13th overall and won the 2-litre class. He also built four special coupés, known as the SLR Morgans with which he came 4th in the 1964 Spa race, and won the second half of the Double 500 race at Brands Hatch. These special cars should not be confused with the Plus Four Plus which was a production coupé of which 60 were built in 1964. The 4-4 is continued, with the 1600cc cross-flow Ford Cortina engine.

A popular sports car was the Sunbeam Alpine. This old name was revived in 1960 for a new integral construction two-seater car powered by the 1,494cc Sunbeam Rapier engine. Maximum speed was 98·4mph. In 1964 the Alpine was available with a 4·3-litre 164bhp Ford V-8 engine, in which form it was known as the Tiger. This model was made until 1967, and the Alpine was continued until 1969. Late in the year this name was applied to a version of the Sunbeam Rapier with an 80bhp 1,725cc engine. This is a Grand Touring rather than a sports car, and is an indication of manufacturers' preference for closed rather than open cars.

We have considered the mass-production sports cars, but a large number of machines were made by smaller firms, of which we can only examine a few. The most significant was Lotus, who grew from the position of an obscure special builder in 1953 to one of the leading makers and exporters of genuine sports cars, as well as three times holders of the Formula 1 World Championship for racing cars. A great expansion of production was initiated by the appearance in 1963 of the Elan. This very successful car had a tuned twin-ohc version of the Ford Classic 116E engine of 1,499cc and 100bhp. It had disc brakes, and a streamlined two-seater body with retractable headlamps. Road holding was excellent, and the Elan was described as one of the finest road-clingers of all time. It was very successful in club racing as well as on the road, and was chosen as a personal car by several well-known racing drivers including Graham Hill and the late Jim Clark. In 1965 engine capacity went up to 1,558cc, giving 105bhp and 122mph. The current range includes the Elan + 2, with longer wheelbase, two rear seats for children, and even better lines than those of the two-seater. Handling is just as good, and top speed only 4mph slower. The Elan has been made in much larger numbers than any other Lotus, production reaching 8,300 by the summer of 1969. Two other sports models are in production. The stark Mark 7 with Ford or Coventry-Climax engines is still available, in kit form if desired, while a new model is the Europa. With this car Lotus join the growing ranks of mid-engined sports car builders. The Europa has a very low coupé body, and is powered either by a Renault R 16 engine for export or by a Cosworth-Ford.

Another small firm which has come to prominence in the 1960s is Reliant. Originally makers of three-wheeled cars and vans only, they are now the largest independent car producers in Britain, coming fifth in production after B.L.M.C., Ford, Rootes, and Vauxhall. Their first sports car was the Sabre, a two-seater with Ford Consul engine, and bizarrely-styled open fibreglass coachwork. Neither appearance nor handling was very satisfactory on the early models, but steady improvement over the next few years resulted in the Scimitar GT coupé of 1965. This used the 2·6-litre Ford Zephyr engine, and had a handsome 2 + 2 seater body styled by Ogle of Letchworth. The 1969 version has 2·5- or 3-litre Ford V-6 engines, the latter giving a speed of 121mph. No open models are made in the current Reliant range.

The kit car fashion lasted for a few years in the early 1960s, but the number of makes in this category has fallen sharply. Two new makes which have achieved considerable fame are Gilbern and Marcos. Both are made far from conventional car manufacturing centres, the Gilbern coming from South Wales, and the Marcos from rural Wiltshire, at Bradford-on-Avon. Gilbern began in 1959 with a neat-looking little two/four-seater fibreglass GT coupé to take B.M.C. or Coventry-Climax 1,098cc engines. From the very first, Gilberns had a much higher standard of finish than most fibreglass kit cars. For 1963 the MGB engine was used, and for 1966 a change was made to Ford units, the 2½- or 3-litre V-6. The latter powers the current Gilbern, known as the Genie. Production is small, about 100 per year being made. The Marcos, designed by Jem Marsh and Frank Costin, was unusual in having a composite chassis and lower body made of marine-type plywood. The first cars had Ford 105E engines, and very ugly appearance, but their light weight

1968 Lotus Elan Plus Two coupé.
(Photo: Lotus Cars Ltd)

1968 Marcos Coupé with Ford V-6 engine.
(Photo: Marcos Cars Ltd)

Above: *A Ginetta G.12 at Mallory Park in 1967.* (Photo: Autosport)

Above right: *The familiar squat shape of the T.V.R. has continued without major change from 1957 to 1969. This is a 1961 Mark IIA with MGA engine.* (Photo: Motor)

helped them to success in racing. J. Sutton won the Autosport Trophy for GT cars in 1961 and 1962 with an early Marcos. In 1963 the firm moved from Luton to Bradford-on-Avon, and the following year a new design appeared with fibreglass body designed by Denis Adams. The same plywood chassis was used with all-independent suspension and Volvo 1800 engine. This shape, with very compact coupé body behind a long bonnet, has remained unchanged up to 1969, but the Volvo engine was replaced first by a Ford Cortina and now by a 3-litre Ford V-6. With this unit, maximum speed is 125mph, allied to excellent road holding. In 1965 the 'big' Marcos was joined by the Mini-Marcos, a fibreglass integral construction unit designed to take B.M.C. Mini components. Maximum speed with 1,275cc engine is 102mph. A French-entered Mini-Marcos was the only British car to finish at Le Mans in 1966. Marcos cars have always enjoyed good sales in France, the first being sold to that country in 1962. Both the Mini-Marcos and the larger car are available in kit form, as well as fully assembled.

The Mini-Marcos was by no means the only sports car to use the famous B.M.C. engine and transmission. With excellent handling and considerable power available from the Cooper-tuned units, the Mini was an obvious attraction for the sports car builder and at least a dozen firms offered Mini-based sports coupés. One of the first was the Ogle SX 1000, a neat little little two/four-seater produced by David Ogle Ltd, the design team who were responsible for the Reliant Scimitar. With 998cc Cooper engine, the Ogle had a top speed of 90mph. Others included the Butterfield Musketeer, Camber GT, and Minijem, while variations on the theme were the rear-engined Deep Sanderson and Unipower coupés. The latter is still in production, with all-independent suspension and 998cc or 1,275cc engines.

Another car available both as a kit and fully-assembled is the T.V.R. The familar squat shape that appeared in 1957 was continued through 1969. Engines included Coventry-Climax, Ford 105E, or MGA. In April 1962 the Mark III appeared with much stiffer chassis which eliminated the cracking of the fibreglass bodies, a drawback of the previous models. For the American market a 271bhp Ford Fairlane engine was available, this model being known as the Griffith-T.V.R. After 1965, this was known simply as the Griffith (see page 307). Another new model for 1965 was the T.V.R. Trident with Austin-Healey 3000 engine, and body styled by Trevor Fiore. This design was sold to T.V.R. agent W. J. Last of Woodbridge, Suffolk, who formed a new company, Trident Cars Ltd. When put into production, it had a 4·7-litre Ford V-8 engine, so can be considered as an English version of the Griffith. Meanwhile, T.V.R. reconstituted once more (they had at least four changes of company organisation from 1962 to 1965), built the Mark IV GT with MGB engine, or the Vixen with Ford Cortina 1600 engine. The same body shell was used for both cars. All T.V.R.s have been successful in club racing and on the road, where they have good handling but a distinctly firm ride. The maximum speed of the Vixen is 105mph.

One of the simpler kit cars was the Ginetta G.4 with fibreglass open two-seater body and Ford 105E engine. It was very successful in club racing, and about 350 were made. More specialised Ginettas were the G.10 and G.11, with Ford V-8 and MGB engines respectively, and the rear-engined sports/racing G.12 with Ford 105E engine. Ginetta still build the latter, as well as a road car, the G.15 with rear-mounted Hillman Imp engine. Other sports cars to use the Imp engine have been the Emery, Davrian, Diva, and the Lombardi-Imp with Italian coupé body originally designed for the Fiat 850.

There have been many other small sports car makers, all using proprietary

1969 version of the Lola GT 70 Group 4 coupé. A road-going version of this was announced but did not go into production. (Photo: Robin Rew)

1969 Chevron-B.M.W. Group 4 coupé. (Photo: Chevron Cars)

engines and components and usually fibreglass bodies. The competition cars became increasingly specialized, but two of the more important should be described. These are Lola and Chevron. The Lola was the work of Eric Broadley who had built small Ford or Coventry-Climax-engined sports/racing cars since 1959. They were extremely successful, winning almost every event in their class, and were more than a match for the equivalent Lotuses. In 1963 Broadley unveiled a totally new car, a GT coupé with mid-mounted 4·3-litre Ford V-8 engine. Ford of America had been working on a similar design, and when they saw Broadley's design they approached him with a view to joint development of a new model. The result was that the Lola GT had a very short career as an independent design, but contributed to the birth of the Ford GT40 late in 1963. The history of the latter is discussed in the American chapter on page 305. In 1965 Lola introduced the Type 70, an open two-seater in the Group 7 category of 'two-seater racing cars'. Engines were the 4·7-litre Ford or 5½-litre Chevrolet. For 1967 a GT coupé version was introduced for racing. It used a 430bhp 5-litre Chevrolet engine, and cost £6,950. The Chevron is the product of Derek Bennett who originally built Ford-engined sports cars for 1172 Formula club racing. In 1966 appeared the Chevron GT, a mid-engined coupé with tubular chassis to which a variety of engines has been fitted. The most popular have been the twin-cam Cosworth-Ford and the 2-litre B.M.W. With the latter unit the Chevron GT was homologated as a Group 4 sports car in April 1968. Other engines fitted to individual cars have included the 2-litre BRM V-8 and the 3-litre Repco Brabham V-8. Chevrons have been very successful in competitions, frequently defeating the equivalent models from Porsche. In the first four months of 1969, they won their class at Daytona, at the BOAC 500 race at Brands Hatch, and the Wills Trophy race at Thruxton. Later in the year, the B8 was succeeded by the Chevron B16. This had a more streamlined body which was 6 inches lower than that of the B8. This was possible because of revised screen height regulations for Group 6 cars.

The Elva began, like the Lola, as a sports/racing car, powered by Ford or Coventry-Climax engines, and was highly successful in club racing. A road-going car appeared in 1958. This was the Courier, with MGA engine and two-seater fibreglass body. From 1963, MGB engines were used, and a GT coupé was available in addition to the open two-seater. An interesting prototype was the GT 160 of 1964 with B.M.W. 2000 engine mounted amidships, and Fiore-styled coupé body. The Mark 4 Courier had a box frame moulded into the body, and was made at least up to 1967, but by that time most of the company's activities were concerned with heavier metal. In 1964 Elva had been taken over by Trojan Ltd of Croydon, Surrey, and in 1966 this company began to make the Group 7 racing cars designed by Bruce McLaren. These were called McLaren-Elvas, but as they are classified as two-seater racing cars they are outside the scope of this book. In late 1969 a new Elva GT coupé appeared, the 3000, powered by the 3-litre Ford V-6 engine.

During 1968 J.W. Automotive Engineering (see page 306) built their first Mirage M2–300, which was intended to replace the GT40 in their racing programme. Initially it was powered by a V-12 B.R.M. engine, but with this unit was not competitive; another version, in open and closed forms and powered by the Ford-Cosworth V-8 showed greater promise. In the same Group 6 category was the Ford F3L, or P68/P69, built by Alan Mann Racing around the Ford-Cosworth V-8. This thinly-disguised Grand Prix car had a singularly unsuccessful racing career.

54. 1969 Porsche 912 1·6-litre coupé. Owned and photographed by Josip Ciganovic.

As we saw in the last section, by 1960 French sports cars were limited to special versions of mass-produced models. This situation has not materially changed up to date, but their performance has increased remarkably, and some really high-powered machines have appeared in the sports/racing class.

The Renault-based Alpine has been developed progressively, benefiting from all the improvements made to the Renault engines. The Alpine *berlinette* had a 998cc engine developing 77bhp in 1961, increased to 1,100cc and 87bhp in 1964 from a Gordini-tuned R 8 engine. Today a wide range of engines is available in the basic body shell, the most powerful being a twin-cam unit giving 115bhp, and a top speed of 127mph. A larger capacity, but lower stressed, engine is the 1½-litre Renault R 16 giving 92bhp. Disc brakes were available on all Alpines from 1967. Development of prototypes for Group 6 racing began in 1964 with a special-bodied coupé powered by a 998cc twin cam engine designed by Amédée Gordini. This won the Index of Thermal Efficiency at Le Mans in 1964. Later Group 6 cars have had engines of 1,150cc, 1,300cc, and 1,500cc, while at the end of 1967 came a 3-litre V-8 with ZF gearbox. The smaller cars use British Hewland gearboxes. The V-8 Alpine finished 8th overall at Le Mans in 1968, while the 1500 won both the Index of Thermal Efficiency and Index of Performance in the same race. For a small firm, Alpine have a surprising number of licence arrangements for manufacture overseas; these include Spain, Mexico, Brazil, and, more recently, Bulgaria. French production is about 600 units annually, the world-wide figure being over 2,000.

The marque D.B. came to an end in 1961 when the partnership of Charles Deutsch and René Bonnet broke up. However, both men continued in car manufacture. Deutsch joined Panhard where he developed a special coupé version of the Dyna-Panhard, known as the CD Panhard. This won the Index of Performance at Le Mans in 1962, and was put into limited production later in the year. It had a streamlined fibreglass body, and cost the equivalent of £1,280. Very few were made compared with the more angular Panhard 24CT which was cheaper, although about 10km per hour slower. The CD was dropped after 1964, but the CT continued as the only Panhard model until production finally ended in 1967.

René Bonnet formed his own company and built a complex range of cars in the former D.B. works at Champigny-sur-Marne. Unlike D.B.s, they used Renault R8 engines and came in three models, the Le Mans with front engine ahead of the front axle, the Missile with front engine behind the axle, and the Djet mid-engined coupé. The Le Mans and Missile had 850cc engines driving the front wheels, while the Djet had a 1,100cc 70bhp engine driving the rear wheels. The front-engined cars were made in very small numbers, but the Djet continued until 1965 when the design was taken over by the rocket firm, Engins Matra of Romorantin. With more capital, production of the Matra Djet, as it was now called, increased considerably. Renault engines tuned to give 70bhp, 94bhp, and 105bhp were used in the various models, the fastest car having a speed of 109mph. In 1967 Matra brought out a new mid-engined car, the M.530, powered by the 73bhp 1,700cc German

55. 1967 Mercedes-Benz 230SL 2·3-litre coupé.
(Photo: Daimler-Benz AG)

*Alpine-Renault 3-litre V-8 on
its first appearance at the Paris
1,000km Race in October 1967;
it finished 7th.
(Photo: Autosport)*

*Matra Djet coupé.
(Photo: Matra Sports Srl)*

Ford V-4 engine. It seated four and was a more refined car than the Djet, but performance was not outstanding, with a top speed of only 95mph. It is probably an interim model, while development is proceeding on a luxury sports car powered by a V-12 engine. This 3-litre unit was originally built for a Formula 1 racing car, and was used in a Group 6 sports coupé which ran at Le Mans in 1968. It held 2nd place for 18 hours before retiring. Matras built for Le Mans in 1969 had open bodies, and finished in 4th, 5th, and 7th positions.

The nearest that a major French manufacturer has come to making a sports car recently has been the Bertone-designed coupé based on the rear-engined Simca 1000. This has an attractive two/four-seater body and engine tuned to give 80bhp. Maximum speed is 112mph. A privately-developed Group 6 coupé called the Moynet Simca ran at Le Mans in 1968. The powerful Simca-Abarth is described in the Italian chapter, on page 296.

A small production sports car is the Sovam which uses front-mounted Renault 850 and 1100 engines driving the front wheels. Fibreglass open or coupé bodies and independent suspension all round by torsion bars are features of its design. Maximum speed is in the region of 100mph for the larger-engined Sovam.

The Matra 3-litre V-12 coupé at Le Mans in 1968. The drivers were Johnny Servoz-Gavin and Henry Pescarolo. (Photo: Autocar)

There has been little sports car activity in Germany since 1960, and the only firm to take an active part in competitions was Porsche. This firm has, however, increased its standing immeasurably, and at the beginning of the 1969 season seemed poised to dominate sports car racing. The biggest change in production Porsches came in 1964 with the introduction of the Type 911. This had a new flat-six 1,991cc engine developing 130bhp and giving a maximum speed of nearly 130mph. For the first time in a road-going Porsche, a 5-speed gearbox was used. The body was new, although having a family resemblance with the old Type 356 shape. The latter was dropped in 1965, but its 1,582cc engine was retained, being installed in the 911 body-shell to make the tamer 912. Even this had a top speed of 116mph. There has been little change from 1965 to 1969; the latest 911S has fuel injection and a speed of 136mph. This car won the Monte Carlo Rally in 1968 and 1969. A new competition car for 1964 was the Carrera 904 with 4-cylinder 180bhp Carrera engine in a new frame with very low fibreglass coupé body. This was replaced in 1965 by the 906 which had the 904 body and a 200bhp version of the new 6-cylinder engine. This in turn was developed into the 907 with 2-litre 6 or 2·2-litre flat-8 engine, and the 3-litre flat-8 Type 908. The 8-cylinder Type 907 came 1st and 2nd at Sebring in 1968, 1st, 2nd and 3rd at Daytona, 1st in the Targa Florio, and 2nd at Le Mans, while one of the 3-litre 908s was 3rd in the same event. As a result of these successes, Porsche came 2nd in the 1968 Constructors' Championship with forty-two points against Ford's forty-five. For 1969 a new car was announced with 4½-litre flat-12 engine developing a claimed 520bhp. Known as the Type 917 it was the fastest car at the Le Mans Test Day, reaching 240mph down the Mulsanne straight. However, handling problems initially made it unpopular with drivers. In the Le Mans Race, all four 917s entered retired, although Vic Elford's car made the fastest lap at 146·2mph. The smaller flat-8 Type 908 had a remarkable record in 1969; before the season was half way through, Porsche had clinched the Manufacturers' Championship through victories at Monza (first three places), Nürburgring (first five places), and in the Targa Florio (first four places) with the Type 908, ably backed up by the smaller Type 907. Late in the season, when Porsche had 'officially retired' from this class of racing, a 917 won the Austrian Grand Prix.

Mercedes-Benz dropped their 300SL in 1963, and since then the only sports Mercedes has been the 230SL and its developments. It used a 150bhp version of the 220 engine, with swing axles at the rear, and hard top or open bodies. It became the 250SL in 1967, with 2,496cc engine, and the latest development is the 280SL. This has a 170bhp 2,788cc fuel injection engine, with optional automatic gearbox and power steering. Top speed is 124mph. A completely new Mercedes-Benz sports coupé appeared in the summer of 1969. This C111 was then made in limited number as an experimental car, and as first shown could hardly have been competitive in racing. It had a three-rotor Wankel engine, rated at 3·6 litres, mounted amidships. This unit developed 280bhp at 7,000rpm, but it would be feasible to add another Wankel chamber to bring capacity to 4·8 litres. The claimed maximum speed in 3·6-litre form was 162mph. A five-speed ZF gearbox was installed in the first cars, partly

Porsche 910 2-litre 6-cylinder coupé seen at the Mittholz–Kandersteg Hill Climb in September 1968.
(Photo: G. N. Georgano)

The incredibly fast and powerful Porsche 917 seen at the Le Mans Test Day in March 1969 when it lapped at 143mph.
(Photo: Motor)

because maximum torque rpm were considerably lower than maximum power rpm. The aerodynamically efficient but heavy coupé body had gull-wing doors.

B.M.W. made no genuine sports cars after dropping the Type 507, but the new series of 4-cylinder saloons introduced in 1962 led to some high performance versions. The original 1500 had an 80bhp engine, increased to 90bhp in the 1800 and 130bhp in the 1800SA. These were all 4-door saloons, but in 1965 came the 2000CS with very handsome coupé body and 120bhp engine. The latest development of the line is the 2800CS with 170bhp 2·8-litre 6-cylinder engine. Before the introduction of the 4-cylinder series, B.M.W.'s production was confined to small cars with flat-twin 700cc engines. A special sporting version of this was developed by B.M.W. agent Willy Martini, and sold under the name Martini-B.M.W. They had fibreglass coupé bodies and engines tuned to give 55bhp compared with 40bhp from the most powerful standard B.M.W. 700. A special sports/racing version developed 78bhp. About ten Martini-B.M.W.s were built between 1963 and 1965, and they achieved several class victories in national events at Nürburgring and other circuits.

A number of semi-sporting cars have been made by well-known German manufacturers, notably N.S.U. and, more recently, Opel. The motorcycle firm of N.S.U. returned to car manufacture in 1958 with the 598cc Prinz economy car and a 30bhp GT coupé version of this, known as the Sport Prinz, appeared in 1959. A roadster version came the following year, and this was available with the revolutionary Wankel engine, being the first production car in the world to use this system. It was made in small numbers from 1964 onwards, although it has been overshadowed by the Ro.80 twin-rotor saloon. Opel is a mass-production firm with little interest in sport, but recently they have produced high-performance GT versions of their Kadett and Rekord range. In 1968 they introduced a new GT coupé with 1·1-litre or 1·9-litre engines, and completely new bodies built in France by Brissonneau et Lotz. The larger car is said to have a maximum speed of 120mph.

Until the Autumn of 1969 Volkswagen had never made a true sports car. But now collaboration with Porsche has resulted in a new mid-engined design known as the 914. This is available with the 85bhp 4-cylinder Volkswagen 1600 engine or the 6-cylinder Porsche 911T of two-litres capacity developing 125bhp. Engines apart, the 914 is more a Porsche than a Volkswagen with integral construction body shell and built-in roll bar above the seats as on the Targa models of Porsche. The 914 is strictly a two-seater. Maximum speed with the 6-cylinder engine is claimed to be over 125mph.

A few small firms have offered sports cars with VW components. These have included the M.C.A. Jetstar roadster and Jetkomet coupé, the latter with 65bhp 1,493cc engine, and the Berlin-built Colani. This was available as a kit, or fully assembled.

26. Italy

As in other countries, one aspect of Italian car development in the 1960s has been the separation of road-going from sports/racing cars. Coupled with this has been the appearance of a number of makers of extremely high-performance cars who have shown no interest in racing. A decade or more ago it would have been unthinkable that two of the fastest cars in the world should never have been raced, or been developed from racing cars, yet such is the case with the Lamborghini Miura and the de Tomaso Mangusta.

Dealing first with sports cars which have been active in competition, Ferrari followed three lines of development in the period. Front-engined V-12s for road and track, rear-engined V-6, V-8, and V-12 competition cars, and the smaller rear-engined Dino V-6. The 250 GT 3-litre V-12 was developed progressively throughout the period, notable milestones being the 250 GTO of 1962 with full Testa Rossa engine and six carburetters, developing 300bhp, the 330 GT with 4-litre 300bhp engine, and the 275 GTB with 3·3-litre engine developing 275bhp at 7,000rpm. In addition to these developments of the 3-litre range, the 500 Superfast with 400bhp 4·9-litre engine was continued up to 1966. Sales were very small, as it was much more expensive than the smaller Ferraris and did not offer all that much greater performance. In 1965 the Superfast was the most expensive sports car in the world, costing £11,519 in England and $24,400 in the United States. The 1969 Ferrari touring car range consists of the 275 GTB and two 4·4-litre cars – the 365 GTC and 365 GTB4 – with 320bhp and 352bhp respectively. The latter is a two-seater coupé with a claimed top speed of 175mph. The 275 GTO was homologated as a Grand Touring car in 1962, and won many events in this category, including the 1962 and 1963 Tourist Trophies. Lately it has been overshadowed by the rear-engined cars which run in the prototype category (Group 6).

The rear-engined sports Ferrari appeared in 1958 under the name Dino 196. This was christened in memory of Alfredino Ferrari, Enzo's only son, who died of leukaemia in 1956. It had a 1,984cc V-6 engine developing 225bhp at 9,000rpm. Neither this nor the larger 2,916cc version was very successful at first, and it was not until 1962 that the rear-engined Ferraris came into their own. In that year, V-8s won the Targa Florio, the Nürburgring 1,000km, and at Le Mans, with front-engined GT cars coming 2nd and 3rd in the latter event. For 1963 the mainstay of Ferrari was the 250P with 2,953cc V-12 engine. This came 1st and 2nd at Sebring, and 1st at Le Mans and the Nürburgring. 1964 was Ferrari's best year in sports car racing, with 1st, 2nd, and 3rd places at Sebring, 1st and 2nd at Nürburgring, 1st, 2nd, and 3rd at Le Mans, 1st and 2nd at Reims, and 1st in the T.T. at Goodwood. Successful drivers included Parkes, Surtees, Bandini, Bonnier, Scarfiotti, and Hill. In 1965 Ferrari were again successful, relying on the 275/P and the new 330/P2 with twin-ohc per bank of cylinders. With these cars, Ferrari won at Nürburgring, Spa, Le Mans, Reims, and the Targa Florio. After 1965 the challenge of the Ford GT and the new Porsche severely shook Ferrari's confidence. In 1966 the new 330/P3 won its first race, the Monza 1,000km, and the Spa 1,000km, while Dino 196s finished 2nd and 3rd at the Nürburgring. The Le Mans race, however, was a fiasco for Ferrari, and

Ferrari Dino driven by
Ludovico Scarfiotti at the
Freiburg Hill Climb.
(Photo: Autosport)

'A thinly-disguised Grand
Prix car.' The Ferrari 312P
driven by Pedro Rodriguez
at the B.O.A.C. 500 in April
1969.
(Photo: Autosport)

during the rest of the season only privately-owned cars were raced. 1967 was
a better year, with a 1, 2, 3 victory at Daytona, 1st and 2nd at Monza, and
good placings at Spa, Le Mans, and Brands Hatch (BOAC 500) to gain
sufficient points to secure for Ferrari the Constructors' Championship.
Ferrari's car this year was the P4, with a new Rocchi-designed 4-litre overhead camshaft V-12 engine, with three valves per cylinder, two inlet and
one exhaust, in place of the two-valve arrangement of the previous 330s.
The P4s were raced by the works, but a number of older cars were sold to
private owners. These had P3 engines, but bodywork, suspension, and brakes
of the P4. Known as the 330 P3/P4, they were raced, among others, by the
Equipe Nationale Belge, North American Racing Team, and the Swiss
Scuderia Filipinetti. For 1968 Group 6 cars were restricted to a capacity of
3 litres, and Ferrari withdrew entirely from this class of racing. However, he
still had a suitable power unit, the 3-litre V-12 Grand Prix engine, and for

*'Birdcage' Maserati: a Tipo 61
with Stirling Moss at the
wheel.
(Photo:Bernard Cahier)*

1969 he announced the 312P for Group 6 racing. This was a thinly-disguised
Grand Prix car with all-enveloping body and off-set cockpit, but using the
same transmission, suspension and wheels as the Formula 1 cars, and a
slightly de-tuned engine. It was closer to a Grand Prix car than any other
Group 6 machine save the Ford F3L, but up to mid-1969 it had not had a very
promising career. Its best performance was Andretti and Amon's 2nd place
at Sebring.

A new line of Ferrari road cars is the Dino 206 GT. This was introduced in
1965, with a mid-mounted 1,592cc V-6 engine developing 190bhp at 9,000rpm.
It has much in common with the Dino sports/racing cars and through them
with the Grand Prix cars, particularly the multi-tube space frame. The body
was a two-seater coupé built by Scaglietti, but designed by Pininfarina. It
went into production in 1967, and the current Dino GT has an engine
enlarged to 1,985cc, giving a maximum speed of 147mph. The 2-litre Dino
engine is also used by Fiat in a front-engined sports car.

Maserati did not sponsor a works team after 1957, but the 'Birdcage'
models (see page 261) were built for private owners to race. These came in
three versions, the front-engined Tipo 60 and 61 of 2 litres and 2·9 litres
capacity, and the rear-engined 3-litre Tipo 63. They were entered in a
number of events by the American Camoradi Racing Team, by Briggs
Cunningham and by the Italian Scuderia Serenissima. Victories included the
Cuban Grand Prix of 1960 (Stirling Moss), and the Nürburgring 1,000km in
1960 and 1961 (Moss/Gurney and Casner/Gregory). Although faster than the
equivalent Ferraris, they were unreliable, and this prevented them from
achieving further success. The last competition Maserati was the Tipo 65, a
rear-engined coupé with 5-litre V-8 engine. A private entry by Colonel
Simone, head of Maserati France, it was actually assembled in France, after
the original car was written off in practice for the 1965 Le Mans race. The
Tipo 65 ran only twice, at Le Mans and Reims, and retired both times. Although Maserati no longer sponsor racing, their road cars have appeared in
considerable variety and increasing numbers. The mainstay has been the
6-cylinder 3500 which carried coupé and convertible bodies by Touring or
Vignale, one of the most popular being the Sebring 2 + 2 coupé by the latter.
The only six being made in 1969 is the 3·7-litre Mistrale, somewhat overshadowed by the V-8s. The first V-8 road cars were very expensive coupé
versions of the Tipo 450S competition car, made to special order only, but a
production V-8 came in 1963 with the 4·2-litre 260bhp Quattroporte, a 4-door
saloon. This was a new development for Maserati (Ferrari have never made a

293

4-door car), and is probably the fastest car with four doors in the world, with a speed of 150mph. A larger V-8 of 4·7 litres and 330bhp is used in the Ghibli coupé, an ultra-streamlined car with five-speed gearbox and top speed of 175mph. The same engine is available in the staider-looking (and cheaper) Mexico coupé.

Lancia produced no specialized sports cars after the D.24s of 1953, but their production cars have been the basis for tuned coupés which have been very successful in rallies. In 1961 came the Flavia saloon with 1,500cc flat-four engine ahead of the front axle, and driving the front wheels. The standard engine gave 90bhp, but a 92bhp version was available in 1962, mounted in sports coupés by Farina and Zagato. In 1964 capacity was increased to 1,800cc and power to 105bhp, while in 1969 capacity went up to 2 litres. The smaller version of the Flavia was the 1,100cc Fulvia, also a flat-four. The current Fulvia has a capacity of 1,300cc and is available with fuel injection, the smallest production car in the world with this system.

Alfa-Romeo finally dropped the Giulietta in 1965, but had already supplemented it with the 1,570cc 92bhp Giulia. This carried coupé bodies by Bertone and Zagato, and a Spyder by Pininfarina, very similar in appearance to those of the Giulietta. More powerful versions of the Giulia engines gave 112bhp, and were available in the saloon and coupés. The larger Alfa-Romeo 2600 was also made in Spyder form. The latest Alfa range is the 1750, with 1,779cc engines giving 113bhp and 118mph. It is a logical development of the Giulia range, and the same coupés and open Spyder models are available. Alfa's sporting activities were organised by the Autodelta concern under the supervision of ex-Ferrari and A.T.S. engineer Carlo Chiti. For several years they concentrated on racing a team of Giulia TZ coupés in Group 4 events, but in 1967 they brought out a completely new car which enabled Alfa-Romeo to enter first-class sports car racing. This was the Tipo 33, a mid-engined coupé powered by a 2-litre V-8 engine. This four-camshaft unit developed 265bhp. Severe handling problems were experienced at first, but several successes have been achieved, including 2nd and 3rd places in the 1968 Targa Florio, and 2nd in the Index of Performance at Le Mans. 2½- and 3-litre versions were introduced for the 1969 season.

The enormous Fiat organisation has shown more interest in sports cars in the 1960s than in any other decade of their history. The Osca-designed twin-cam 1600 introduced in 1959 was continued until 1966, and was joined by the 2300S, a GT coupé capable of 120mph. In 1965 came the 850 saloon and sporting versions of this were soon available. They were a spyder and a coupé. The latter has become very popular, about one in seven of all 850s made being this model. The larger Model 124 Sport has a 1,438cc twin-cam engine, with camshafts driven by cogged belts, and a maximum speed of just under 100mph. The most sophisticated Fiat is the Dino coupé which uses the four-camshaft 2-litre V-6 engine of the Ferrari Dino. This engine is manufactured by Fiat to Ferrari design. So far Fiat have not joined the fashion for mid-engined sports cars, but a straw in the wind was the mid-engined coupé exhibited at the 1968 Turin Show on the stand of Autobianchi, who are a Fiat subsidiary.

Closely allied to Fiat development in the 1960s was Abarth, almost all of their cars being based on Fiats. The Abarth range was very complex, but two lines of development can be traced: tuned versions of Fiat saloons, and coupés using Fiat-based engines with distinctive coachwork. The saloons varied from a 'hot' 500 giving 38bhp and 87mph to an incredible machine with twin-cam 1,600cc Abarth engine mounted in the Fiat 850 hull with front-mounted radiator. Maximum speed was 137mph. The coupés used Fiat

Alfa Romeo Tipo 33 at Le Mans in 1968. Driven by Galli and Giunti, it finished 4th. (Photo: Motor)

1964/65 Abarth 850 coupé at the Mittholz–Kandersteg Hill Climb in September 1968. (Photo: G. N. Georgano)

500, 600, and 1100 engines, usually bored out to give greater capacity, and highly tuned. Twin-cam heads were used in the 600 and 1100 derivatives, the former having a capacity of 982cc (97bhp) and the latter 1,300cc (110bhp and 140mph). One of the fastest models was the Simca-Abarth with 1,946cc engine developing 202bhp, and a claimed maximum speed of 168mph. It had a similar coupé body to the smaller cars. For 1968 Abarth announced that a Group 6 competition car would be available to special order. This had a centrally-mounted 982cc engine and was known as the 1000SP. In 1969 came the 2-litre 2000, to take among other race successes, 1st and 2nd places on the demanding 41-mile Mugello road circuit.

The great success of Abarth has tended to overshadow all the other small Fiat-derived cars. Moretti and Cisitalia shrank to the position of special coachbuilders on tuned Fiat chassis, and the latter ceased production altogether in 1965. Osca continued to 1967, using the 1600 twin-cam engine that they designed for Fiat in a series of cars of their own, with bodies by Fissore, Vignale, or Zagato. In 1963 the Maserati brothers sold out to the MV motorcycle firm who closed down car building altogether four years later. Like Moretti, Siata have concentrated on special versions of 1100 and 1500 Fiats, with 94bhp twin carburetter engines. In 1968 they introduced the Spring, a 1930s style roadster with Fiat 850 engine, and this is the only car produced in 1969.

Two interesting new marques to appear in the 1960s were A.S.A. and A.T.S. The former was a high quality small coupé based on a baby Ferrari which had been designed by Giotto Bizzarrini. Ferrari never put it into production, and the design was acquired by the wealthy de Nora family who formed a new company, Autocostruzione SpA, to make it. The engine was a 1,032cc single-ohc unit developing 91bhp, mounted in the rear of a coupé body. Maximum speed was 113mph. It was very expensive and production has never reached a scale where the car is commercially viable. In 1966 a 1,292cc 6-cylinder car ran at Le Mans without success. This was offered to the public as the Rollbar GT Spyder, with open fibreglass two-seater body. The A.T.S. was an even more expensive car financed by the Scuderia Serenissima, a racing stable backed by Count Volpi and Bolivian tin millionaire Jaime Ortiz-Patino. A 1½-litre V-8 Grand Prix car designed by Carlo Chiti appeared in 1963, but did not distinguish itself. Chiti's second design was a GT coupé powered by a 2½-litre V-8 engine mounted ahead of the rear axle, in what has become the conventional position for competition cars. Two stages of tune were available, 210bhp for the road car and 245bhp for the competition version. Four Weber carburetters or fuel injection could be had. Two of these coupés ran in the 1964 Targa Florio, but both retired. Volpi soon abandoned the idea of a production car, but persevered with the competition version which he called the Serenissima from 1965 onwards. This had the same engine, but with two camshafts per bank of cylinders, compared with only two altogether on the A.T.S. Capacities were 3 or 3½ litres. The former ran at Le Mans in 1966, but retired. Hardly any cars have been produced since 1966, although a Ghia-bodied coupé appeared at the 1968 Turin Show.

A significant group of high-performance Italian cars has had little or no connection with the sporting world. The best known of these are the Iso and its derivative the Bizzarrini, the de Tomaso, and the Lamborghini. The Iso Rivolta appeared in 1962 as a four-seater saloon powered by a 5·4-litre Chevrolet Corvette engine developing 260bhp. It was not a sports car, but the Italian equivalent of the Gordon-Keeble or Facel Vega. In 1963 came the Iso Grifo, a two-seater GT coupé with 365bhp Chevrolet engine, and 160mph

56. *1969 de Tomaso Mangusta 4·7-litre coupé. (Photo: Automobili de Tomaso SpA)*

57. *Overleaf, above left: 1965 Lamborghini 350 GT 3½-litre coupé. Owned by C. W. P. Hampton. (Photo: Charles Pocklington)*

58. *Overleaf, below left: 1969 Saab Sonnett V4 1½-litre coupé. (Photo: Saab Aktiebolag)*

59. *Overleaf, above right: 1968 American Motors AMX 6·4-litre Hard Top Fastback Coupé. (Photo: American Motors Corporation)*

60. *Overleaf, below right: 1968 Mazda 110 S coupé. (Photo: Toyo Kogyo Co Ltd)*

maximum speed. The 1968 model Grifo had the option of a 410bhp 7-litre Chevrolet engine, giving a claimed maximum speed of 180mph. Both Iso cars were designed by Giotto Bizzarrini who set up an independent firm in 1965. Special-bodied Grifos prepared by Bizzarrini had run at Le Mans in 1964 and 1965, and this became the Bizzarrini Strada GT 5300 which went into production in 1966. It had lower lines than the Grifo, but the same chassis and engine. Also in 1966 Bizzarrini built a small prototype coupé with Fiat 1500 engine, and this went into limited production in 1968 with a 1,900cc Opel engine. Production of Bizzarrinis is very small, not exceeding 20 per year, compared with about 200 per year for Iso.

Alessandro de Tomaso was a racing driver from the Argentine who built a number of prototype sports and racing cars before beginning actual production of sports cars in 1964. The first of these was the Vallelunga, a GT coupé powered by a rear-mounted 1½-litre Ford Cortina engine. About 50 of these were made before de Tomaso turned his attention to a much more powerful car which he called the Mangusta. This was also a rear-engined coupé but had a 4·7-litre Ford V-8 engine tuned by Carroll Shelby to give 305bhp. It had an exceptionally low body made by Ghia, the coachbuilding firm in which de Tomaso acquired a majority interest in 1967. The Mangusta has a maximum speed of about 145mph, with acceleration from 0–60mph in 6·1 seconds. Production models have the Shelby-tuned engine giving 306bhp, or a 5-litre V-8 giving 265bhp, and complying with the latest air pollution regulations for the American market. Production of Mangustas was running at 20 per month in the spring of 1969. It has made no competition appearance yet, but de Tomaso is said to be considering the matter.

The last new Italian marque to be described is also the most dramatic. Every decade has its glamour car *par excellence*, and that of the 1960s is undoubtedly the Lamborghini Miura. Ferruccio Lamborghini is a manufacturer of tractors, oil-fuelled central heating equipment, and air-conditioners, who turned to car manufacture as a sideline. To call it a hobby might imply a charge of amateurism which Lamborghini certainly does not deserve, but it is undoubtedly a labour of love. The first car to bear his name appeared at the Turin Show in 1963. It was a front-engined GT coupé powered by a 3½-litre V-12 engine with two camshafts per bank of cylinders, and six Weber carburetters. This engine was designed by Bizzarrini and the entire project was supervised by a young ex-Ferrari engineer, Gian Paolo Dallara. The car attracted a great deal of attention, for although new makes are familiar at Turin completely new V-12 engines are not. There were many admirers on the Lamborghini stand, but few who predicted a future for the new car which was appearing at a time of economic crisis in the Italian motor industry. Also, Lamborghini was challenging Enzo Ferrari in a field in which he was virtually supreme. The 350 GT, as the new car was called, was slow to get into production, owing to difficulty with body suppliers, but by the end of 1965 over 150 had been made. Meanwhile a new and more exciting Lamborghini had appeared. Christened the Miura after the fiercest breed of Spanish fighting bulls (the bull was Lamborghini's reply to the prancing horse of Ferrari), this had a 4-litre V-12 engine mounted transversely behind the passenger compartment. It developed 420bhp at 8,000rpm, giving a maximum speed of 180mph. Power is transmitted to the clutch by a pair of spur gears, and thence to a 5-speed gearbox. From there another pair of gears transmit power to the differential. The Miura is a remarkably original car, but it is surprisingly untemperamental and suffers from none of the plug fouling or irregular idling often associated with such exotic machinery. Consequently it is not only dreamed about by thousands, but has been

61. 1968 Auburn 866 7-litre Replica Speedster. Owned by Glen Pray. (Photo: William S. Jackson)

301

ordered by several hundred people who are not necessarily die-hard motoring enthusiasts. Even at a retail price of over £10,000, demand for the Miura exceeds supply. The 350 GT was replaced by the 400 GT with larger engine and available with four-seater bodywork. This has now been replaced in turn by the Islero 4-litre 2 + 2 coupé with restyled coachwork. The latest Lamborghini, and the most expensive, is the Espada. This is a full four-seater, with 4-litre V-12 engine and a claimed top speed of 152mph.

1964 A.T.S. 2½-litre V-8 coupé. (Photo: Automobili Turismo Sport)

Iso Grifo 5·4-litre coupé. (Photo: Carrozzeria Bertone S.A.S.)

Lamborghini Miura 4-litre V-12 coupé. (Photo: Carrozzeria Bertone S.A.S.)

27. Other European Countries

Very few sports cars have been produced in the smaller countries in recent years. Sweden and Holland have developed flourishing native industries since the war, but only the former has produced anything near a sports car, the Volvo P.1800S. This is a GT coupé powered by a 1·8-litre 4-cylinder engine developing 115bhp, and giving the car a maximum speed of 107mph. At one time the body was built in England by Jensen, while another English connection has been the use of Girling disc brakes on the front wheels. It was introduced in 1960, and has continued with very little change up to 1969. A fast tourer rather than a sports car, its makers have shown no inclination to develop a higher performance version or to enter it for any class of racing. The other Swedish manufacturer, Saab, have for a long time been experimenting with sports cars based on their 748cc 3-cylinder 2-stroke saloon. A prototype of a low, two-seater sports car appeared in 1958, and various other open and coupé versions appeared over the next few years. In 1966 a production sports model was introduced, the Sonett with two-seater fibreglass coupé bodywork. In 1968 Saab abandoned their 2-stroke engine for the 1½-litre German Ford V-4 4-stroke unit. This gave the Sonett a greatly improved performance, maximum speed of the current version being nearly 100mph.

Apart from the Enzmann mentioned in the last section, the only Swiss sporting machines have been the work of Peter Monteverdi. He began car construction in 1959 at the age of twenty-five with Formula Junior racing cars, and then produced a two-seater sports car powered by an 1,100cc Osca engine, with disc brakes and de Dion rear axle. The twin-ohc engine developed 100bhp at 7,500rpm, and maximum speed was over 130mph. Unfortunately such a car was bound to be expensive, and the price was 29,000 Swiss francs, or about £2,200. Very few were sold, and Monteverdi's next sports car used a Ford 105E engine, being made in open or coupé form.

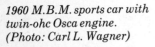

1960 M.B.M. sports car with twin-ohc Osca engine.
(Photo: Carl L. Wagner)

This was built from 1961 to 1962, again in very small numbers. These sports cars were sold under the name M.B.M., but when Monteverdi next essayed car manufacture he gave the product his own name. The Monteverdi GT coupé appeared in 1967, and was a typical Euro-American hybrid of the Iso Rivolta type. The power unit was a 7·2-litre 375bhp Chrysler V-8, coachwork was a two-seater coupé by Frua of Italy, and the cars had de Dion rear axles. A four-seater version, the 375L, has since been added to the range. At $21,000, it is one of the most expensive GT cars in the world.

Belgium has produced two small makes, A.P.A.L. and Méan. The former was a low GT coupé powered by an Okrasa-tuned Volkswagen engine, which has been replaced by a Renault 16TS unit in the latest model. The Méan is a kit car available with an incredible variety of engines. These include British Ford Cortina, German Ford V-4 or V-6, Renault R 8 or R 10, Peugeot 404, Volkswagen, Porsche, or N.S.U. By January 1969, a total of eighty-five Méans had been made, with twenty-two different power units.

28.The United States of America

American interest in the sports car has continued unabated during the 1960s, and the cars have been a varied selection. They have ranged from tuned personal cars from major manufacturers, such as the Ford Mustang and Rambler AMX, on the one hand, to sports/racing cars of international fame on the other, such as the Ford GT40. The latter was really an Anglo-American car, with development initiative changing from one side of the Atlantic to the other with confusing speed. Ford made the decision to enter sports car racing early in 1963, and a design team headed by Roy Lunn started work on a mid-engined car. This was to be built around the 350bhp 4·2-litre light alloy power unit developed by Ford for Indianapolis, driving through a 4-speed Colotti transaxle (combined gearbox and rear axle unit). At the same time, Eric Broadley was developing his Lola GT in England along very similar lines (see page 282), and consequently a liaison – which amounted to a take-over of Lola for a limited period – was arranged by Ford. The American company was to put vast sums of money into the enterprise, and without such resources Lola could never have achieved great success.

A subsidiary company, Ford Advanced Vehicles Ltd, was established at Slough, Buckinghamshire, under John Wyer and Roy Lunn, to handle the project. The first GT40 (so-called because the roofline was exactly 40in from the ground) was completed in the spring of 1964 and, without adequate preparation, two cars were run in the Le Mans trials. Both crashed, an inauspicious start on the circuit where they were later to be so successful. During 1964 GT40s were raced at the Nürburgring, Le Mans, Reims, and Nassau, demonstrating great potential but failing to finish in any race.

At the end of the year the GT40 programme was re-arranged. Ford Advanced Vehicles became primarily responsible for production while in racing development the emphasis shifted to the U.S.A. During 1964 the blocks of all the available light-alloy engines cracked, so the Cobra version of the 4·7-litre (289 cu in) Fairlane V-8 was substituted, and the transmission, brakes, and aerodynamics improved. The first success came early in 1965, with victory in the Daytona 2,000km race and a second place at Sebring.

Meanwhile another Ford subsidiary, Kar Kraft, was developing the Mk II at Detroit, using rolling chassis built at Slough. The main difference was the use of a 445bhp 7-litre (428 cu in) engine derived from the Galaxie unit. Two of these cars were completed in time to run at Le Mans. However, neither of them, or the four normal GT40s in the race, completed the twenty-four hours. In order to qualify the model as a production sports car, Ford Advanced Vehicles produced 50 GT40s during 1965 and 1966, selling them at £7,254 in England and about $20,000 in America, and also developed a road-going version. Apart from the chassis shipped to Kar Kraft for completion as Mk IIs, most of the Slough cars were delivered to private owners, by whom the GT40 was increasingly raced. Confusingly, a handful of cars were also built by Alan Mann Racing at Byfleet, for Ford-sponsored teams such as Shelby American.

In 1966 the investment in the Mk II paid substantial dividends. Fords came 1st, 2nd, and 3rd at Daytona, 1st and 2nd at Sebring, 2nd at Spa, and, triumph of triumphs, 1st, 2nd, and 3rd at Le Mans. The winning car, driven by Bruce McLaren and Chris Amon, averaged 125mph for the whole twenty-four hours. For 1967 another new version, the Mk IV, was developed through the interim J-car. This used the 7-litre engine, but had a new and completely novel hull built up of aluminium honeycomb sandwich. With it, Ford again won Le Mans, Gurney and Foyt averaging over 135mph, and also won the Sebring 12 Hours. During the year private owners with GT40s also gained for Ford the Group 4 Championship. Immediately after their second Le Mans victory Ford withdrew from this class of racing, and the Mk II and Mk IV cars were retired.

By this time the FAV operation at Slough had closed down, and succeeded by J.W. Automotive Engineering which was licensed by Ford to carry on the production of homologated and road-going GT40s. Under John Wyer, and with the backing of the Gulf Oil Corporation, the company also continued to run GT40s in front-line racing. During 1967 the J.W. Automotive team had raced the Mirage, in effect a GT40 with a lighter, smoother body, slightly modified chassis and 4·7-, 5-, and 5·7-litre engines. Changes in the international regulations meant that this was not eligible for Championship events in 1968, so the team reverted to the GT40, refined in detail and with a 400bhp 5-litre engine to keep it competitive. Whereas Ford had concentrated on Le Mans, the Gulf programme was spread more evenly over the Championship, and with victories at Brands Hatch, Spa, Monza, Watkins Glen, and Le Mans, the team gained the Constructors' Championship.

Because of delays with their 3-litre Mirage (see page 282), J.W. Automotive had to depend on the GT40 for their 1969 racing programme, although in the world of competition the basic design was ageing. During the season they gained two more first-class victories, at Sebring and Le Mans, before retiring their GT40s. After the Le Mans race, the drivers of the winning GT40 were awarded the prize for the highest-placed *British* car, an award for which the GT40 had not hitherto been considered eligible!

In the road-going GT40 the engine was detuned to give some 335bhp and other modifications, to suspension, brakes, and cockpit, incorporated. The maximum speed was about 165mph. Thirty-one of these cars were built, selling at £6,428 (a specially-prepared model with greater comfort for road use was offered by Performance Cars of Geneva at 110,000 Swiss francs, or £9,130). The road-going GT40s had many deficiencies from the touring point of view, though few as a sports car in the finest tradition (one was driven from England to Portugal in 1969, to compete in, and finish in, a 6-hour race). These deficiencies were admitted, and in the Mk III many were overcome. But this model was built only in a left-hand drive version, which meant that the gear lever had to be moved from the right-hand side of the cockpit to the centre, and this proved to be its Achilles heel, as a precise gear linkage could not be devised. In any case, the sale of cars of this type for use on American highways was discouraged, so only seven Mk IIIs were built. Production of road-going cars came to an end in the spring of 1969, and of Group 4 racing GT40s during the summer of that year.

No other American sports car was built for international competition, with the exception of the Chaparral which is a Group 7 car and outside the scope of this book. Nevertheless, a number of other sports cars have been made, of which the best known is the Chevrolet Corvette. This is a very fine two-seater sports car in the old tradition, and has provided healthy competition for the Cobra. For 1963 the design was completely revamped, having a new body with retractable headlamps à la Cord, and a 5·3-litre 360bhp engine. This new model, called the Stingray, was available as a fast-back or open two-seater. Different engine/transmission/rear axle combinations gave speeds varying

Above: *Ford GT40 Mk III with 7-litre (428 cubic inch) engine.* (Photo: Autocar)

Above right: *Not all competition Mustangs were Shelby-prepared. This is a Ford Mustang in action at Brands Hatch.* (Photo: Autosport)

from 115mph to 185mph. For 1968 the Corvette was restyled again, and engine options were 5·3 litres or 7 litres. This 1968 Corvette resembles a General Motors dream car of a few years ago, and in the autumn of 1968 GM showed another dream car, the Astro 2. This was a low coupé with engine mounted amidships, and some observers have professed to see in this the Corvette of 1972.

There have been a number of smaller firms making sports cars in the 1960s, though nothing like so many as in the previous decade. One of the most distinctive looking was the Fitch Phoenix, built by former racing driver John Fitch. It was powered by the Chevrolet Corvair air-cooled flat-6 engine, tuned to give 170bhp, and had a distinctive two-seater body built in Italy by Intermeccanica of Turin. Comfort and individuality were Fitch's aims rather than performance, although the Phoenix was capable of 135mph. Price was high, at $9,160, and production never started. Another small-production sports car builder is Fiberfab of Santa Clara, California. Their main business is in making fibreglass bodies for Volkswagen and other chassis, which are mounted by the car's owners. One model is available either as a body only, or as a complete car. This is the Valkyrie, powered by a 450bhp 7-litre Chevrolet engine mounted amidships, with five-speed ZF transaxle. Performance is among the highest of any car in America, with a maximum speed of 180mph, and acceleration from 0–60mph in 3·9 seconds. For 'primary braking' from speeds of over 140mph, a Simpson drag parachute can be used. Price of the Valkyrie complete is $12,000. American sales of the T.V.R. led to an interesting Anglo-American hybrid, the Griffith. Ford and Cobra dealer Jack Griffith wanted a high-performance GT coupé to add to his line, and decided to install a Ford 289 engine in the squat but distinctive T.V.R. body. The result was called the Griffith 200 and was shown at the New York International Auto Show in 1964. About 265 were sold in a little over a year, when the project was hit by one of T.V.R.'s many changes of ownership.

1968 Chevrolet Corvette Stingray coupé. (Photo: Motor)

Griffith then planned to buy body/chassis units from Intermeccanica of Turin, but ran out of money after only thirteen cars had been delivered. The project was taken over by Stephen Wilder who changed the car's name to Omega. Another Italo-American car was the Apollo, a GT coupé slightly reminiscent of the E-type Jaguar in appearance, powered by a 3½-litre Buick engine. Bodies again came from Intermeccanica, and the car was offered first by International Motor Cars of Oakland, California, and then by Apollo International Corporation of Pasadena. Sales were disappointing, and after a change of name to Vetta Ventura the car disappeared.

One of the most remarkable cars of the 1960s was the Ford Mustang. It was not a sports car, but a four-seater personal car more compact than the average American sedan, appealing particularly to the young single man or woman who represent an increasingly wealthy section of the market. It was available with 6- or 8-cylinder engines, in four sizes, from 2,781cc and 101bhp to 4,728cc and 210bhp. The latter was the famous 289 cu in engine used in the Cobra and Ford GT 40. Speeds of the Mustangs varied from 95–120mph. It would not have found its way into this book had not Carroll Shelby taken

1964 Studebaker Avanti. This was the last year of the Studebaker-built Avanti but the car was continued by an independent company. (Photo: Studebaker Corporation)

it up and produced his own version, the Shelby GT 350. This used the '289' engine and Mustang fastback body shell. Appearance was superficially similar to that of the stock Mustang, but almost every part of the car was modified by Shelby in some way. In particular, attention was paid to engine, brakes, and suspension, while the body was lightened and the metal bonnet was replaced by fibreglass. The road version gave 306bhp, while a competition version with free-flow exhaust gave 350bhp. In 1967 came the GT 500, using the 427 cu in (7 litres) engine giving 360bhp in the road version, and 400bhp in the competition version. The road car had a speed of 135mph. Shelby's Mustangs are now called Cobras, as the two-seater A.C.-based Cobra is no longer made. Since 1968 a much closer cooperation between Shelby and Ford has been reached, and most of Shelby's modifications can be bought through Ford dealers. Thus an enormous variety of tuning and lightening is available to any Mustang owner.

Another personal car is the American Motors Javelin, a Mustang-type four-seater coupé with choice of engines up to a 5·6-litre 280bhp V-8, giving a maximum speed of 119mph. The Javelin was introduced in 1967, and was joined the following year by the AMX, a shorter wheelbase two-seater coupé. Engine options on the AMX are 4·7, 5·6, or 6·3 litres, the latter giving 315bhp and a speed of about 135mph. A specially-tuned AMX driven by Craig Breedlove reached 175mph, with 0–60mph acceleration in 6½ seconds. Apart from the Corvette, the AMX is the only two-seater sports car currently made by a major manufacturer.

One of the most individual-looking cars made in America was the Studebaker Avanti, introduced in 1962. This was a four-seater close-coupled coupé powered by a 4,737cc V-8 engine similar to that used in Studebaker's Lark V-8 and Hawk models, but tuned to give 240bhp. An unusual option was a supercharger, which boosted power to 290bhp. In 1962 the Avanti took twenty-nine stock car records, including the flying mile at 168·15mph. These figures were of course achieved by a special car. The stock Avanti had a speed of 124mph. In 1964 Studebaker closed down production of all their cars, but the Avanti was continued by a small independent company called Avanti Motor Company. The new car had similar styling, but used a 5·3-litre Chevrolet Corvette engine giving a speed of 118mph.

A new type of car that appeared on the American scene in the 1960s was the replica, based on the classic cars of thirty or forty years ago, but using modern engines and running gear. The true sports car enthusiast may recoil with horror from the replicas, but they undoubtedly offer a very sporting type of motoring. The most striking is the Excalibur SS, built by Brooks Stevens who had made the three prototypes of the Excalibur J in 1952. The SS was styled to resemble the SS Mercedes-Benz of the late 1920s and came with two- or four-seater open bodies. Originally a Studebaker engine with optional supercharger was used, but when Studebaker went out of business this was replaced by a Chevrolet Corvette unit. Maximum speed is in the region of 130mph, and price over $10,000. Other replicas are a very handsome one of the Auburn 851 speedster and one of the Cord 810. The Auburn is known as the 866 Speedster and is built by Glenn Pray of Broken Arrow, Oklahoma. It is powered by a 7-litre Ford engine giving a maximum speed of 135mph. Pray also built the original Cord replica. This was a four-fifths size replica, which meant that the fine lines of the original were spoilt by a foreshortened appearance. The first replica Cord used a Chevrolet Corvair engine, but later models had a Ford V-8 unit. These, alas, strayed even further from the appearance of the original, for they abandoned the retractable headlamps.

The rise of the Japanese motor industry in the 1960s has been phenomenal; she now stands sixth in world production of private cars, and in 1967 made more commercial vehicles than any other country, including the United States. Sports cars did not attract Japanese manufacturers at first, but over the past few years a number have appeared, two of which have attracted international fame because of their unusual character. They are the little Honda and the twin-rotor Wankel-engined Mazda coupé.

Honda had been making motorcycles for twelve years when they introduced their first car in 1962. It had a minute 4-cylinder twin-ohc engine of 360cc capacity, which developed 33bhp at the remarkably high speed of 9,000rpm. On early models, the rev counter read up to 14,000rpm. A five-speed gearbox transmitted power to the differential, whence drive was by separate chains to each rear wheel. The engine was canted at an angle of forty-five degrees to give a low bonnet line. An alternative model had a 492cc 40bhp engine. Subsequently the small model was dropped, and the larger was increased to 606cc and then to 791cc on the 1968 model. This developed 78bhp at 7,800rpm, and gave the car a top speed of 95mph. In other ways it became more conventional; the five speeds were replaced by four, and an ordinary hypoid bevel rear axle took the place of the chain drive. Interestingly enough, although the Honda S.800 sells well in Europe and the United States very few are sold in Japan. The sporting young Japanese prefer highly-tuned versions of baby saloons such as the Daihatsu Fellow, Suzuki Fronte 360, or Honda's own N.360.

The Mazda 110 S is a much more expensive car than the Honda, and on the British market has to compete with such cars as the E-type Jaguar. This has severely restricted its sales, but it is a most interesting machine. Toyo Kogyo Ltd, makers of the Mazda, were the second firm in the world (after

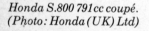

Honda S.800 791cc coupé.
(Photo: Honda (UK) Ltd)

N.S.U. of Germany) to take out a licence for production of the Wankel engine, and the 110 S was their first car to use this system. It was the first, and still is the only, proper sports car to be powered by a Wankel engine. The twin-rotor engine develops 128bhp, and drives the two-seater coupé at 116mph. It has a de Dion rear axle, and road holding is excellent. William Boddy, editor of *Motor Sport*, called it 'the Elan of Japan' when he road tested it. The company have gained competition experience with the Wankel engine in saloon car races, two M10A coupés finishing 5th and 6th in the 24-hour race at Spa in 1969.

Although much more conventional, a car in the same class as the Mazda is the Toyota 2000 coupé. Toyota is one of the largest car manufacturing concerns in Japan, and made a sports version of their Publica 700cc 2-cylinder light car as early as 1962. However, their first high-performance model was the 2000, introduced in 1966. It is a sleek GT coupé not unlike an E-type Jaguar in appearance, powered by a 2-litre twin-ohc 6-cylinder engine developing 150bhp at 7,000rpm. Maximum speed is 130mph. Although designed

Toyota 2000 GT 2-litre coupé. (Photo: Toyota Motor Company Ltd)

Nissan R380 2-litre Group 6 coupé. (Photo: Nissan Motor Company Ltd)

by Toyota, the 2000 GT is built by the Yamaha motorcycle firm, who are also responsible for the construction of the Toyota Group 7 racing cars.

In the competition field the most striking Japanese cars have been in the Group 7 category, the Toyota 7 and the Nissan R381. However, two Group 6 sports/racing cars appeared during 1968, the Daihatsu P5 and Nissan R380. Daihatsu are now part of the Toyota empire, so the two major Japanese firms compete in Group 6 racing as well as in Group 7. The Daihatsu has a 1,298cc twin-ohc 4-cylinder engine developing 140bhp, mounted amidships in a space frame. It is the most outstanding smaller sports/racing car made in Japan. The Nissan is a more formidable proposition, with a 6-cylinder 1,996cc engine with twin-ohc and 24 valves, developing 250bhp. Like the Daihatsu, the engine is mounted amidships in a space frame. It has proved exceedingly reliable, as well as fast. In the 1968 Japanese Grand Prix Nissan R380s finished 3rd, 4th, and 5th, behind a 4½-litre V-8 Nissan R381 and a Porsche 910.

Index

Miller, Capt Alistair, 45, 78
Minerva, 134
Minijem, 280
Mirage, 306
Momberger, Alfred, 122
Monopol, 249
Monopole, 245
Monte Carlo Rally, 105, 114, 119, 133, 154, 163, 176, 179, 196, 209, 219, 229, 239, 255, 289
Monteverdi, Peter, 303–4
Montlhéry, 75, 90, 104, 153, 196, 251
Montpensier, Duque de, 139
Mont Vertoux, 117
Monza Autodrome, 75, 105, 106, 121, 223, 289, 306
Moretti, 265, 296
Morgan, 15, 20, 76, 167, 217, 278
Morris (cars), 16, 86, 87
Morris, Mme Violette, 99
Mors, 23, 39
Moscovics, F. E., 110, 146
Moss, Mrs A. E., 189
Moss, Stirling, 225, 229, 232, 238, 253, 261, 265, 293
Moveo, 184
Moyet, Edmond, 93
Moynet-Simca, 287
Mugello, 296
Mulford, Ralph, 58
Mulliner, H. J. (coach-builders), 234
Mullner, 48
Muntz, 270
Mussolini, Benito, 124, 204
Mussolini, Bruno, 207

N

Nacional, 140
Nadal, 139
N.A.G., 41, 121
Napier, 11, 24, 44
Naples Grand Prix, 265
Nash (engines), 183, 221
Nassau Grand Prix, 305
National, 54, 61
Naudin, Louis, 32
Nazzaro (cars), 123
Nesselsdorfer, 41

Neubauer, Alfred, 136
Newns, E. J. (coach-builders), 180
Newton-Ceirano, 129
Niedermayer, H., 252
Nissan, 312
Noma, 145
North American Racing Team, 292
N.S.U., 122, 290, 304, 311
Nürburgring, 234, 236, 249, 253, 255, 261, 289, 290, 291, 293, 305
Nuvolari, Tazio, 154, 204, 265

O

Ogle, 279, 280
Oldsmobile (engines), 219
O.M., 129
Omega, 308
Opel, 41, 198, 203, 290, 301
Ormond Beach, 53
Orsi, Omer, 208, 260
Ortiz-Patino, Jaime, 296
Osca, 263, 265, 295, 296, 303
Otto, 121

P

Packard, 150
Paget, Hon Dorothy, 69
Paige-Daytona, 143–4, 146
Panelcraft (coach-builders), 221
Panhard, 106, 245, 249, 285
Paris-Madrid Race, 23
Paris-Nice Rally, 196
Paris-Rouen Trial, 23
Parkes, Mike, 291
Parry Thomas, J. G., 83, 89
Pateley Bridge, 28
Paul, Cyril, 80, 90
Pearce-Jones, G. D., 72
Peerless, 231
Pegaso, 267–8
Perl, 137
Perrin, John G., 58
Perrot (brakes), 74, 99, 108
Peugeot, 12, 53, 106–7, 197, 304
Phänomobil, 48
Phoenix Park, 83, 168, 208
Picardie, Circuit de, 99
Pikes' Peak Hill Climb, 143, 148

Pininfarina (coach-builders), 205, 207, 221, 254, 256, 259, 260, 265, 293, 295
Pio Arate di San Pietro, Duke, 132
Pipe, 11
Pitt, Major W. T., 37
Plus-Power (engines), 86
Pluto, 94
Poch, Jacques, 268
Poege, Willy, 27
Polish Grand Prix, 210
Polish Mountain Race, 210
Pomeroy, Laurence, 28, 72
Porporato, 103
Porsche (cars), 20, 251–2, 289, 290, 304, 312
Porsche, Ferdinand, 27, 115, 135–7, 251
Portago, Marquis de, 259
Porter, F. R., 55, 56
Posthumus, Cyril, 11
Prado, 63
Pray, Glenn, 309
Prescott Hill, 233
Prince Henry Tours, 24, 27–8
Puch, 41
Pullen, Eddie, 56

R

Rabag, 113, 121
Rabe, Karl, 135
R.A.C. Dewar Trophy, 75
R.A.C. Rally, 162, 231
Radley, James, 41
Railton (cars), 15, 16, 179–81
Railton, Reid, 84, 89
Rally, 101
Ramponi, Guilio, 124
Rapier, 189
Rawlence, L. G., 129
R.E.A.C., 245
Rédéle, Jean, 248
Reims 12 Hour Race, 226, 261, 291, 293, 305
Reliant, 279
Remi Danvignes, 191
Renault, 239–40, 245, 248, 279, 285, 304
Renwick, W. S., 85
Repco Brabham (engines), 282
Revere, 145
Ricart (cars), 140